RESOURCE HANDBOOK FOR
ACADEMIC DEANS

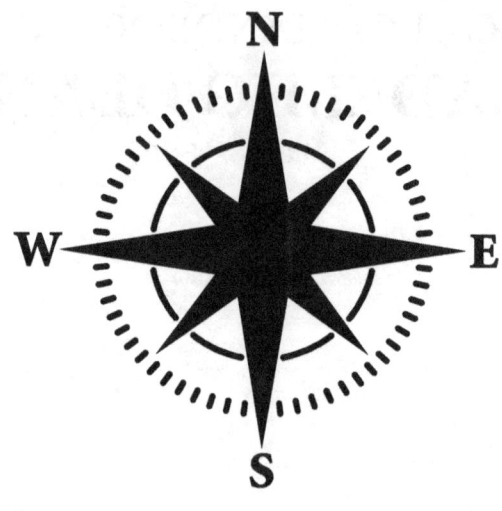

RESOURCE HANDBOOK FOR
ACADEMIC DEANS

THE ESSENTIAL GUIDE FOR COLLEGE AND UNIVERSITY LEADERS

FOURTH EDITION

edited by ANDREW ADAMS

JOHNS HOPKINS UNIVERSITY PRESS

BALTIMORE

Johns Hopkins University Press
2715 North Charles Street
Baltimore, Maryland 21218-4363
www.press.jhu.edu

Library of Congress Cataloging-in-Publication Data

Names: Adams, Andrew (Pianist) editor.
Title: Resource handbook for academic deans : the essential guide for
college and university leaders / Edited by Andrew Adams.
Description: Fourth edition. | Baltimore : Johns Hopkins University Press,
2022. | Includes bibliographical references and index.
Identifiers: LCCN 2021055017 | ISBN 9781421444512 (hardcover) |
ISBN 9781421444529 (ebook)
Subjects: LCSH: Universities and colleges—United States—Administration. |
Deans (Education)—United States.
Classification: LCC LB2341 .B42 2022 | DDC 378.1/11—dc23
LC record available at https://lccn.loc.gov/2021055017

A catalog record for this book is available from the British Library.

Special discounts are available for bulk purchases of this book.
For more information, please contact Special Sales at specialsales@jh.edu.

Contents

I. Leadership Insights

II. Leadership and National Contexts

III. Leadership and Partnerships

IV. Leadership and the Institution

V. Leadership and the College

FOR ACADEMIC LEADERS

Founded in 1945, the American Conference of Academic Deans (ACAD) is an individual membership organization dedicated to the professional development of academic leaders. Recognizing that provosts, deans, and other academic administrators undertake academic leadership as their "second discipline," ACAD's mission is to assist these leaders as they advance in careers dedicated to the ideals of liberal education. Through meetings and workshops relevant to the current and future directions of higher education, ACAD facilitates professional networking across institutional types in order to promote collaboration, innovation, and effective practice.

VISION

ACAD will be recognized as a leader in promoting the effective practice of academic leadership in higher education. Our professional development and networking opportunities will not only expand the expertise of academic leaders but will also advance inclusive excellence in order to meet the changing needs of students, faculty, staff, and society and to foster their success. To these ends, we will also partner with other organizations whenever such partnerships serve the needs of our constituency.

VALUES AND GUIDING PRINCIPLES

In fulfilling its mission, ACAD will be guided by certain values. We will:
- Uphold the highest ethical standards in our work and promote ethical development in our academic communities.
- Foster and support academic freedom.
- Promote within academic communities equity, diversity, and inclusion.
- Encourage innovation by faculty.
- Promote responsible stewardship of resources.

Preface

In his book *Integrity*, Henry Cloud made the case that as we go through life, we leave behind us a wake in the lives of the people around us. The wake has two sides: results and relationships. For academic leaders, results are important—we manage change, move our institutions forward, and build teams. The changes in higher education and the world at large that we have had to contend with in the last several years have been unprecedented. On top of a global pandemic, we have dealt with student demographic shifts, institutional financial stresses, and strong cultural and political crosscurrents at the national level. Managing this change has demanded deep wells of perseverance and wisdom. We also move our programs and institutions forward. This involves a commitment to excellence, shared governance, and shared credit. I am fortunate to have a highly talented leadership team, and we are moving our institution forward thanks to the hard work, skill, and dedication of every team member. I believe that the most important thing that we do as leaders is attract and build strong teams. I find amazing team members, then release, support, and develop them to do their jobs.

On the other side of the wake is relationships. It is crucial that we as leaders build trust, invest in people, and affirm those we serve. Building trust involves being trustworthy. That, along with competence, is what builds trust with senior leaders, faculty, staff, and students. These two ingredients go a long way in creating a culture of trust. We also invest in our team members, faculty, and students. These investments pay dividends into the future that we may or may not see for ourselves. Finally, we affirm those around us. As the CAO of an institution or academic unit, we are the Chief Affirmation

Officer. As we encourage others and provide an example of positivity, we create a healthy relational environment.

This fourth edition of the *Resource Handbook for Academic Deans* provides many contributions that will help you develop both sides of your wake. I have learned so much from my ACAD colleagues, both in person and from their written contributions to the *Resource Handbook, ACAD Leader,* and the ACAD list serve. I hope that you will continue to benefit from the incredible learning resources in this handbook and from interacting with your peers at ACAD conferences. ACAD is thriving because of the many rich contributions of time and talent that numerous members make.

I want to especially thank Andrew Adams and Laura A. Best. Andrew has demonstrated surpassing commitment to ACAD as editor of this volume. His attention to detail, tenacity, and devotion of countless hours have made this an outstanding resource for academic leaders. I am thankful to Laura A. Best, executive director, for her service to ACAD, which now spans seventeen years. Her dedication to ACAD is unparalleled and she has demonstrated great fortitude during a season of change for ACAD.

MIKE WANOUS
Northern State University, Aberdeen, South Dakota
Chair, ACAD Board of Directors

Acknowledgments

ACAD is deeply grateful to the dedicated staff of Johns Hopkins University Press for their expertise and support. This volume was begun and completed during a difficult time for leaders in higher education. Greg Britton, Juliana McCarthy, freelance copyeditor Steven Baker, Adriahna Conway, and others in the Hopkins Press team expertly and sensitively guided ACAD through the process and saw this edition through to its final form. From the leadership and membership of ACAD, our deepest thanks and sincerest appreciation go to our colleagues at Johns Hopkins Press.

Introduction

ANDREW ADAMS

In the first three editions of the *Resource Handbook for Academic Deans*, the American Conference of Academic Deans (ACAD) published nearly eight hundred pages by more than one hundred academic leaders from across the country. The first handbook, printed in 1999, presented twenty-six authors on a range of topics in forty-two chapters. The second edition, in 2007, offered the experience of twenty academic leaders who crafted twenty-seven chapters. And in 2014, our tradition for excellence led to the greatly expanded third edition published by Jossey-Bass. That sprawling 425-page volume of sixty-three chapters contained the work of fifty-one writers.

This small library is a significant accomplishment for any organization, but our passion for leadership continues. Now, with this fourth edition, we're proud and honored to partner with Johns Hopkins University Press, whose reputation for excellence is recognized around the world.

The preparation of this volume began in the spring of 2019 with a rigorous review of our first three editions. A steering committee met that summer and considered the structure for the new volume. Many academic leaders are inspired by the work of Lee Bolman and Terrence Deal and their well-known frames of leadership: structural, human resource, political, and symbolic.[1] Following a similar approach, we sought to examine how leaders engage with national and international events that shape our institutions and how they collaborate with colleagues on and off campus. As detailed below, our principal frames became "Leadership and National Contexts," "Leadership and Partnerships," "Leadership and the Institution," "Leadership and the College," "Leadership and the Units," and "Leadership in the Future and in the Past."

Our work has been a labor of love through challenging times. We solicited ideas for chapters in the early fall of 2020 when the COVID-19 pandemic was in its sixth month. One year later, as the vaccine became available, the future looked brighter. But through the summer of 2021, when writing and editing were at their peak, the virus's Delta variant began to spread rapidly. In the fall of 2019, less than two years ago as I write these words, our most pressing concern was a demographic cliff. Now the sagging lines on enrollment charts are offset by the soaring graphs of infection rates.

But our own anxieties are insignificant. In the past year and a half, our campus and local communities have lost colleagues, students, and neighbors. And in our personal lives we have lost, or know those who have lost, parents, children, family, and friends. Some in higher education may have been personally untouched by the virus but were nonetheless devastated by its effects. Institutions have closed or merged, budgets cut, early retirements encouraged or mandated, faculty lines reassigned, and contingency positions eliminated.

MEMBERSHIP AND AUDIENCE

At the founding meeting of ACAD in Atlantic City in January 1945, our first members compiled a list of duties common to most deans. The items were discussed and refined at the January 1946 conference, and in September of that year ACAD's first secretary-treasurer, Ruth Loving Higgins (1895–1979), drafted a survey of twenty-six open-ended questions and mailed more than four hundred copies across the country. The survey results were presented in the May 1947 edition of the bulletin published by the Association of American Colleges (now the Association of American Colleges and Universities [AAC&U]).[2]

Of particular interest in the report is the way the word "dean" was used. Many of the founding members, like Higgins herself, were provosts in all but name. This can be easily explained: many were dean of *the* college rather than dean of *a* college. In the *Educational Directory of Federal and State School Officers*, published by the Federal Security Agency in 1947, Higgins is listed directly after the president of the institution she then served.[3] The word "provost" does not appear in Higgins's article, and the 1947 directory has only two entries with that title.

If our founding deans were provosts in 1947, who are ACAD members today, almost eight decades later? At its spring meeting in 2019, our board voted to retain the acronym ACAD as an important historic artifact of our organization but to change our logo to read "ACAD: For Academic Leaders." While many ACAD members currently serve as deans, they—like many readers of this book—were once program directors, department heads, or associate deans. Some first became excited about academic leadership by chairing an important committee or serving as faculty members in an institution-wide capacity. Several chapters in this volume are addressed specifically to deans, but there are frequent references throughout these pages to "leaders." ACAD is devoted to leadership as a second discipline, and the challenges and opportunities of leadership often transcend job titles. For decades, ACAD has been proud to offer training sessions and other services for leaders in an array of positions at a broad range of institutional types.

FOCUS AND TONE

In the preface to the first edition of the *Resource Handbook*, editor George Allan wrote, "The handbook should be practical. There are plenty of other venues for providing interpretive frameworks, historical perspectives, psychological analysis, and hortatory expectorations regarding deanliness. . . . [This book] aims at the middle ground: more general than the nitty-gritty, more specific than the theoretical."[4] Two decades later, our goal for the fourth edition is to continue this tradition by crafting a volume that is both helpful and inspiring—offering helpful advice that can be studied in relatively short chapters, and inspiring content based on personal experience that can help academic leaders seeking insights. All of this is accomplished in prose that is professional yet conversational. The dress code for ACAD's conferences is "business casual," and that phrase can also describe the tone of this volume. We embrace writing from the first person, and as you'll see, contractions add to the informal atmosphere.

STRUCTURE AND CONTENT

This volume is divided into seven parts—or seven frames, again to acknowledge the influence of Bolman and Deal. In Part I, "Leadership Insights,"

Philip Glotzbach sets the tone by observing that the authors in this book "have sailed the administrative waters before you and are eager to share their experiences, observations, and insights." Courtney Smith then presents an overview of the theories on leadership by Simon Sinek.

Part II, "Leadership and National Contexts," focuses on our pressing work with diversity, equity, and inclusion. As O. John Maduko notes, these writers "consider how academic leaders can use personal reflection and emotional intelligence to shape concepts and interpretations surrounding diversity, equity, and inclusion in higher education." The final chapter in this section offers insights into "identifying, administering, and revising or creating" campus policies.

In the first chapter of Part III, "Leadership and Partnerships," Margaret Hunter states that "educational institutions are interacting with one another in more and different ways that require new relationships for student success." Each of the chapters in this part explores how colleges and universities collaborate with their surrounding communities or with regional and state educational entities.

The first chapter of Part IV, "Leadership and the Institution," describes how deans work with their provosts; the second offers techniques for building relationships with the development office. The remaining six chapters examine how leaders have collaborated on particular projects that impact entire institutions.

Part V, "Leadership and the College," considers a range of topics such as the dean serving as a role model for wellness, data-informed decision making, working with salaries and the college budget, accreditation processes, and communication. Finally, James M. Sloat's advice in chapter 28 will be invaluable for associate deans.

Part VI, "Leadership and the Units," begins by examining the mentorship of department chairs, then moves to building effective leadership teams, and includes innovative leadership ideas for reframing difficult conversations.

The last section, Part VII, "Leadership in the Future and in the Past," begins with a chapter by Lisa Jasinski on leaving the deanship and charting a future that embraces leading in new ways. This volume concludes with a speech given by William C. DeVane at ACAD's national conference in 1964. Reflecting in part on "the care and feeding of the faculty," DeVane's observations mirror those in the opening chapter by Philip Glotzbach.

* * *

The ACAD Board of Directors and I would like to extend our deepest thanks to Laura A. Best, Executive Director of ACAD. Laura is the organization's bedrock in the best of times; during the pandemic, she has steered us forward with unflagging faith in ACAD's mission. Academic leaders throughout the country have, whether knowingly or unknowingly, been influenced by her expertise for almost two decades. This volume is a testament to her commitment and vision.

NOTES

1. See Lee G. Bolman and Terrence E. Deal, *Reframing Organizations: Artistry, Choice, and Leadership*, 6th ed. (Hoboken, NJ: Jossey-Bass, 2017).
2. Higgins's survey was republished in the April 2021 edition of *The ACAD Leader* and can be found at https://acad.org/newsletter_issue/april-2021/.
3. See Office of Education (Federal Security Agency), *Educational Directory, Part 1: Federal and State School Officers, 1947–1948* (Washington, DC: United States Government Printing Office, 1948), 102.
4. American Conference of Academic Deans, *The Resource Handbook for Academic Deans*, ed. George Allan (Washington, DC: American Conference of Academic Deans, 1999), vi.

PART I

Leadership Insights

CHAPTER 1

A President's Letter
to a New Dean
or Academic Leader

PHILIP A. GLOTZBACH

Leaders see everything with a leadership bias. Their focus is on mobilizing people and leveraging resources to achieve their goals rather than on using their own individual efforts. Leaders who want to succeed maximize every asset and resource they have for the benefit of their organization.

John C. Maxwell

Congratulations on your appointment as academic dean or associate dean, or to *another academic leadership position!*[1] May any feelings of uncertainty or trepidation associated with your arrival in this brave new world be offset by the promise of new opportunities in the unfamiliar landscape that now extends before you. Above all, I hope you are eager to do all you can in your new position to help your institution become an even better place for its students and faculty.

Your life truly has changed—at least for the duration of your administrative tenure and probably for the remainder of your academic career. From this point forward, you'll view both the academic world and your own institution from a different perspective, and don't be surprised when others cast you in an unfamiliar or unexpected light. This certainly will be true if you have just arrived at a new institution. But even if you're continuing at your previous one, you'll notice a change in the attitudes of at least some faculty colleagues and others (perhaps including even some longtime friends). People will expect new things of you. It's now your job to live up to those expectations that are reasonable and to challenge the ones that are not. Above all, as a dean, you'll find yourself in a prime institutional position to help advance the mission of your college or university to achieve its desired learning outcomes for your students.

A dean is, first of all and by historical definition, *the leader of the faculty*. Given faculty members' typical predisposition to resist authority and set their own course, that statement may sound oxymoronic; however, it remains a meaningful description of your new role. Your president is the head of your institution. But they[2] will expect you to live up to your title: to focus on leading your faculty with grace and skill. The responsibility of leadership can revert to the president by default if the dean fails to fulfill it. Don't let this happen on your watch.

The deanship provides a platform from which you can influence an entire institution, or at least an academic division. By working effectively with others, you'll be able to

- Consistently remind your faculty members (and others, including the board of trustees) of your institution's fundamental values and highest strategic priorities
- Play a leadership role in articulating a new academic vision or refining an existing one
- Strengthen curriculum and pedagogy
- Reaffirm and, if necessary, raise academic standards
- Direct resources where they can be used most strategically
- Provide professional development opportunities and other forms of support for your faculty
- Help to shape your faculty for the next twenty to thirty years by influencing hiring, tenure, and promotion decisions
- Play a key role in developing your institution's short- and long-term strategic agendas

Along the way, you'll encounter obstacles that will challenge your intellect and test your spirit. Nevertheless, the position of academic dean can be an incredibly rewarding administrative post.

* * *

The purpose of this fourth edition of the *Resource Handbook for Academic Deans* is to provide useful guidance in fulfilling the many responsibilities of these crucial administrative jobs. If you feel that the task ahead of you is daunting and that you have a lot to learn, you certainly aren't alone. Most incoming deans experience such feelings—and if they don't, they *should*. One inconvenient reason for this fact is that, although your experience as a faculty member was essential to attaining your new position—and doubtless will continue to serve you well—it most likely didn't fully prepare you to succeed in it.

In important ways, faculty work is *analog*: many parts of it are infinitely divisible and extendable. By contrast, much of your administrative work will be *digital*: you'll face an unending series of decisions (many, though by no means all of them, binary) that must be made to meet fixed guidelines. Faculty work today is much more collaborative than in the past; even so, many dimensions remain highly individual. Administrative work, when done well, is primarily collaborative. It involves leadership responsibilities far beyond those typically required of a faculty member. Accordingly, you'll need to adopt a new mind-set and acquire new skills. And odds are, you'll not have the luxury of time in doing so.

In the early days of European oceanic exploration, before longitude could accurately be fixed while at sea, a ship's pilot had to depend on a *rutter*: a highly specialized log that included detailed observations of the currents, weather patterns, physical features, and hazards (e.g., shoals, reefs) one was likely to encounter on a voyage. In short, it provided a wealth of essential information that enabled a pilot to steer his ship (back then, they were all males) safely to its destination and then home again. The rutter was a record of the journey from someone who had successfully traveled there before and *returned*. You might think of this handbook in a similar way. Its authors have sailed the administrative waters before you and are eager to share their experiences, observations, and insights. They offer guidance on conditions and potential hazards you're likely to come across in your own journey.

Of course, no rutter could account for all contingencies on the ever-changing oceans. Pilots always had to rely on their own experience, judgment, and creativity to deal with whatever situation might arise in the moment—especially those occurrences that could place their ship and the lives of those depending on them in peril. So, too, for you. On the storm-tossed and unpredictable seas of academe, there are no administrative algorithms. To cite just one obvious example, no one foresaw the COVID-19 pandemic, much less its enormous implications. Everyone pretty much had to throw out their previous plans and make up new ones on the spot. Deans, especially, had to lead their faculties to develop almost overnight the radically different pedagogical tool kit required to work in an unfamiliar (to say the least) virtual environment. The more general implication is that you should regard virtually every piece of advice you'll encounter as a *heuristic*—a short-cut in reasoning based on experience that can greatly increase your likelihood of attaining success but that can't guarantee it.[3]

In the end, you, too, will be called upon to master each new situation by relying on your own experience, creativity, and judgment, augmented by the advice of trusted colleagues. But always take even the best advice—including my own—with a healthy measure of skepticism. (During the Cuban Missile Crisis, John F. Kennedy was reputed to have remarked that "there is something immoral about abandoning your own judgment."[4]) Past experience won't always prove a reliable guide to present challenges. But this handbook does give you the incomparable advantage of hearing from experienced voyagers who have journeyed there and back before you. Writing as one who made the transition from faculty to administration nearly thirty years ago and, more recently, from the perspective of a president with specific expectations for the academic administrators who served under him, I hope the reflections offered here can be helpful as you embark on this new and exciting stage of your professional life.

This handbook is divided into seven parts organized around different structural aspects of leading in an academic institution and reflecting various dimensions of the portfolio of the dean's office: I. Leadership Insights; II. Leadership and National Contexts; III. Leadership and Partnerships; IV. Leadership and the Institution; V. Leadership and the College; VI. Leadership and the Units; VII. Leadership in the Future and in the Past. Each of these sections explores important aspects of your job, aspects that you'll need to consider as you go about your work and, from time to time, perhaps revisit as circumstances dictate.

Moving our conversation to a more personal level, I offer some practical advice about taking advantage of the opportunities and overcoming the challenges you'll encounter as a new academic leader.

TWO PILLARS OF DECANAL SUCCESS: COMMITMENT TO INSTITUTIONAL VALUES AND EARNING TRUST

Leadership is the art of enabling people to accomplish together what they cannot do individually. Easily said; not always so easily done. To succeed in your new position, you'll need to think more seriously about leadership than ever before: you'll need, in effect, to become a *student of leadership*. Specifically, you must actively develop your own leadership abilities and intentionally cultivate leadership within both your own administrative team and the faculty—especially among department and committee chairs but also among both new and established faculty members at large. You'll be the administrative point person in dealing with problems that arise within the academic division. At the same time, you must be the primary cheerleader for your faculty members, their principal advocate within the administration, and a leading proponent of the intellectual life of your institution. To achieve these ends, you'll need to care deeply about what the faculty is thinking, saying, and doing.[5]

Before going any further, let me pose two fundamental questions: First, *Why did you want to become a dean in the first place?* There really is only one good response: *Becoming an academic administrator should be an act of service to your institution, based on your internalization of its core academic values.* Period.

Above all else, the mission of your college or university should serve as the polar star of your work. Always place your institution first, other people second, and yourself third. If you focus instead on advancing your career, you'll make decisions that adversely affect both your division and its people—and, ultimately, your professional prospects. Your faculty and administrative colleagues are intelligent. Be assured that, sooner or later, they'll discover your real agenda and judge you accordingly.

In other words, *this job is not about you; so check your ego at the door.* Don't expect people to appreciate your many admirable traits; instead, work intentionally on appreciating *theirs*. And if their virtues aren't readily apparent, look harder until you find them. *Share the credit; take the blame.* The legendary football coach Bear Bryant used to say, "If anything goes bad, I did it. If anything goes semi-good we did it. If anything goes really good, then you did it."[6] Grammar aside, these are words to lead by. Remember that the more you praise yourself, the less others will feel the need to do so.

Always look for things to appreciate in what others are doing; write lots of thank-you notes and e-mails. People will appreciate receiving them, and it's a great way to reinforce good behavior. Sometimes people will let you know when they value something you've done. It's useful to keep a file of thank-you messages you receive. They'll help to remind you that some people do, in fact, notice what you're doing, and glancing at them from time to time can help to revive your spirits on a tough day. Just don't accept everything you read at face value. Ultimately, you need to take satisfaction from the results of your efforts, not from the recognition of others. *To be a successful dean, always concentrate on doing what's best for your institution, and your career will take care of itself.*

And now the second basic question: *Why should anyone be willing to follow you?* Here, too, there is one overriding answer: *trust.* If you enable them to trust you, people will be prepared to follow your lead—even when they might not fully agree with the course you're setting. Your position does carry significant authority, and you shouldn't hesitate to use it appropriately. But a skilled dean exercises effective leadership in a variety of ways—most importantly through persuasion and less frequently through the application of power. Weak and ineffective leaders want the power to tell everyone what to do; strong and effective leaders find ways of bringing people together to advance a common agenda. Indeed, a shared vision that has been developed collaboratively is the one most likely to be realized.

Effective administration, therefore, is fundamentally about relationships, not transactions. Robust, enduring relationships enable people to work together. No matter how well intentioned you are or how brilliant your ideas, you will fail as a leader if people refuse to work with you. As the cliché has it, people will not care how much you know until they know how much you care. You don't need to be the smartest person in the room or the one with all the good ideas—and no one *ever* has all the good ideas. You'll succeed as a leader if you facilitate effective collaboration and shared decision making that take full advantage of the collective wisdom of your colleagues. You and your fellow collaborators won't always see eye to eye. The working relationships you cultivate need to be strong enough to survive disagreement.

Relationships ultimately stand or fall on the basis of trust. Many things will come with your new title. Unfortunately, trust is not necessarily one of them. You'll need to earn it—initially, perhaps, in the face of cautious faculty skepticism or even outright distrust. The atmosphere you initially encounter will be shaped in large part by the actions of your predecessor(s), over which you quite obviously have no control.

Start by being generous in offering your trust to others; withhold it only when someone has demonstrated that they'll abuse it. This doesn't at all mean you should be naïve. Ronald Reagan was right to say, "Trust but verify."[7] In other words, never trust blindly; it's appropriate to look for evidence that your trust is well placed. But always open by offering trust and assuming the competence and goodwill of those with whom you are interacting. Then be prepared to decide when someone has subverted your trust.

Develop a reputation for fairness, honesty, and consistency, and trust will follow. Your institution (indeed, the academic world as a whole) is a small village. Assume that what you say about someone will get back to them. In fact, when talking about a third party, a good heuristic is to imagine them to be present in the conversation. Never play favorites. Be especially transparent and clear in your reasoning when you need to make an exception to a rule, or when you have to do something that might appear inconsistent with your previous practice or statements. Never fail to consider the way an action or decision will look from the perspective of whomever it will most directly affect. Ask yourself how *you* would feel if you were in their situation. Consider, as well, how your decision will look to others who can't know all the inside details.

Always mean what you say, and internalize the following mantra: "I am *never* not the dean (associate dean etc.)." There are no throwaway lines in your script. Every sentence you utter always comes from the dean. As a professor, you could brainstorm with colleagues, try out crazy ideas, and make immodest (or even outrageous) proposals with relative impunity. In your new role, and especially at the beginning of your deanship, you'll need to do such blue-sky thinking most often with other administrators and much less frequently with faculty colleagues—and only in settings where everyone understands and accepts the ground rules about what can and can't be more broadly shared. Remember that the half-baked thought you toss off and immediately forget may be remembered by someone else as a promise (or threat) and repeated to others. Prepare to have your most benign, innocuous, or well-intentioned statements and actions scrutinized, overinterpreted, sometimes misinterpreted, or blown out of proportion. It goes with the territory. *So pay close attention to what you say. Always.*

People must know they can trust you with extremely sensitive information. As a dean, you will encounter facts to which most people in your institution can't have access—including details about some of your faculty or staff colleagues that you would rather not know. Dealing with this burden of confidential information is an inescapable dimension of your job. Develop a track record for absolute reliability in respecting confidences. And understand that some of your most significant achievements as a dean will involve matters that can never be discussed, much less celebrated, beyond a very small inner administrative circle.

People must be able to trust you to keep your promises. Few actions build trust more effectively than keeping promises. If people see that you follow through on the commitments you make, they'll come to rely on you. Never forget that the inverse is equally true. Failing to keep promises destroys trust, and, unhappily, it takes much less time to lose trust than to build it. Therefore, resolve to do what you say you'll do.

Be impatient with yourself but patient with others. Paradoxically, some of the very strengths you relied upon as a faculty member and that brought you to this juncture—especially mental quickness and facility in driving a discussion forward—can undermine your success as a dean. Stephen Covey advises that one "seek first to understand, then to be understood."[8] Take this advice to heart. Demonstrate to people that *before* proffering your own opinion, you'll *actively* listen to them. Acknowledge and credit what others are saying *prior to* articulating a contrary perspective. Make doubly sure you fully understand what you're about to oppose. Your position gives you access to data and information not readily available to those outside the administration. So, when sharing that information, give people a chance to catch up and process what has become familiar to you but may be new to them. Concentrate on giving others the time they need to think through an issue at their own pace, not yours. Let them finish expressing their thoughts, even when it seems clear to you where they are heading. (Sometimes they'll surprise you.) Value their participation in the decision-making process and honor their contributions to it.

Be mindful of your own fallibility. Even when you're convinced you're right, you still might turn out to be wrong. Descartes to the contrary, very strong feelings of certainty never guarantee that one actually knows. As Wittgenstein observed, "One always forgets the expression, 'I thought I knew.'"[9] In this spirit, be tolerant of disagreement and strive to create a climate—especially within your leadership team—in which contrasting views can be explored constructively. Remember, your colleagues will take their cues not necessarily from what you say but from what you *do*.

Even if your thinking is correct as far as it goes, someone else may still have a better idea or one that takes the conversation in a different, more helpful direction. Be open to those possibilities. There are many worthy goals and even more pathways to reach them. Develop the art of encouraging others to collaborate with you in thinking through problems; when possible, engage them early in the process. Earn a reputation for valuing the ideas of others. Show that you have a tough skin, can tolerate criticism, enjoy vigorous discussion, and can hold your own in fierce conversations. Model staying in the room. Always be grateful when someone shows you a better way to think about an issue. Displaying a willingness to acknowledge when you were wrong—and to change your mind in light of new facts or superior arguments—is a powerful way to build credibility and, once again, trust.

Cultivating awareness of your own fallibility will also help you *practice genuine humility.* No one expects a dean (not even you) to be perfect. More administrators crash and burn because of hubris than from lack of intelligence or ability. Own up to your mistakes and learn from them. Just try to avoid having to do so often. Always strive to make *new* mistakes as you go forward; people will have little patience if you keep making the same ones over and over. Indeed, "making *new* mistakes" is a good working definition of *learning*.

Finally, *maintain your sense of humor.* Being able to lighten up a tense moment and, more significantly, to laugh at your own foibles shows that you aren't overly impressed with yourself and encourages others to relate to you as a human being—not as someone defined entirely by their position.

EFFECTIVENESS AND EFFICIENCY MATTER

People will judge your performance as an administrator by what you are able to accomplish—or, more tellingly, by what your academic division or institution as a whole is able to accomplish during your administrative tenure. Leaders get no style points for trying.[10] *It is far better to complete a few high-priority projects than to work on many and finish none.* Finish what you start.

Look to begin your administrative term with some early successes, even if they're mostly symbolic or don't necessarily reflect your institution's long-term strategic priorities. Pick one or two objectives you can accomplish that will be perceived as making an immediate difference. Let people see that you are able to get things done. Similar advice applies later in your administrative term. Identify those specific initiatives that will make the most progress toward realizing strategic goals. Focus on what is most readily achievable *now*. Remember the motto of the Navy Seabees: "The difficult we do immediately; the impossible takes a little longer." An objective may be strategically important but unrealizable at a given moment. If so, defer it. You can always return it to your agenda later on—when people are ready to consider and help achieve it, or when necessary resources are in place. Allow time for conditions to change: what previously seemed impossible may then be conceivable.

Efficiency really does matter. *Peer administrators, faculty members, and others will judge your effectiveness, in part, by the efficiency of your office.* In other words, they'll ultimately ascribe the efficiency—or *lack* of efficiency—of your staff and subordinates to you.

They'll begin by observing how well you manage your staff and by how effectively you and your people move work along. In transitioning from the faculty to administration, your effectiveness will be determined in no small part by how well you *turn over to others* much of the paperwork and other tasks (e.g., keeping up with your correspondence, managing your calendar) that for so long, as a faculty member, you had to do for yourself.

Be intentional about sharing authority and power with your staff. Develop strong working relationships with them. Help them earn your trust and find ways to expand their sphere of autonomy. If you can't trust a team member implicitly and without reservation, then you need either to discover (or build) a basis for that trust or replace them. Clearly articulate the specific responsibilities of everyone in your office, so people will know to whom they should direct their questions and requests. Then provide your colleagues with the resources—and delegate the *authority*—they need to do their jobs. But always be aware that *you can't delegate responsibility*; ultimately, responsibility percolates up to you.

See to it that information flows effectively in and out of your office and is managed well in between. Never let your office become an institutional black hole into which communications vanish, never to be seen again. *The worst possible use of your time is searching for a misplaced piece of paper.* Discipline yourself to touch a piece of paper (or e-mail) once. Think *RFRR: Respond* to it; *File* it (if necessary, create a new file or duplicate and consolidate them later); *Refer* it to your assistant or to a subordinate; or *Relegate* it to the trash. Alternatively, think *OHIO*: Only Handle It Once.

Taming the office paper monster requires more than just your personal attention and action.[11] You need to ensure that you and your staff employ an effective paper management and filing system—one that is organized according to the central recurring tasks in your portfolio (e.g., curriculum, departments, faculty, diversity and inclusion, shared governance, personnel and tenure reviews, student matters, board of trustees, accreditation, assessment). Make sure your executive assistants understand the importance of having an effective document management system—especially for tracking and managing your correspondence. If necessary, collaborate with them to design one. You may find it helpful to distinguish the various categories through color coding your files. (Color-coded files are easier to distinguish and locate than homogenous manila folders.) Determine which system makes the best sense to you and your team. But do it. You may have only a brief window in which to accomplish this (re)organization early in your tenure; alternatively, after having served, say, for a year, you might be better positioned to understand and implement any required changes. You'll need to make that call. But, either way, you're ultimately responsible for how your office functions. So take the time to ensure that your processes are effective and that everyone is on board in using them. Then give ongoing attention to your office's workflow and include it in your staff members' annual evaluations. It's extremely difficult, if not impossible, to achieve what you're unable (or unwilling) to measure and assess.

Give your executive assistant(s) the guidelines they need to manage your calendar and your daily workflow. Agree on rules for prioritizing meetings and schedule regular desk time for yourself. Make sure everyone's priorities are aligned. For example, if your assistant's top priority is to schedule everyone who wants to meet with you ASAP, you'll soon find your days fully booked with meetings, with no time to do the other work that falls to you—a formula for disaster. Also try to reserve some time in each day to deal with the unexpected and unplanned problems that inevitably crop up.

As part of this process, make sure your assistant is skilled in communicating with those outside your office clearly and in ways that reflect your values. Remember that everything *they* say—and *how* they say it—will be attributed directly to *you*. For example, *never* let your assistant tell someone that "the dean is too busy" to respond immediately to their question or issue. Collaborate with your staff to develop language for them to use in letting people know you'll attend to their concerns and that someone (not necessarily *you*) will get back to them before too long. It also helps to set a deadline for this return; even if it's just a date for your assistant to initiate a follow-up tracking contact. Enable your staff to guard your time without walling you off from—and annoying—those people who want to see you. Overall, the objective is for your staff to manage your schedule without making people feel unimportant, even when they can't gain immediate access to you.

Decide how to process the notes from all the meetings that will occupy such a large portion of your time, and follow your system religiously. As you take notes, identify follow-up items to which you must attend personally and distinguish them from those you'll delegate to others.[12] Develop a system for your assistant to create and manage your project follow-up list to ensure that nothing gets lost and to keep you on schedule in meeting commitments. Your assistant then can inform others on the progress of key tasks, letting people know that you haven't forgotten about their concerns.

Your efficiency and effectiveness as a leader begin with learning to resist upward delegation. Don't assume you have to solve every problem someone wants to deposit on your desk. Most problems, in fact, turn out to belong to someone else—usually the one who is trying to delegate them to you. Your first task, therefore, is to identify the right person or group to address the issue. *Always* ask, "Whose problem is it; who should own it?" *Always* stop before you commit to assuming a task and ask yourself the following, "Is this something I *can* and *should* do?" "How does it fit in with my preexisting priorities and commitments?" "If I *am* going to do it, then by *when?*" *Never* take on responsibility for a project that legitimately should belong to someone else.

As I said above: mind what you promise. It's much easier to explain in advance why you can't (or shouldn't) do what someone wants, than it is to explain after the fact why you failed to fulfill a carelessly made commitment. Once you've determined whose problem it is, collaborate with that person to identify the next step(s) in the process and encourage the owner to return later and report on *their* progress. This way, you are coaching them on resolving their issue, as opposed to allowing them to hand it off to you—and then expecting you to report back to them on the progress you've made. Always be clear about who reports to whom.[13]

Through both your own leadership and the composition of your leadership team, demonstrate that diversity matters to you. I'm certain I don't need to emphasize the importance of being knowledgeable about the issues of social and racial justice that recently have received increased attention in both our society at large (especially among white populations) and on our campuses. But you also need to make sure that your colleagues are well versed in this area. Also ensure that your office is free from sexual harassment and other forms of toxic behavior.

Beyond having theoretical expertise, also show that you're aware of the power of leading a diverse team—diverse across a variety of dimensions of social identity. Creating such a team demonstrates to all members of your institution (especially to your faculty and students, two groups that will be watching) that you value the contributions of a broad range of individuals. Certainly, a knowledgeable and diverse leadership team is better positioned to deal with diversity-related issues as they arise on your campus. And make no mistake, such issues *will* arise during your term in office.

A growing body of research has shown that diverse teams are better at making good decisions generally—across all areas of their portfolio—than more homogeneous groups. Having a variety of backgrounds represented on your leadership team increases the probability that your people can draw upon a wider range of expertise, experience, metaphors, and analogies than would otherwise be the case. Scott Page has referred to this as the "diversity bonus," and realizing its power can provide a crucial edge to your effectiveness as an academic leader.[14]

BE PREPARED TO GIVE "TOUGH LOVE"

People want to know *who you are and what you stand for*. They'll need to understand your academic vision, of course, and sometimes you'll need to talk about your values. But, as I've already emphasized, the most significant messages will come through your actions. Following Machiavelli, understand that it's far more important for a dean to be respected than to be liked—or loved.[15] There will be times, especially, when you need to make and *own* a difficult decision or take a tough or unpopular action in the face of opposition.

One key way you establish your values is by saying "no." It's almost never a good idea to say "no" just for the sake of doing so. But be very clear—first, to yourself, and then to others—about what you are and are *not* prepared to accept. Others will notice. If you operate with integrity and transparency about your decision-making processes and the justifications for your judgments (to the extent that confidentiality allows), others will respect you, even if they disagree with your conclusions.

You also establish your values by what you praise. It usually feels good to complement someone, but always do so thoughtfully and judiciously. Keep in mind that it's much easier to step up your praise later on, if and when it is merited, than to take back unwarranted praise once you've gone too far. If you're too casual with what and whom you praise, you'll devalue your words, and people will learn to ignore them.

* * *

Conflicts happen, and you must be prepared to fight when necessary. The most experienced and effective leaders consistently strive to anticipate possible conflicts and take steps to prevent them from becoming actual. It's helpful to remember Sun Tzu's observation that "a skillful general must defeat the enemy without coming to battle."[16] By thinking ahead and having awareness of the institutional environment, the truly strategic leader is able to diffuse problems in advance or neutralize opposition before it can coalesce into an effective force. To do so requires experience and judgment, combined with a robust information network—people who are willing to let you know of potential issues that are out there. For a dean, this network starts with effective associate dean(s); they can frequently be your best eyes and ears regarding the faculty. Combining good information with experience allows you to think several moves ahead of a potential adversary. Not an easy assignment, yet it needs to be another of your professional objectives.

I've emphasized that developing positive relationships and fostering collaboration are crucial elements in your success as a leader. But even the most experienced and competent dean can't avoid every conflict. Despite your best efforts, on (one hopes) rare occasions, relationships can break down and collaboration can become impossible. At that point, you need to employ alternative tactics.

Part of earning people's respect is showing them they can't cross you with impunity. Let me emphasize that I'm not talking about mere disagreement. Rather, I'm talking about someone who "crosses" you in a moral sense: who reneges on an important promise, lies to you or about you, violates a confidence, deliberately ignores an important process protocol, or does something else that damages your institution. In such instances, people will look to you to gauge your response, and what you say and do will speak volumes about your integrity and about what kind of leader you are prepared to be.

Therefore, *it's essential to know what you're willing to fight for and what you're prepared to do to preserve a core institutional or personal value.* Deciding when to do battle and when to let something go is always an act of judgment. Once again, there's no algorithm to help you make such a decision—other than to say that you must *never* compromise on your basic values. Always pick your battles carefully. Even if you are in the right, some fights are just not worth the collateral damage—to the institution, to your relationships, or to you personally.

Next, *if you must fight, always fight to win.* As Viper (played by actor Tom Skerritt), the commander of the training squadron in the movie *Top Gun,* informs his new class of hotshot fighter pilots, "In combat there are no points for second place."[17] When it becomes necessary to call people on unacceptable behavior, fighting and winning might simply mean having a frank but difficult conversation.[18] Of course, it's better to do this privately, but on occasion it will need to happen in public. Other situations may require more aggressive tactics. And sometimes it's just a matter of staying in office long enough for an adversary to take a job elsewhere or retire. In any event, remain mindful of your basic values; always fight hard but fair. Make sure you could defend each of your actions in the public arena if you were called upon to do so.

Finally, *when it's over, remember you're still on the same team.* From time to time, we all need "a shot at redemption."[19] Be prepared to forgive and forget what's now in the past, and work to rebuild any damaged relationships. Then return to collaborating. Develop a long memory for good deeds and a short recall for transgressions. Cultivating a generous spirit will serve you well by encouraging others to trust you, willingly work with you, and enjoy doing so.

PRACTICE ADMINISTRATIVE INTEGRITY

Administrative privileges entail corresponding responsibilities—another obvious point but one worth reflecting upon. Your position gives you access to the highest levels of institutional decision making, and with that seat in the room where it happens comes a capacity to influence policy that no one outside administrative circles (e.g., on the faculty) can possess. Yet this level of access comes with a price. As a dean, you relinquish any right to complain to the faculty about administrative matters—for example, about not carrying the day in a budget or policy decision or about the bad behavior of an administrative colleague. In fact, you now have three options, as you participate in administrative deliberations: (1) Persuade others to adopt your position, be persuaded by them to accept their views, or collaborate in crafting a compromise; (2) accept and implement a decision with which you disagree but can live with because it doesn't violate some fundamental value, without communicating your disagreement beyond the administration; or (3) resign your position.

There simply is no legitimate fourth option—for example, going back to the faculty (or any other person or group outside the administration) to continue fighting a lost battle. Nor can you publicly blame your president, provost, vice-provost for academic affairs (VPAA), or the board of trustees for an unpopular decision. And you certainly can't blame a staff member who, after all, reports to *you*.[20] *Never* bring an internal administrative conflict back to the faculty or publicly position yourself with the faculty (or any other group) in opposition to your president (or your dean, if you're an associate dean) or to the trustees. Doing so may provide you a short-term advantage with some constituency, but in the long run it can only fragment the faculty itself or divide it from the administration or the board. No president (or provost) worth their salt will countenance such behavior. Nor should you countenance it in anyone who reports to you.

Be proactive in supporting your boss. Anticipate the information they're likely to need from you, and provide it before you're asked. Alert them if they're about to make a damaging misstep. Make sure they hear bad news from you first, and as soon as you come to possess it. Your boss needs to know that you'll be honest in telling them what they need to hear, as opposed to what they might *want* to hear. And if your boss isn't prepared to talk honestly with you or hear inconvenient facts, then I suggest you begin looking for another position.

Never bring your boss a problem without also suggesting at least one or two possible solutions. Regardless of whether you report directly to your president, never surprise them in a meeting where others are present. Most emphatically, *never* do so in front of the board of trustees. Remember, just as your primary constituency is the faculty, your president's is the board. These principles reflect common administrative courtesy. But following them also will give your superior(s) confidence—that is to say, *trust*—both that you know what you're doing and that you're a reliable colleague.

Prepare a yearly written plan of goals and major projects. Review the plan with your immediate superior and refer to it throughout the year. On an ongoing basis, collaborate with your boss to set priorities and manage your workload. It can be helpful, when facing a new potential addition to an already overfull plate, to ask your boss to help you decide which other priorities to defer or remove from your agenda altogether. Track your progress in achieving your goals and prepare an annual written self-assessment. Keep a file of accomplishments. It'll be useful when you prepare your annual report to your boss, which you should do whether you're asked for one or not, or when you revise your CV. Require your staff to do these things as well, and make them the basis for their annual evaluations.

TAKE CARE OF YOURSELF AND
REMAIN TRUE TO WHO YOU ARE

As a dean, you are still a teacher. In your administrative role, instead of students, you're now responsible for teaching members of your faculty (especially department chairs, program directors, committee chairs, and the like), other administrators, and even your president and members of the board. You might think of yourself as running an extended graduate seminar on shared governance, diversity and inclusion, curriculum, pedagogy, institutional history, and leadership, along with other key dimensions of your portfolio.

An essential part of your job is to advocate for the academic programs in your college or university, but this advocacy can never go in just one direction. You also need your faculty members to understand the larger institutional context in which they serve, just as you help other administrators understand the academic perspective.[21] Similarly, you must help department chairs learn to function as mediators between their departments and the overall school or college in which they're located. Effective mediation requires one to understand—and acknowledge—legitimate concerns occurring on *both* sides of the relationship and a willingness to advocate in both directions. Sometimes doing so entails giving people unpopular news and, therefore, requires courage. A telling dimension of your decanal responsibilities is to model that kind of courage (e.g., for department chairs) and then to expect and inspire others to display it as well in dealing with their faculty colleagues.

Don't sacrifice your body to your job. Unlike a faculty position, in which the year is broken up by academic terms and breaks that give time to recover and shift focus, administrative responsibilities are relentless and ongoing. Despite the rhythm of the academic year, which will be reflected in differing demands on your time and attention, the dean's office sees precious little downtime. In truth, it's easier for faculty members to organize their schedule than it is for a dean. As busy as they are, professors simply do not face the range of unrelenting demands that accompany an administrative position—the demands now falling to you. It's essential to prioritize what you take on, and to be proactive in preventing your to-do list from becoming overwhelming to the point of failure.

It's a good idea to become more intentional about self-care than you might have been in the past. Discipline yourself to eat well, remain physically active, and get enough sleep.[22] (If you need a brief daily nap, have your assistant build it into your schedule.) Let the person who manages your calendar in on the secret; have them include regular time for exercise (or runs, yoga, or whatever), if possible. Take vacations that get you out of the office for blocks of time during which you can reconnect with yourself and the significant others in your life—times for personal renewal. Vince Lombardi frequently remarked that "fatigue makes cowards of us all." Granted, the demands of your job as a dean can easily override your best intentions and attempts at self-preservation. But overly tired deans make mistakes. You'll be no good to anyone if you let your physical condition deteriorate. Care enough for yourself (and for your friends and family members who love you) to do what it takes to stay physically healthy.

Don't sacrifice your mind to your job. Reserve regular time in your schedule to plan and reflect; again, let your assistant know that this is a priority because it's necessary to your success. If you don't make time on your calendar, you won't do it. Make it a point always to be reading something that interests you that is not directly related to your administrative job. It'll keep your mind alive, and you never know when you'll encounter an idea or metaphor that will contribute to a project or suggest a solution to a problem you're working to resolve. As your schedule permits, attend intellectual and cultural events on campus. In addition to broadening your mind, it's always helpful to have others see you participating in the life of the institution.

If possible, stay connected to your academic discipline and keep your hand in teaching. But if this proves impossible—and it frequently is impossible in these administrative positions—you still can (and must) stay connected to current developments in the broader world of ideas. Try to devote some time every day (even just a few minutes) to learning something new. Your faculty colleagues need to respect what you bring to discussions. Talk with them about what's on *their* minds—not just about what's on yours.

Don't sacrifice your spirit to your job. As you're probably tired of hearing, deans face relentless demands. Issues arise without warning and beyond your ability to control. Facing these challenges year in and year out can wear anyone down. Your position also calls upon you to be at your best when the stakes are highest, precisely when a misstep could prove most costly. It's easy to feel isolated and even fearful. In truth, many (if not most or all) leaders in every line of work experience such feelings, though few admit it. Your experience is not likely to be different from theirs. In the end, to serve effectively, you'll have to find the resources to overcome your anxiety and manage your overall mental health. But, in doing so, realize that you are never alone. Seek counsel from your administrative colleagues and superiors. Asking them for advice or assistance is a sign of your respect for them. They, in turn, should respect you for doing so, and they should be more than willing to offer suggestions and support. Admitting your difficulties to others also helps you to remain humble.

No matter how crazy or idiosyncratic they may seem to you, the challenges you encounter will be familiar to your counterparts at other institutions. Build relationships with both regional and national professional colleagues, and develop a network of deans (or associate deans) at other institutions whom you respect and trust. Seek their advice. Become a resource for them. Create opportunities for mutual professional support and renewal. If you're not already a member, join the American Conference of Academic Deans (ACAD). Attend professional meetings regularly. Talk about your most difficult problems, and share success stories as well. You should be able to trust that what is discussed in these circles will remain within those circles.

CONCLUDING UNSCIENTIFIC POSTSCRIPT

Always remember why you entered the academy in the first place—presumably for a love of learning in general and your own discipline in particular, along with the intrinsic values you discovered there. An institution should nurture a flourishing life of the mind, body, and spirit, and its ultimate success is measured in the educational and personal development of its students. Your job is to help make it so. Therefore, always consider the following two questions when deliberating a course of action: *Will this decision serve to enhance or diminish my institution's values and its capacity to fulfill its fundamental educational mission?* And, more specifically, *How will this decision affect our students?*

To be an excellent dean, you need to respect and, yes, *love* your institution, its faculty, and its students. No one expects a college, faculty member, or student to be perfect. In the end, we're all just poor, dumb, fallible human beings. But these relationships should be marked by love all the same—even if you're sometimes called upon to provide some "tough love," as I say above. If you can't find it in yourself to develop such a profound level of caring and affection for your faculty, students, and institution, you need to find another job. But, assuming you do experience these emotions, take the risk of letting others know how deeply and powerfully you feel connected to your school and its people. As the leader of the faculty, you need to demonstrate the depth of your personal care.

In sum, as an academic dean or administrative leader, you're called upon to be efficient, patient, ethical, courageous, visionary, witty, and wise, among many other things. A daunting list, to be sure. But if others didn't see these traits in you, you wouldn't have been appointed to your position in the first place. Even so, no one (reasonably) expects you to be perfect in your decision making or, much less, a moral saint. Truth be told, there were too many times in my own administrative career when I failed to heed some of the advice I've been passing along so assertively to you.

The important thing is not to never fall but always to get back up again. Babe Ruth once said, "It is impossible to beat someone who never gives up."[23] Resolve to display that level of determination in the face of whatever obstacles are thrown in your way. You'll need it. And even as you remain cognizant of your own limitations and practice humility, be honest in affirming your strengths. Just as you must know your faculty, follow the Socratic imperative and make sure that you know yourself best of all.

In the final analysis, as I've emphasized, no one can tell you how to make the key decisions that will shape your deanship. You have to develop your own capacities for judgment and then trust your instincts. Approach challenging situations as experiments whose success or failure will be determined not *a priori* but after the fact—by the results your decisions and actions produce. In making these inductive judgments, you'll find that an abiding commitment to the core values of your institution and a steadfast focus on the importance of the work you have taken on will serve you well. If you persist in maintaining that focus and commitment throughout your tenure in office, you'll have a profound and lasting influence on the direction of your division and institution.

Virtually all of our schools are dealing with profound challenges—financial, regulatory, political, ideological, and other trials that place in question not only our institutions' core values but also, in some cases, their very survival. Not to mention the enormous issues created by the COVID-19 pandemic and its effects, which will linger long after this book's publication. Moments of great adversity also present great opportunities. It's a good bet that you have within you the capacity to provide the leadership your institution requires. If those opportunities aren't obvious, make it part of your job to help bring them to light.

In the end, recognizing the difference you've made will provide you an enormous sense of professional and personal satisfaction. Indeed, many people who've moved from a deanship to other positions (e.g., a presidency) will tell you they enjoyed their time in the dean's office more than in any other administrative position. That certainly was true for me. My final and fondest hope is that you, too, will have just such an experience: May your own time in the dean's office become one of the enduring highlights of *your* professional career!

— *Takeaways* —

- Place the highest importance on your institution and its values, and build robust relationships of trust that will encourage people to follow you. Be the kind of dean *you* would like to work with or for.
- After your integrity and your intelligence, your time and attention are your most important assets. Ensure that you and your staff collaborate effectively to make the best use of these essential resources. Never take on a project that legitimately belongs to someone else.
- To succeed as a dean, you must be respected. Avoid conflict whenever possible. But when you must fight, always fight to win. Remem-

ber that in combat there are no points for second place. If you really want to be loved, get a dog.

- It's as important to build trust with your superior(s) as it is with your staff inside the dean's office and your colleagues beyond it. Give all of them numerous reasons to trust you and respect your work.
- Even as you place yourself third (behind your institution and its people), remember to take care of yourself. You need to bring your best and most resilient self to this complex and demanding position.

NOTES

1. Earlier versions of this article appeared in the second and third editions of the ACAD *Resource Handbook*; it has been revised and expanded for this edition. Although almost everything I say applies to deans, associate deans, and other academic administrators, for the sake of efficiency I'll primarily reference the position of dean.
2. Here and throughout the handbook, the other authors and I follow the convention of using "they" instead of gendered pronouns.
3. See, for example, Thomas Gilovich, Dale Griffin, and Daniel Kahneman, ed., *Heuristics and Biases: The Psychology of Intuitive Judgment* (Cambridge: Cambridge University Press, 2002). See also Daniel Kahneman, *Thinking, Fast and Slow* (New York: Farrar, Straus and Giroux, 2011). As the literature on this topic makes abundantly clear, heuristics necessarily incorporate systematic biases that which one needs to take into account.
4. The quotation is from the film *Thirteen Days* (Beacon Pictures, 2000).
5. General George S. Patton remarked that a leader needs to command one echelon down but know what is happening two echelons down. This is a useful way to think about the dean's job. Though Patton's style didn't necessarily represent a good model for an academic dean, he was an astute student of leadership, and one can learn a great deal from studying him.
6. Paul W. Bryant with Gene Stallings, *Bear Bryant on Winning Football* (New York: Simon and Schuster, 1983).
7. Reagan repeated this phrase frequently—especially in the context of arms negotiations with the Soviet Union. Ironically, as he was aware, Reagan was quoting one of Lenin's favorite Russian proverbs.
8. Stephen Covey, *The Seven Habits of Highly Effective People* (New York: Simon and Schuster, 1989), chapter 5.
9. Ludwig Wittgenstein, *On Certainty*, ed. G. E. M. Anscombe and G. H. von Wright, trans. Denis Paul and G. E. M. Anscombe (Oxford: Basil Blackwell, 1969), 12.
10. John Maxwell has made this point. If you are a *Star Wars* fan, Yoda's celebrated injunction to Luke Skywalker provides another useful mantra: "Try not! Do. Or do not. There is no 'try.'" *Star Wars Episode V: The Empire Strikes Back* (Lucasfilm / Twentieth Century Fox, 1980).

11. There is a book by this title: Amy Beth Miller, Jessica Fagerhaugh, and Neil Griffin, *Taming the Paper Monster* (New York: National Institute of Business Management, 2002).

12. Levenger's "Annotation Ruled" note pads (which come in various sizes and colors) represent one commercial product that makes it easy to differentiate a to-do list from informational notes. There certainly are other options—including creating your own unique note-taking structure. But it really is worth the effort to decide how you want to do this. So create an effective system and then employ it consistently.

13. A *short* book on this topic that should be required reading for any new administrator is *The One Minute Manager Meets the Monkey* by Kenneth Blanchard, William Oncken Jr., and Hal Burrows (New York: HarperCollins, 1989).

14. See Scott Page, Earl Lewis, and Nancy Cantor, introduction to *The Diversity Bonus: How Great Teams Pay Off in the Knowledge Economy* (Princeton, NJ: Princeton University Press, 2019).

15. Discerning readers will note that I've taken a liberty here. In *The Prince*, Machiavelli considers the merits of a prince's being loved versus his being *feared*—probably the right contrast for sixteenth-century Italy, but certainly not the right one for the twenty-first-century dean's office. Today, a dean who is feared by the faculty (or others) is most likely dysfunctional and destined for a limited term of office. On the other hand, a dean who is *respected* can lead effectively and serve long enough to accomplish important work. Cf. Niccolò Machiavelli, *The Prince*, in *The Portable Machiavelli*, ed. and trans. Peter Bondanella and Mark Musa (New York: Penguin Books, 1979), chapter 17, pp. 130–33.

16. There are multiple translations and editions of Sun Tzu's classic text, *The Art of War*. One of the most beautifully done and informative, because it also includes a number of historical case studies, is *The Art of War Illustrated*, trans. James Trapp (London: Amber Books Ltd., 2018). The cited passage appears on p. 29.

17. *Top Gun* (Paramount Pictures, 1988).

18. Not surprisingly there's a whole literature on this topic. One of the best is *Fierce Conversations: Achieving Success in Work and in Life, One Conversation at a Time*, by Susan Scott (New York: Viking Press, 2002). See also *Difficult Conversations: How to Discuss What Matters Most*, by Douglas Stone, Bruce Patton, and Shelia Heen (New York: Penguin Random House, 2010).

19. Paul Simon, "You Can Call Me Al," on *Graceland*.

20. Think of Captain John Miller's (Tom Hanks) injunction to his platoon in *Saving Private Ryan* (Amblin Entertainment, 1998) that complaints always have to go *up* the chain of command, not down.

21. See Richard Morrow, *Strategic Leadership: Integrating Strategy and Leadership in Colleges and Universities* (Westport, CT: Praeger, 2007).

22. Getting a good night's sleep on a regular basis turns out to be much more important to one's general health than many of us might previously have believed. For an informative and highly readable summary of the latest research on the positive effects of sleep (and the negative effects of too little sleep), see Matthew Walker, *Why We Sleep: Unlocking the Power of Sleep and Dreams* (New York: Scribner, 2017).

23. Baseball Hall of Fame, Cooperstown, New York.

CHAPTER 2

Purpose-Driven Leadership

The Value in "Finding Your *Why*"

COURTNEY B. SMITH

The chapters in this volume reveal two immutable truths. First, the challenges facing academic leaders are wide ranging and complex and require solutions that must be developed in environments of incomplete information and insufficient time. Second, every leader brings a different set of skills and characteristics to their role: no individual has all the talents necessary to manage all situations effectively. The disconnect between these dual realities is the impetus for studies that explore a wide range of leadership styles and stress management techniques.

When I by chance discovered the work of Simon Sinek and his advice to "start with why," I immediately saw the relevance of his ideas to my own role as a rising higher-education leader. I completed the "finding my why" process while serving as an associate dean in January 2019, and it had practical relevance when our school unexpectedly entered a leadership transition six months later. The value of focusing on my *why* and *hows* became further evident when I was an acting dean, especially in a time of significant turbulence, including our own leadership transition, the COVID-19 pandemic, and calls for greater racial justice across the United States and beyond.

This chapter offers an overview of what "finding your why" entails and a discussion of my own *why* with examples of how it has impacted my leadership across all three areas of turbulence. Purpose-driven leadership as described by

Sinek is one path academic leaders can take to effectively navigate the challenges of their positions. Those who have found their *why* understand the motivation underlying their work and are better positioned to develop strategies that marshal their unique strengths as they perform their duties effectively.

THE WORK OF SIMON SINEK AND MY *WHY* STATEMENT

Simon Sinek first introduced the importance of "starting with why" in a 2009 TED Talk that quickly became one of the most watched videos in the series. He followed with a 2011 book that explored how leaders who understand their purpose are better able to motivate their colleagues to perform well.[1] His concept of the "golden circle" is illustrated in a bulls-eye representation of his key point: having a clear sense of *why* you do *what* you do will make you a more inspirational leader who enjoys the trust and commitment of those around you. He describes your *why*, which lies at the center of your "golden circle," as your purpose, cause, or belief. Put another way, he asks, "*Why* do you get out of bed every morning? And *why* should anyone care?"[2]

The appeal of *why* as a concept prompted Sinek and two colleagues to release a practical guide to "finding your why" in 2017.[3] They articulate three steps: gather stories of standout memories and defining moments, identify key themes and insights about ourselves, and draft and refine our *why* statement.[4] The *why* statement is one sentence that takes the following format: *to* make some type of contribution to the lives of others *so that* we will have a particular type of impact.

Given that the *why* statement is fundamental to each of us as a person, it should have relevance in both our personal and professional life. Once our *why* has been articulated, the next step is to look at the other themes from our stories that didn't quite make the cut as our *why* but are nonetheless important to who we are as a person. These become our *hows*, which lie in the middle ring of our "golden circle" and "are the actions we take when we are at our natural best to bring our *why* to life."[5] Finally, in the outer ring of the "golden circle" lie our *whats*, which "are the tangible manifestations of our *why*, the actual work we do every day."[6]

My own *why* statement helps demonstrate the utility of purpose-driven leadership in a more concrete way: My *why* is to build environments with others so that we all can make a positive impact on our world. This statement has direct relevance for my professional life as one of the first four faculty members hired in a new academic program and as a faculty member and administrator working to build that school from the ground up for more than two decades. It also captures the mission of our institution, which is to educate servant leaders who are prepared to make a difference in their local, national, and international communities. This *why* statement also relates to my personal life, capturing my role as a husband and father, as well as my volunteer work through church, Boy Scouts, Music Boosters, the local nature conservancy, and the community food bank.

A few days after completing the "finding my why" process, I was working an all-day event with a recruitment component, and my meeting with one family stretched into the evening. Although it was the type of event I had done hundreds of times, this time felt different. All of us have moments in which we feel "in the zone"—at first I attributed my sense of the evening to nothing more than that. However, on the drive home I had a different realization: the conversation with that family was different because I had a deeper appreciation of *why* my work mattered, so I was doing it better, with more passion, energy, and commitment. As we talked, I was building an environment with the family that demonstrated how their daughter would grow her knowledge and skills in our program to be ready to act on her passion and interests throughout her future career.

MY FIVE *HOW*s OF PURPOSEFUL LEADERSHIP

Five *hows* accompany my *why* statement, and each captures a different action or behavior that I exhibit when acting as my best self to build the environments that embody my *why*. These *hows* include (1) take responsibility for others, (2) learn to solve problems, (3) explore what is possible, (4) use data to plan, and (5) seek consensus when feasible. Taken collectively, they help ensure that the decisions I make and the actions I take represent the best possible way to prioritize my work in light of the competing trade-offs I face. Put another way, acting in line with these *how* statements helps determine which choices and options build a better environment for all constituencies in our school. Their utility is further reinforced by the extensive overlap with the many lessons and themes articulated by the other academic leaders in this volume. Each of the five *how* statements cited above is illustrated in the following paragraphs.

Take responsibility for others. Responsibility is the heart of leadership—being responsible for assuring the well-being of your faculty, staff, and student colleagues; being responsible for bringing a team together to accomplish shared goals; being responsible for hearing the concerns and suggestions of others; and being responsible for doing what is right even when that is not the easiest path available. I strive to embody the Golden Rule ("Do unto others as you would have them do unto you") and act based on the principles I learned as an Eagle Scout. Concrete manifestations include fostering the success of students through advising and experiential learning, fostering the success of faculty through hiring and mentoring, and fostering the success of colleagues through professional development.

Learn to solve problems. Like many leaders, my administrative portfolio has expanded and changed over time, which has offered me the opportunity to learn new skills. Initially my responsibilities were typical of a department chair, including curriculum development and course scheduling, faculty development and evaluation, and adjunct hiring. They quickly expanded to those common for an associate dean or dean, including student services, recruitment, personnel, budget management, building partnerships on and off campus, and stewardship. Writers in this book effectively show the challenges and potential pitfalls of learning each area, some of which are more daunting than others. A key objective with each new task is to ask questions of those around us. This is an effective way to determine whether to work within the existing system or to change the system itself.

Explore what is possible. I've worked as an associate dean for five deans and as an acting dean for two provosts. That translates into six transitions in fifteen years. Each one was a time of uncertainty but also a period of opportunity for innovation and exploration of new things to do and new ways to do them. My *why* is about building environments, and exploring what is possible can generate results that weren't previously considered. This includes, for example, developing new programs with diverse audiences and new revenue streams; recruiting faculty with professional experience and allowing them to interact with students in unique teaching formats; and mentoring students to create new clubs and organizations that best reflect their own interests and leadership skills.

Use data to plan. Chapters in this book describe how our work as academic leaders has been transformed by data. It has impacted academic leaders in at least three ways. First, we analyze more data about our own programs and operations at all levels across campus. Some of this data is generated in house; other information is provided by a growing array of outside consultants. Second, membership in key professional associations and service on numerous external review teams have opened windows on the data and best practices used at other institutions and have sparked valuable self-reflection. Finally, linking these data to positive change through strategic planning is essential yet challenging. My time on campus includes several periods of intense strategic planning at the school and university level, with our current effort having succeeded in moving from a strategic "laundry list" toward actual implementation.

Seek consensus when feasible. My natural goal in each situation is to create mutually beneficial solutions through consultation, listening, and consensus building that are guided by integrity and a commitment to treating people with fairness and respect. This goal is consistent with my scholarly focus on the United Nations (where most decisions are made by consensus) and translates well into the shared-governance environment of academia. Seeking consensus has both internal and external dimensions, and the implications are distinct. The areas we lead offer a range of situations in which we have the formal authority to decide unilaterally based on our position and title. The same power, however, is not present in most interactions with partners (or potential partners), either on or off campus. Regardless of whether consensus is necessary or not, attempting to build it can have positive benefits even when it remains elusive. Colleagues are more likely to engage with, or at least acquiesce to, decisions they didn't initially agree with if they feel their ideas were given consideration through a fair and (as much as possible) transparent process.

CONCLUSION: PURPOSE-DRIVEN LEADERSHIP IN ACTION

Defining *hows* such as these can help you gain a clear sense of purpose in your leadership. This can be especially helpful in periods of turbulence, such as three current examples facing my own school: a leadership transition, the pandemic, and our efforts to enhance diversity, equity, inclusion, and justice (DEIJ). Managing our leadership transition has necessitated my taking responsibility, solving problems, and seeking consensus. Entering my new role eight months after "finding my why," I held one-on-one meetings with all administrators and full-time faculty to listen to their goals and develop a stronger mentoring relationship with each one. I set up four Microsoft Teams (one for faculty, one for administrators, one for our Joint Leadership Team, and one for all faculty and administrators together) to foster transparency, inclusive discussion, shared governance, and efficiency. Having this culture of collaboration in place facilitated the move to remote learning seven months later, because our team had a strong foundation of trust. Our sense of community is also evident in our impressive yield rates for undergraduate and graduate recruitment and in the series of town halls held with students in person and via Teams.

Leading during the COVID-19 pandemic has necessitated learning to solve problems, exploring what is possible, and using data to plan. As evident throughout this volume, a plethora of related yet distinct issues had to be addressed simultaneously, and some of the most challenging involved contingency planning. I served on two different university contingency groups during this process, one of which planned for the end of fiscal year 2020 and the other prepared for the early months of fiscal year 2021. These campus-wide efforts highlighted how effective leadership involves working well with peers and superiors, not just the people you manage. This is especially true in crisis situations where the problems we need to solve impact the entire institution, perhaps in different ways, and where exploring what is possible must be judged using data that reflect the interests and goals of all units on campus.

As challenging as these efforts have been, leading our school toward a robust DEIJ agenda has necessitated using all five of my *how* statements. When students first shared their concerns after the murder of Mr. George Floyd, we sought to provide an environment of respect where all constituencies of the school could feel safe sharing their perspectives. This encompassed two summer listening sessions, each lasting three hours or longer, that shifted between moments of hope and frustration. As our learning progressed, we identified five areas of action and formed a committee around each to explore avenues of potential action. This involved assessing the data related to our existing DEIJ initiatives and exploring ideas about how to enhance each one in the midst of the pandemic and the associated budget reductions. At some moments, consensus was elusive—especially regarding the unique priorities of our Black and international students. Ultimately, each committee found areas of common agreement, which made tangible progress possible.

This volume explores a wide range of skills and experiences that foster successful academic leadership. While "finding your why" is a personal endeavor, the benefits of purpose-driven leadership can be positive for our colleagues around us. In the words of Simon Sinek: "Leaders don't have all of the great ideas; they provide support for those who want to contribute. Leaders achieve very little by themselves; they inspire people to come together for the good of the group. Leaders never start with what needs to be done. Leaders start with *why* we need to do things. Leaders inspire action."[7]

Your actions will be all the more effective when guided by insights from the other writers in this book and by a personal exploration of the *why*s and *how*s of your own purpose-driven leadership.

— *Takeaways* —

- Purpose-driven leadership helps academic leaders meet the complex challenges we face.
- Leaders who have found their *why* understand the motivation underlying their own work and are better positioned to inspire the trust and success of colleagues.
- Developing your *how* statements can help you use your unique strengths in designing strategies that effectively navigate difficult decisions.

NOTES

1. Simon Sinek, *Start with Why* (New York: Portfolio, 2011).
2. Sinek, *Start with Why*, 39.
3. Simon Sinek, David Mead, and Peter Docker, *Find Your Why* (New York: Portfolio, 2017).
4. Sinek, Mead, and Docker, *Find Your Why*, 30–37.
5. Sinek, Mead, and Docker, *Find Your Why*, 152.
6. Sinek, Mead, and Docker, *Find Your Why*, 152.
7. Sinek, *Start with Why*, 228.

PART II

Leadership and National Contexts

CHAPTER 3

The Critical Role of Historically Black Colleges and Universities in Higher Education

HIDEKO SERA AND KENDRICK T. BROWN

The unique role that Historically Black Colleges and Universities (HBCUs) have long played in higher education is receiving national attention with prominent graduates such as Vice President Kamala Harris, Senator Raphael Warnock, Atlanta mayor Keisha Lance Bottoms, and politician Stacey Abrams—to name only a few in a long and august list of HBCU alumni. In the context of the racial reckoning inspired by the Black Lives Matter conversations and activism across the United States and around the globe after Mr. George Floyd's murder in 2020, HBCUs have also garnered philanthropic contributions from donors desiring to exhibit their commitment to social justice. These donations provide funds to various HBCUs at a time when many Predominantly White Institutions (PWIs) face financial hardships and academic disruptions amid the global COVID-19 pandemic and declining numbers of first-time full-time students.

Although mainstream America has finally begun hearing about HBCUs, these exceptional institutions remain a mystery, disconnected from their rich histories and the diversity that exists within them. This chapter provides a brief overview of HBCUs and applies a well-known psychological racial identity development model to explain how HBCUs offer a unique and critical refuge for Black students. We are intentionally using the term "Black students" as opposed to "African American students" to be inclusive of individuals whose origins and identities are not specific to Africa (e.g., the Caribbean, Central America).

A BRIEF HISTORY OF HBCUs

According to the US Department of Education, the Higher Education Act of 1965, as amended, defines an HBCU as a "college or university that was established prior to 1964, whose principal mission was, and is, the education of black Americans, and that is accredited by a nationally recognized accrediting agency or association determined by the Secretary [of Education] to be a reliable authority as to the quality of training offered or is, according to such an agency or association, making reasonable progress toward accreditation."[1] The first higher-education institution for Black people, known as the Institute for Colored Youth, was founded well before the US government defined HBCUs.[2]

The first HBCU, Cheyney University, opened in Cheyney, Pennsylvania, in 1837 and was originally known as the African Institute.[3] In 1856, Wilberforce University in Ohio became the first college run by African American people. Currently, there are more than one hundred HBCUs in the United States, most of them located in the South, with Alabama having the highest number. HBCUs range from two-year community colleges to four-year liberal arts colleges and to universities that extend into graduate education. About half of the existing HBCUs are public institutions, and the other half are nonprofit private institutions. They can be single-gender or coeducational entities, as well as religiously affiliated or nondenominational schools. They also incorporate different scopes and domains of scholarly expertise, including STEM education, the arts and humanities, and agriculture.

DIVERSITY WITHIN HBCUs

Although approximately 75 percent of all HBCU students rely on the Pell Grant, there are also multigenerational legacy students whose family members fully finance a student's education.[4] HBCUs make up only 3 percent of higher-education institutions in the United States; however, they enroll 10 percent of all Black students and produce 20 percent of all Black graduates.[5]

The socioeconomic diversity within and amongst HBCUs is comparable to what one would observe at PWIs. This often-overlooked reality leads to perplexing ranking systems that determine, for instance, "Top 10 HBCUs" (e.g., *U.S. News & World Report*, Best Colleges, College Consensus), when in fact no ranking system for PWIs deliberately ignores niches and intentionally clusters all institutions into one category. Indeed, PWIs are ranked according to private versus public sectors, regions and locations, various types of student support, known academic domains and majors, faculty-to-student ratio, recognized athletic teams, and many other characteristics.

Listings of "Top 10 PWIs" would fail to consider their many distinctive qualities. If so, why do they exist for HBCUs? This different regard for HBCUs epitomizes the "cross-race effect" (also known as cross-racial bias, other-race bias, and own-race bias). One way the cross-race effect manifests lies in the tendency to easily recognize faces of people of one's own race.[6] It is evident in higher education when an empowered group that has historically been the predominant presence in higher education (i.e., white Americans) can or will recognize their own unique differences but cannot or will not do the same when considering disempowered groups (i.e., Minority-Serving Institutions [MSIs] such as HBCUs). Those who are unable to recognize the rich diversity within HBCUs are less likely to accord them the same regard or respect that PWIs receive, reinforcing a bias that further disadvantages institutions of higher education that have served Black students for almost two hundred years.

HBCUs AS A COLLECTIVE REHUMANIZATION PROCESS

The most critical difference between PWIs and HBCUs is the latter's clarity of mission regarding Black individuals—originally specified as Black Americans—and focus on their education. Although approximately 25 percent of students at HBCUs self-identify as non-Black,[7] there is a keen understanding and expectation that HBCUs offer rare critical spaces for Black college students to have transformational experiences, such as those contributing to identity formation. These trajectory-building opportunities extend beyond the salience of ethno-racial qualities. HBCUs enable students to (1) interact with peers who share similar qualities; (2) learn from faculty and staff who share similar qualities; and (3) most important, experience being respected and honored, not treated simply as minoritized individuals in the United States.

As Hideko Sera and Andrew F. Wall have noted, "Educational institutions in the U.S. mirror a history of the country where, from its inception, racialized injustices, systemic racism, and racialized violence have been deeply woven into the fabric of the system."[8] Juxtaposed to this norm of everyday dehumanizing experience, HBCUs offer an affirmative, rehumanizing process for many Black students. This is particularly true when the student's experiences outside the college campus provoke self-doubt about their own capabilities and potentials. Their personhood and safety are always a step away from serious threat or harm. Regardless of the diversity within all HBCUs, the commitment to appropriately educate and prepare Black college students for success is a shared vision cutting across institutional differences and histories. Because most HBCUs began their operations by educating formerly enslaved people and providing opportunities for gainful employment, this mission to nurture Black communities serves as the institutions' backbone.

Recently, this cross-cutting commitment has gained momentum through encouraging former HBCU students who have not completed their degrees to return to their college or university to finish their education. Prominent stakeholders are creating student success pathways to strengthen the HBCU pipeline with access, quality of student experience, and graduation as prominent goals. For example, the United Negro College Fund (UNCF), an organization representing thirty-seven private HBCUs, launched a campaign to convince 4,000 students who left without their degrees to return to ten HBCUs or Predominantly Black Institutions (PBIs), with a program of student success coaching designed to fit their needs and ensure degree completion.

UNCF president and CEO Michael Lomax noted, "The work that HBCUs do daily is essential to building a more inclusive and equitable system of higher education in this country. HBCUs are not only cornerstones of educational access and attainment, but fixtures of the Black experience in America, whose students develop meaningful and lifelong connections to the institutions they attend."[9] The success of HBCUs is driven by and shared across different stakeholders, all of whom work for the common purpose of advancing Black communities in the United States. Indeed, a coalition of collaborators, supporters, and resources rally around Black students who pursue their education at HBCUs. This common purpose often appears as a reminder on many HBCU campuses in the form of artifacts that tell stories about countless collective sacrifices that have been made for students to pursue their education (e.g., the *Lifting the Veil* statue of Booker T. Washington, a formerly enslaved man; the Dr. Martin Luther King Jr. statue at Morehouse College). There is a sense and awareness at HBCUs that the students' success stands on the shoulders of those who came before them.

The rehumanizing process fostered by HBCUs is crucial to understanding why they are top choices for Black students. Often cited in explaining the choice to attend an HBCU are the various support systems dedicated to attracting and retaining students.[10] The multiple ways HBCUs promote psychological well-being beyond programming and student experiences are often overlooked, however. Considering that student well-being has become a heightened focus for all of higher education since the global COVID-19 pandemic, it's not surprising that Black students are intentionally choosing to attend HBCUs. Envision a space where a student's personhood is not questioned or attacked, where their sense of belonging is enhanced and affirmed, where the educational and social environment is filled with people who fundamentally believe in them, and where regular reminders are present of investment in the student becoming who they are meant to be. In this respect, HBCUs serve as a psychological refuge from daily threats and offer systemic encouragement. These qualities give students the strength and hope to transform themselves during their college years, a pivotal phase in many people's lives.

CROSS'S NIGRESCENCE MODEL AS A FRAMEWORK FOR UNDERSTANDING THE HBCU EXPERIENCE

The benefit Black students may gain from attending an HBCU can be explained psychologically. Cross's Nigrescence Model (also known as the Black Racial Identity Development Model) maps the unique transformative and affirmative processes fostered within HBCUs for Black students.[11] In his model, Cross discussed five stages through which Black individuals in the United States pass in navigating confusing, often hurtful messages about their self-worth and eventually forming their own individualized, unique identities of reclaimed personhood, rooted in Black experiences. Cross's word for becoming Black was "nigrescence."[12] Cross further argued that, in the United States, it is challenging for a Black person to go through formal education without being exposed to historical distortions about Africa and Black experiences in the United States. When Black people express self-doubt or self-hatred due to these education-based distortions, Carter G. Woodson argues, the socialization process turns into "mis-education," which can further dehumanize Black people.[13]

Cross's racial identity development model can explain how many Black individuals choose to pursue education at an HBCU. He explains that in the first stage, "Pre-encounter," Black people experience a strong desire to assimilate into dominant white-based values and practices or even develop self-hatred. As mainstream, white-dominated culture surrounds Black people with its standards for beauty, intelligence, intellectual and other aptitudes, and success, anyone who is not reflected and included in these standards and images begins, explicitly or implicitly, to question their sense of worth.

Research indicates that children as young as three or four years old notice racial differences and social meanings attached to these differences.[14] For instance, Black children surrounded by white children and teachers could come to question their own value and begin favoring white-based standards, especially when teachers don't provide the same type and amount of encouragement for Black children and their academic aptitudes. However, this admiration and assimilation can shatter when Black people have pivotal experiences that prompt the realization that they will never wholly fit white-based standards, no matter how hard they try to assimilate into the dominant norms. This negative experience and powerful realization is what Cross calls "Encounter," the second stage in his developmental model.

For Black students who choose HBCUs over PWIs, their Pre-encounter and Encounter experiences could have occurred during childhood. However, a significant racial incident, such as being stopped and searched by police for no justifiable reason or being called a racial slur by classmates, can frame a decision to seek educational opportunities that would reduce such occurrences or provide additional support when these transgressions happen. We argue the racial reckoning that has occurred nationally and internationally in the past few years can be a critical factor in choosing HBCUs over PWIs for many Black students. A student's selection of a preferred college or university is heavily influenced by their loved ones, who are invested in their safety while pursuing education.

Following the Encounter stage, individuals often retreat to and seek to be surrounded by others who possess similar physical and life experiences. Cross describes this "Immersion-Emersion" as a stage that many Black people go through to connect with their histories, experiences, and worldviews, and further characterizes it as "the most sensational aspect of Black identity, for it represents the vortex of psychological nigrescence."[15] Immersion-Emersion is filled with intense involvement and pride in Black aspects of life, leading Black people to become invested in and well informed about matters related to their histories and experiences.

However, Black people in Immersion-Emersion cannot create their lives simply by completely dissociating from the white presence in the United States. Every activity in daily life involves some degree of involvement with white people. Cross also noted that this stage might bring on intense psychological experiences for Black people in the form of anxiety, rage, hurt, and sadness (as well as all the positive outcomes) associated with delving deeply into learning about Black history and experiences. Such experiences are necessary for Black people to form an *internalized* Black identity. This identity critically differs from one based on often-negative images and narratives promulgated in white-based standards. Also, the sense of self emerging at this stage is not solely based on reactions to whiteness and racialized inequities in the United States, which cultivate Black identity only as an opposite to a white norm. Instead, this internalized identity comes after thoughtful and substantive reflections about what it means to be a holistic Black person and to reclaim that sense of self.

What HBCUs promote and offer often overlaps with this critical stage of racial identity development for Black individuals. Scholars featured as main contributors to academic disciplines influence how students consciously and implicitly understand their self-worth. HBCUs spotlight, perhaps for the first time in many Black students' lives, the significant contributions made by Black scientists, thinkers, and artists. According to the Gallup–USA Funds Minority College Graduates Report (2015), Black students at HBCUs reported significantly higher satisfaction with the support they received than their peers who attended PWIs—a finding closely related to feelings of being cared for as people by mentors and professors who got them excited about learning.[16]

In the last two stages of Cross's model, "Internalization" and "Internalization-Commitment," Black people undergo complex processes of change through which they achieve a sense of freedom from society's stereotypes. They come to consciously acknowledge the intersectionality of Black identities, whereby Black people see themselves in a holistic manner that brings in factors other than race as critical components of their identities. Further, this is where Cross's view of Black nationalism becomes sharpened as the goal for Black experience becomes achieving the same civil rights in political, educational, and financial and economic arenas as their white counterparts. While trying to dismantle inequities that impact them, Black people in the last stage also become intensely involved in addressing injustices that other oppressed groups face. This new way of focusing on inequities becomes further developed when a Black person sees many facets of their complex intersectional identity, beyond simply race: gender, sexual orientation, age, ability, and other critical components of difference serve as vehicles for extending their humanity to others who experience systemic oppression. Many Black students at HBCUs engage, for example, in social justice activism and allyship with other minoritized and oppressed individuals. Being in the HBCU environment enables Black students to explore various aspects of their identity while being grounded in Black history and culture. This exploration can solidify the ways Blackness intersects with other social statuses, intersections that mark the Internalization and Internationalization-Commitment stages in Cross's model.

FREEDOM FROM JUSTIFICATION
FOR WHY BLACK PEOPLE MATTER

In light of this analysis of Cross's racial identity development model, which describes intimate, internalized reactions and complex Black experiences, it seems that many Black students who seek HBCUs have experienced the Pre-encounter and Encounter stages before their arrival at HBCU campuses.

In fact, some may have chosen explicitly and intentionally to pursue their education at HBCUs because of those experiences. For Black HBCU students who are going through Cross's Immersion-Emersion stage, their college experiences offer curricular and cocurricular activities that highlight essential Black histories, figures, innovations, and contributions that are not often taught in predominantly white spaces. This is where the primary rehumanization process can begin, while their intelligence, beauty, potentials, and successes are not constantly measured against a white-based norm.

During and since the racial reckoning inspired by the murder of Mr. George Floyd in the summer of 2020, many universities and colleges across the United States have fostered dialogues about why diversity, equity, inclusion, and justice are critical components of the education they offer. HBCUs offer a distinct, fundamental understanding that these ideals undergird their institutional existence. With that clarity already affirmed for them, Black students entering HBCUs do not need to justify their racial status and identity while on campus. Whereas Black students entering PWIs often spend enormous energy and time convincing others why their educational experiences matter, HBCUs offer students an explicit and implicit understanding that the institution exists for them to succeed. Freed from the exhausting effort of repeatedly explaining why their existence and experiences matter, Black students at HBCUs can freely explore their education, much as white students at PWIs can focus on their development. The traditional college experience lasts four years and is one of the most transformational in a person's life. Away from the constant anxiety of trying to find a sense of belonging in spheres where they have to fight for their existence, Black students at HBCUs experience transformational changes to become the people they are meant to be, both for themselves and for their communities.

— *Takeaways* —

- There are more than one hundred HBCUs, each with prominent and unique contributions to educating Black students. Yet the diversity within HBCUs is often ignored (as in listings of "Top 10 HBCUs"), whereas various niches are detailed for PWIs.
- HBCUs offer a rehumanization process for Black students who explore educational and relational experiences that reflect rich Black

contributions to society. No longer racially minoritized, Black students at HBCUs are able to build trajectories without constant comparisons against white-based norms.

- Black students encounter at HBCUs a strong sense of collectivistic respect for those who came before them. Experiences of historical injustice, inequity, and oppression that were endured by their ancestors and communities are deeply woven into the fabric of HBCU experiences. Because of this awareness, a sense of community and belonging is a critical component of students' tenure at HBCUs.
- Context matters for Black students' development. Frameworks such as Cross's Nigrescence Model can help higher-education leaders and educators to understand Black students' identity development processes. These frameworks also explain what happens when Black students' identity development meets challenges, such as racial tension in white-dominant spaces, that differ from the affirming environments of HBCUs.

NOTES

1. See "What Is an HBCU?" White House Initiative on Advancing Educational Equity, Excellence, and Economic Opportunity through Historically Black Colleges and Universities, U.S. Department of Education, accessed 31 October 2021, https://sites .ed.gov/whhbcu/one-hundred-and-five-historically-black-colleges-and-universities/.
2. Nicole A. Taylor, "Institute for Colored Youth," in *Unsung Legacies of Educators and Events in African American Education*, ed. Andrea D. Lewis and Nicole A. Taylor (London: Palgrave Macmillan, 2019), 123.
3. Taylor, "Institute for Colored Youth," 123.
4. "About HBCUs," Thurgood Marshall College Fund, accessed 25 June 2021. https:// www.tmcf.org/about-us/member-schools/about-hbcus/.
5. "HBCUs Make America Strong: The Positive Economic Impact of Historically Black Colleges and Universities," United Negro College Fund, https://cdn.uncf.org/wp -content/uploads/HBCU_Consumer_Brochure_FINAL_APPROVED.pdf?_ga=2 .80581908.223413501.1625866490-13011803.1625411706.
6. See Gwendolyn M. Combs and Jakari Griffith, "An Examination of Interracial Contact: The Influence of Cross-Race Interpersonal Efficacy and Affect Regulation," *Human Resource Development Review* 6, no. 3 (2007): 222–44; Siegfried L. Sporer, "Recognizing Faces of Other Ethnic Groups: An Integration of Theories," *Psychology, Public Policy, and Law* 7, no. 1 (2001): 36–97; and James W. Tanaka, Markus Kiefer, and Cindy

M. Bukach, "A Holistic Account of the Own-Race Effect in Face Recognition: Evidence from a Cross-Cultural Study," *Cognition* 93, no. 1 (2004): B1–B9.

7. "About HBCUs."

8. Hideko Sera and Andrew F. Wall, "Ichigo-Ichie: How Impactful Racial Justice and Transformational Changes Begin with the Urgency of Making Each Encounter Meaningful in Higher Education," in *Handbook of Research on Leading Higher Education Transformation with Social Justice, Equity, and Inclusion*, ed. Clint-Michael Reneau and Mary Ann Villarreal (Hershey, PA: IGI Global, 2021), 1–18.

9. "UNCF Launches Nationwide Campaign to Re-enroll Former HBCU and PBI Students through Coaching," *Globe Newswire*, 19 May 2021, https://www.globenewswire .com/news-release/2021/05/19/2232476/0/en/UNCF-Launches-Nationwide -Campaign-to-Re-Enroll-Former-HBCU-and-PBI-Students-through-Coaching.html.

10. See Bryan J. Cook and Diana I. Córdova, *Minorities in Higher Education Twenty-Second Annual Status Report: 2007 Supplement*, project report, accessed 13 November 2021, https://www.acenet.edu/Documents/Minorities-in-Higher-Education-2007 -Supplement-22nd.pdf; and Sean Seymore and Julie Ray, "Grads of Historically Black Colleges Have Well-Being Edge," *Gallup*, 27 October 2015, https://news .gallup.com/poll/186362/grads-historically-black-colleges-edge.aspx.

11. William E. Cross, "The Negro-to-Black Conversion Experience," *Black World* 20, no. 9 (1971): 13–27.

12. See William E. Cross, *Shades of Black: Diversity in African-American Identity* (Philadelphia, PA: Temple University Press, 1991).

13. Carter G. Woodson, *The Mis-education of the Negro* (Trenton, NJ: Africa World Press, 1990).

14. Jessica Sullivan, Leigh Wilton, and Evan Apfelbaum, "Adults Delay Conversations about Race Because They Underestimate Children's Processing of Race," *Journal of Experimental Psychology* 150, no. 2 (2020): 395–400.

15. Cross, *Shades of Black*, 201.

16. Seymore and Ray, "Grads of Historically Black Colleges Have Well-Being Edge."

CHAPTER 4

How Academic Leaders Can Bend Their Institutions toward Racial Justice

PAULA O'LOUGHLIN AND JEFFREY RATLIFF-CRAIN

Diversity, equity, and inclusion (DEI) efforts among US higher-education institutions are not new. There is, however, heightened urgency for meaningful racial justice reforms in response to highly visible events in our society (e.g., the murder of Mr. George Floyd by a Minneapolis police officer; the systematic killings of Asian American women in Atlanta on March 16, 2021), high-profile debates about symbols honoring the Confederacy on university campuses (e.g., the "Silent Sam" statue at the University of North Carolina), and continued instances of apparent racial profiling of Black, indigenous, and people of color (BIPOC) students, among other examples. Student affairs and chief diversity officers are the traditional champions for this work, but they need help.

If transformational DEI change is to happen, academic leaders will have to be much more heavily involved. This chapter offers advice for the many academic leaders who seek to address DEI but are unsure how to begin. As deans embrace this work, they need to reflect on the changing demographics of higher education and how campus cultures, policies, and practices align. Recognizing that different institutions, departments, and units are at varying stages of DEI progress, we focus on several key areas where deans can have meaningful influence for continuing change. Individually, we also need to acknowledge who *we* are within the campus context. Based on recent statistics, the majority of us will be engaging with the triple privileges of being white allies, seated as academic leaders (over 87 percent white), and working at predominantly white institutions (PWIs).[1] Before continuing, take a moment to consider your own institution's circumstances, including your role and responsibilities.

CULTURAL CHANGES THROUGH SYMBOLIC AND TRANSFORMATIVE ACTIONS

It's first worth thinking about the kind of change you want to make. Symbolic and transformational actions are both needed for shifts in institutional culture that establish true inclusivity. Confronting symbols of historic oppression, such as changing building names or publicly acknowledging a complicated institutional history as a PWI, is necessary but not sufficient for pervasive cultural shifts. Focusing on symbolic modifications doesn't necessarily alter people's daily experiences for the better, but these battles matter.

None of our institutions exists in a vacuum. If you wish to start with symbolic change, we advise partnering with your broader community, given the challenges to culture and tradition inherent in taking such steps. A mascot may be considered racist by some, but is part of university identity and, by extension, personal identity for alumni, donors, and others with deep commitment to the institution. Instead, most deans may be better situated to focus first on substantive changes in policies, practices, and what the department does and let the broader symbolic modifications wait for another day. Your work will not completely change institutional culture regarding DEI, so focus on the areas of progress you *can* achieve in your college or unit.

Timing affects when a dean can be most successful at introducing and completing initiatives. Generally, academic leaders have the greatest opportunity to make headway in moving their institutions forward around DEI-related initiatives when they're at the beginning of their terms. Even with strong commitment to DEI efforts, outside forces, governance boards, and even individual faculty can create headwinds based on perceived threats, economic or effort costs, political fights, and the like. Whatever the position one holds, the political capital needed to make change is never higher than in one's honeymoon phase. When we're nearing the end of our term, we have usually spent all our capital. Therefore, start off with quick wins (e.g., remove racist or sexist language from department materials; introduce discussions and reading groups on inclusive teaching) that will help build momentum and allies for the harder conversations around DEI. Every smaller goal attained helps build the momentum for larger transformation. This approach doesn't mean certain critical areas for modification (e.g., making general education more inclusive) are unimportant, but the glacial pace can slow overall momentum for DEI across the range of your influence.

If an academic leader is not just starting off in a position and yet wants to significantly move their institution forward, two other factors can help achieve success. First, you will not have to expend as much capital getting DEI-related issues on the agenda if you link your efforts with broader mandates or strategic plan goals. Secondly, change is easier when DEI objectives are not buried underneath multiple competing priorities. Clearly defining goals and making them attainable increases salience and facilitates moving forward on racial justice.

RESOURCES SUPPORTING CHANGE

Many deans believe new resources are needed to advance DEI initiatives, but we disagree. A lack of new funding is a red herring: you're in higher-ed administration—there will never be enough resources. Beyond reprioritizing your budget, you have multiple tools that do not require funding. For example, academic leaders can keep DEI goals uppermost in mind for their institutions by showing up to events. The impact on supportive action is magnified when we show up as people and as the representative of our college or unit. When we, as academic leaders, articulate our commitment to DEI efforts by our visible presence, our governing boards, supervisors, colleagues, direct reports, students, and others in our community are more likely to see those efforts as sincere. Adjusting a scheduled faculty retreat so it no longer competes with the Martin Luther King Jr. holiday is supportive. Conversely, that support and affirmation of importance is mitigated by *not* showing up.

Collaborative relationships offer another resource-neutral way to elevate the significance of DEI efforts. A critical element of these relationships is reinforcing DEI priorities at discussions in which we are included and other people are not. If your role places you in cabinet meetings, ask yourself how a discussion item furthers your unit's commitment to DEI. Where there are relationships with community partners outside the institution, raise the significance of DEI for these organizations by making your commitment to inclusion a central part of your connection.

There are also multiple resource-neutral ways you can draw on the adage "What gets measured matters" in moving your part of the institution forward. A learning outcome at the course or unit level that focuses on DEI-related goals doesn't depend on the interests of individual faculty.

If you're lucky enough to have modest resources to use, lead DEI change by beginning with the academic program or your part of it. Academic leaders can carefully and sometimes quickly push for curricular updates without usurping the faculty's historic power. Certainly, you can encourage the development of courses that address or connect to domestic diversity. This change usually occurs at the undergraduate level through general education reform and the inclusion or expansion of a domestic diversity course category. Academic leaders may also free up staffing resources so that faculty with expertise in DEI-related subjects can provide more courses that appeal to student interest in this area. By capitalizing on institutional priorities, you might be able to get a new teaching line devoted to DEI concerns.

If adding courses that bring diversity to the curriculum isn't possible, you can encourage faculty to add new content or adjust existing material to make their courses more inclusive. For example, a music course can include works by underrepresented composers as a medium for studying basic theoretical concepts. This kind of approach requires delicacy on an administrator's part because it could easily raise concerns about impeding academic freedom. However, if done carefully by encouraging more inclusive course content, apprehension will be reduced. Where curriculum development minigrants are available, note the priority of addressing inclusive pedagogies (e.g., inclusive grading strategies) or including units that incorporate domestic diversity into existing courses. When faculty express interest in creating an academic program such as a major or minor in a DEI-related field, you can help mentor the faculty members involved and connect them with colleagues at other campuses so they craft the best possible curricular proposal.

If faculty are uncertain how to address student interactions surrounding race, consider sponsoring professional development on how to approach difficult and divisive topics in classroom conversations. Advising practices offer another arena in which to sponsor change. A dean can support faculty interest in advising students from historically underserved populations and sponsor trainings that draw attention to privilege and how it affects these mentoring relationships. For example, you could offer workshops to reframe advising so that it acknowledges what students bring to the relationship and emphasizes culturally responsive mentorship.

HIRING AND RETENTION FOR CHANGE

Significant long-term movement toward your DEI goals requires strategic talent recruitment, hiring, and retention. As with student recruitment, hiring objectives are sometimes set as numeric goals (e.g., based on demographics that reflect the broader population). However, we should first clarify the goals that underlie "increasing diversity." We all need to critically assess how open those in the conversation are to being challenged in how we work, starting with ourselves. Simply hiring to meet numeric representation will not achieve a truly diverse faculty and equitable workplace if we aren't also inviting and listening to every voice in our discussions, decisions, and planning. Examine your own motivations, and challenge statements made on your behalf as a representative of the institution. For example, be sure you know what upper administrators and unit-level leaders mean by "equity" or "diversity" and that you have a shared understanding.[2]

Next, put that understanding into ongoing action. Be sure you and other leaders undertake building diversity through recruiting and hiring practices with the intentionality it deserves. The starting point in any position request is to ask how it will contribute to this core campus goal. Resist pressure to replace positions as they come open without first considering how they support where the unit is going rather than where it's been. Then work with human resources, your equity and diversity office or committee, or other resources to analyze position descriptions to assure inclusive language. This is harder than it sounds, and it means search teams cannot just copy and paste. Hiring is for building the future, not for replicating the past.

As a new dean, save yourself some trouble by starting the analysis prior to the first search. Ask your HR department about the diversity in similar search pools. Are they meeting the institution's goals? If not, consider where and how positions are advertised and which networks the unit is tapping into. Professional organizations exist for BIPOC scholars and professionals in most fields. For example, consider attending and recruiting at the Institute on Teaching and Mentoring, offered each year by the Southern Regional Education Board—accurately described as "a four-day conference that has become the largest gathering of minority doctoral scholars in the country."[3]

Reinforce your commitment through the search process. Of course, the search committee needs to be as diverse as possible. It also needs to be structured so that every voice is heard. Share clear expectations with the chair. As the CAOs for our respective campuses, the authors visit with every search committee to reinforce the importance of what we're doing and to unequivocally state the significance of our collective roles in building diversity in our faculty and staff. Over the years, we've successfully shifted the culture norms of search committees on our campuses through clarity and consistent application of procedures. Be sure your search team is holding to the stated qualifications (and not adding hidden ones) when initially reviewing candidates for further consideration. If a pool lacks diversity among candidates and finalists, extend or cancel the search and analyze *why* the pool lacks racial, ethnic, and other aspects of diversity.

The goal is to recruit talented people to add not only to your unit but also to your community. We recommend providing all position finalists, whether BIPOC or not, with firsthand information or, where possible, individual contacts to learn what living in the community is like. If the thought of doing this for BIPOC job candidates produces anxiety, interpret that as motivation for getting to know community leaders and organizations that align with the institution's goals for inclusion. The university is an extension of the community and vice versa.

HIRING ALONE DOES NOT CREATE A CULTURE SHIFT

True shifts in the culture of higher education necessitate challenging what already exists. This idea can make many of us who have advanced into leadership uncomfortable. Key questions that require nondefensive inquiry and that you should raise as a dean committed to moving your institution forward toward inclusion and racial justice include: What is your department's record on *retention* of BIPOC colleagues? What conditions in the university or the surrounding community, or both, lead people to leave or prevent them from receiving tenure? The psychological tendency is to look to the individual as the source of the problem, but first ask what you know about the context. Identify changeable aspects. The effective solutions will vary; however, foresee a need for deep analysis. Deans have a responsibility to eliminate additional baggage and share the emotional work that our existing and new BIPOC colleagues carry as they navigate the already-difficult pretenure and other professional advancement waters.[4]

Academic leaders may struggle with balancing competing institutional commitments for BIPOC faculty and staff. To ensure fairness, protect a new faculty member's time without being paternalistic. However, if tenure and promotion codes, for example, don't include DEI work, attempts at institutionally defined "fairness" might be anything but. For example, a relatively new tenure-track faculty of color at a PWI may end up with significant, uncredited mentoring and advising work.[5] Viewing this type of situation as an individual workload problem is insufficient. We need to go further in tenure and promotion policies and annual review practices and consider the cultural taxation our BIPOC faculty experience.[6] Ensuring inclusivity and equity requires thinking differently about how faculty work is quantified.

As these efforts of hiring and retaining BIPOC faculty succeed, consider how to mentor the next generation of BIPOC academic leaders. Nationally, developing this new generation of leaders will take time and effort. It has taken a major shift in the number of women entering academia for the levels of equity evident today to emerge in the professoriate, but higher-education leadership lags. Only 30 percent of all presidents are women, a figure bolstered by the portion who are presidents of two-year colleges, where women make up 36 percent of the leadership.[7] For all of your faculty, but particularly your BIPOC faculty, make intentional efforts to connect them to administrative opportunities and academic leadership programs. Unless faculty feel that they have strong support, anyone who has experienced impostor syndrome is much less likely to apply for such opportunities.

CONCLUSION

Academic leaders are best positioned to bend institutions toward racial justice. To do this work, the first step is to recognize our own identities and the privileges that come with them. However, a dean's ability to make change will depend on both the institutional environment and what is within their portfolio. Multiple approaches and continued efforts are needed to achieve this. Based on the authors' own experiences and lessons learned, with a heavy dose of listening to those around us, we've identified immediate and long-term actions to achieve transformative progress on DEI initiatives.

— *Takeaways* —

- For educators with an investment in our institution and society, transformational DEI change is our work.
- Think holistically from the individual to the institution and to the community; from the symbolic to the deep, structural change.
- Keep in mind wisdom shared by Matt Reed, CAO at Brookdale Community College: Identify what's controllable; seek the small wins and build from them; lead with diagnoses, not solutions.[8] We would add three more actions: assess, adjust, and persist.
- Identify and use the resources at your disposal, including nonfungible ones such as time.

NOTES

1. Adam Pritchard, Sarah Nadel-Hawthorne, Anthony Schmidt, Melissa Fuesting, and Jacqueline Bichsel, "Administrators in Higher Education Annual Report: Key Findings, Trends, and Comprehensive Tables for the 2019–20 Academic Year (Research Report)," CUPA-HR (College and University Professional Association for Human Resources), April 2020, https://www.cupahr.org/surveys/results/.
2. Tia Brown McNair, Estella Mara Bensimon, and Lindsey Malcom-Piqueux, *From Equity Talk to Equity Walk: Expanding Practitioner Knowledge for Racial Justice in Higher Education* (Hoboken, NJ: Jossey-Bass, 2000).
3. See the Institute on Teaching and Mentoring at https://instituteonteachingandmentoring .org/.

4. Eva Michelle Wheeler and Sydney Freeman, "'Scholarling' while Black: Discourses on Race, Gender, and the Tenure Track," *Journal of the Professoriate* 9, no. 2 (2018): 57–86.
5. Social Sciences Feminist Network Research Interest Group, "The Burden of Invisible Work in Academia: Social Inequalities and Time Use in Five University Departments," *Humboldt Journal of Social Relations* 39 (2017): 228–45.
6. Chanté Griffin, "Managing 'Cultural Taxation' and Combating Burnout: Tips and Resources for Underrepresented Faculty and Staff," HERC: Higher Education Recruitment Consortium, 24 June 2019, https://www.hercjobs.org/managing-cultural -taxation-and-combating-burnout-tips-for-underrepresented-faculty-and-staff/.
7. Elizabeth Howard and Jonathan Gagliardi, "Leading the Way to Parity: Preparation, Persistence, and the Role of Women Presidents," American Council on Education, Washington, DC, 2018, accessed 23 July 2021, https://www.acenet.edu/Documents /Leading-the-Way-to-Parity.pdf.
8. This reflection is inspired by Matt Reed's presentation "Where Do We Go from Here? Lessons from 2020," given on 20 January 2021, at the (virtual) 9th Annual ACAD Deans' Institute.

CHAPTER 5

Navigating the Civil Rights and Social Justice Landscape

O. JOHN MADUKO

The year 2020 was an explosive and transformational one for American society, academia, and the world. The confluence of social media platforms that enable users to project their voices and compete with institutional rhetoric has undone the separation of civil rights and social justice from standard higher-education operational practices. As a result, a dramatic shift has occurred within the postsecondary landscape, with educators now having to see through an equity-minded lens and maneuver through an emotional environment.

Provosts, vice-presidents, deans, and other academic leaders are accustomed to preparing for and executing common responsibilities, such as determining faculty rank and tenure; assessing pedagogical needs of disciplines and programs; adhering to institutional and programmatic accreditation standards; monitoring enrollment and student success metrics; leveraging fiscal acumen to balance departmental budgets; and mitigating the dynamics (and egos) of both the president's office and the faculty senate. The tragic and heartbreaking murders of Mr. George Floyd and Ms. Breonna Taylor were not the first instances of racial injustice in the United States to have sparked civil rights challenges. Coupled with the COVID-19 pandemic, the 2020 protests revealed the boiling temperament of marginalized and systemically oppressed communities.

Colleges and universities relying on human resources–mandated compliance and cultural sensitivity training have encountered an unapologetic BIPOC, LGBTQIA, international, low-income, and first-generation student body; frustrated faculty and staff from underrepresented communities; and an angry general public demanding change from a historically lukewarm higher-education sector that, when prompted, at best placates stakeholders.

The rapid evolution of diversity, equity, and inclusion within higher education has placed academic leaders who typically oversee major divisions or departments at the forefront of equity work that demands intentionality and resiliency. This chapter considers how academic leaders can use personal reflection and emotional intelligence to shape concepts and interpretations involving DEI in higher education.

ANTIRACIST AND EQUITY-AND-INCLUSION FRAMEWORKS

Before embarking on DEI commitments, academic leaders are wise to review antiracist and equity-and-inclusion frameworks from five perspectives. First, consider the amount of authentic support the institution and leadership (i.e., board of trustees and president) are willing to provide. Equity work without direction can be costly in the long run. Division between the president and provost or chief academic officer (CAO) can cause further conflict within an institution. Gauging the amount of autonomy one can yield while providing oversight on how a unit will adopt best practices through an equity lens offers a greater sense of confidence when dealing with a layered scene.

Second, reflect on your intestinal fortitude, stamina, and awareness of past traumas and biases. Academic leaders are often required to remain objective when managing people and processes, but DEI work brings with it current and past experiences that are difficult to ignore. Reliving past traumas related to discrimination and marginalization is common when attempting to implement equity frameworks or navigating tense relations on campus. The challenging dynamics of leading equity from a personal standpoint can derail one's efforts or delay beginning the process of guiding these initiatives.

Third, determine where to place the focus on equity: working to close student equity-and-achievement gaps; addressing the institution's disparity in diversity and inclusion among faculty and staff; or engaging with the surrounding underserved communities. Leaders are accustomed to putting out fires and immediately providing solutions, but equity and inclusion require identifying the problem, understanding its impact, determining its scope, and disaggregating data to unearth DEI problems concealed in aggregate data. Endeavor to secure trustworthy and vetted resources to lead equity efforts and visualize desired success.

Fourth, identify allies to partner with in your equity work. Gwenyth Wallen, chief nurse officer and senior investigator in the National Institutes of Health (NIH) Clinical Center, defines an ally as "an individual who unites themselves with another to promote a common interest where both benefit."[1] It's not about "paving the way" for new investigators with common goals but, rather, walking the walk with them. Goals pursued across these alliances have included sharing lessons learned and developing methodological strengths from bench to bedside, to the community and back.[2] Go beyond working with others to address social justice on campus: develop allies who are willing to encounter resistance or face backlash from stakeholders who present a different viewpoint on equity issues or disagree entirely with inclusivity measures.

Fifth, acknowledge the complexity of equity initiatives and the political pressure from internal and external stakeholders. We have witnessed tense, emotional, and public disputes surrounding critical race theory challenges to the paucity of African American women being granted tenure; student athletes boycotting scheduled games due to conflicts with the president's office; and state systems prohibiting use of taxpayer funds to support travel to states with anti-LGBTQIA legislation. Public and private universities, community and technical colleges, and tribal colleges can all experience campus decisions that spill into the surrounding communities, in some instances making waves nationally. Academic leaders perform and maneuver on a stage with internal and external audiences. One can never know how prepared one really is until faced with public or political animus that stems from supporting or opposing social rights matters that are perceived as divisive.

Adopting antiracist frameworks begins with understanding, at both the concept and the system level, the necessity of dismantling inequitable norms within academia. An antiracist framework interconnects concepts and strategies that first acknowledge inequality among racial groups and the existence of racial policies (and how they cause inequities), and then go further to confront racist policies through action to advance equity.[3] Scholars and researchers committed to DEI and to leveraging antiracist frameworks have challenged historically accepted interpretations of research data. For example, Nichole M. Garcia and Oscar J. Mayorga coupled critical race theory with convergent mixed-methods secondary data that question normative educational research practices by acknowledging that racism permeates educational institutions and marginalizes communities of color.[4] Critical race scholars are deepening our comprehension of research data collection by scrutinizing decisions based on sampling. Academic leaders have witnessed DEI work evolving into complex systems of practices, programs, responsibilities, and expectations.

Institutions of higher education are typically driven by operations and results: key performance indicators such as student learning outcomes or graduation rates dominate institutional priorities. But problems arise when higher-education institutions and other academic organizations strive to achieve compositional (numeric) diversity without reflecting on and examining their own histories, policies, and practices or relying on expert support to guide and advance equity and inclusion. Simply increasing the numbers of nonwhite individuals without actively responding to structural impediments or developing equity and inclusion goals is grossly insufficient. Moreover, this practice has the potential to intensify rather than lessen campus and organizational climate issues and dissatisfaction among students and employees alike.[5] Leaders are now required to have a strong grasp of antiracist frameworks so that they may move beyond facilitating mandatory and stagnant diversity.

FROM THEORY TO APPLICATION

Transitioning from equity and inclusion theory to evidence-based application is the core challenge for equity-minded academic leaders. As a leader navigating your DEI efforts to align with your institution's equity north star, you may need to function between obligatory and aspirational dynamics. This is not a debate about whether an institution should adopt inclusive and equitable methodologies to close the equity gaps related to student learning outcomes or hiring practices. Rather, this is a guide from the perspective of an academic leader who will often encounter challenges in adopting, implementing, and sustaining equitable ideals while leading a college's largest division (i.e., academic affairs) or an academic unit.

Lee G. Bolman and Terrence E. Deal speak to the challenges higher-education leaders experience within their institutions.[6] On the surface, the intent of equity and inclusion efforts appears to be pure, as both are necessities for systemically oppressed stakeholders. But structural, political, symbolic, and human resource frames within academia's walls can potentially hinder any form of DEI progress. Through the political frame, a new academic leader will need to determine how to engage faculty who express concern that their academic freedoms or contractual rights are in direct conflict with an institution's equity framework. Human resources may be devoid of allies and supporters due to the hesitation on the part of the board of trustees and institutional leaders to embrace equity.

Risks and adverse challenges are constants in the everyday encounters of equity-minded academic leaders. Adopting tactful, pragmatic, and trans-formative strategies—while maintaining a substantial level of emotional intelligence—is crucial.

Analyze the environment of the institution's personnel landscape, including senior leadership, student outcomes, and a baseline of equity competencies. Getting a clear take on the institution's position on DEI will help you envision the scope of your work. Adopt an equity assessment for staff and faculty, such as an IDI (intercultural development inventory)—a theory-based assessment of intercultural competence that allows individuals to focus on effectively engaging diversity—to establish a collective and individual baseline for those involved.[7]

Map the desired outcomes to the institution's mission and values. These might be incompatible with DEI, complicating this work. What does DEI success look like at your institution or for you as an academic leader? Examples of desired DEI success goals include equitable outcomes in admissions or student graduation rates; an increase in diversity among tenured faculty and academic leaders; and the adoption of curricular and cocurricular high-impact practices that foster an environment of belonging for marginalized students.

A plan can be useful in establishing an institution-specific vision for equity. Attainable DEI outcomes can be defined that are tied to intentional actions. Accountability is often a hurdle with planning: failure typically ensues for leaders who do not assign specific goals to responsible parties. Institutional change and endorsement require many collaborators and cannot be obtained through the efforts of one person. Regular updates provided to the involved stakeholders, regarding breakthroughs and setbacks alike, offer real-time transparency and reinforce the premise of proposed changes.

Carefully consider resources, allyship, and pace. Will financial and human capital be available to support and sustain DEI efforts? Doing more with less as it pertains to equity often results in lukewarm results and resentment among change drivers. Serving as an army of one can lead to emotional fatigue: those who champion equity—and come from marginalized groups—burn out emotionally and mentally through shouldering most of the work. Allies should invest professional and personal capital in projects that academic leaders from minoritized backgrounds are typically forced to pursue alone, thereby risking their institutional standing.

DEI work is a series of marathons, not sprints. There are no quick fixes when attempting to address systemic inequities within higher education. Leaders must encourage their campus and teams to record their development with complete transparency and unassumingly recognize the unavoidable mistakes along the way. Academic leaders will need to monitor the pace of their equity commitments, knowing that maintaining patience will be a struggle. Investing in a network of trusted institutional leaders, mentors, and allies is the best insurance against DEI fatigue.[8]

Finally, compare your own professional and personal ethics with those of the institution. The most important guideline for academic leaders beginning to dedicate themselves to DEI is to consider their personal morals related to equity and how they correlate with the institution's. Room might exist for growth and atonement on the part of the college or university, but an academic leader might also foresee compromises that they will be unable to make.

CONCLUSION

Academia is the canvas that academic leaders dedicate their careers to by creating a sustainable environment that supports the pursuit of academic excellence and provides a safe space for all stakeholders. The triumphs and perils of the civil rights and social justice landscape generate a litany of emotions and realities for leaders. Conscious devotion to self-care and emotional intelligence strategies can lessen the blow of DEI work for academic leaders. Emotional intelligence is the ability to reason about emotions and manage them in order to facilitate problem solving. It includes the abilities to accurately perceive emotions, to access and generate emotions to assist thought, to understand emotions and emotional knowledge, and to reflectively regulate emotions to promote emotional and intellectual growth.[9]

Emotional intelligence is required for leaders to be effective in reflecting on experiences, understanding environmental signals, connecting to stakeholders, and developing relationships.[10] The evolving and charged civil rights and social justice realities that confront academic leaders in the twenty-first-century demand an unprecedented roadmap. Leaders are expected to take on these personal matters without hesitation, but failure is imminent for those unwilling to develop new competencies to take on these daunting challenges. Strategic planning, promoting allyship, developing emotional intelligence, determining an institution's equity vision, encouraging cultural awareness, defining success, and identifying marginalized stakeholders or communities that demand DEI reforms are all components of the new normal for academic leaders.

— *Takeaways* —

- Find ways to become a student of DEI reform both locally and nationally. Find a mentor who can serve as a sounding board and ally throughout your journey of leading equity work.
- You will be surprised and disappointed by the institutions you serve, by some of the people you consider close colleagues, and by the very systems you assumed were in place to support all stakeholders and causes. There are many who verbally support and sign on to what's publicly expected, but ultimately will not align themselves with intentional DEI stances.
- As an ally for marginalized, minoritized, and underserved groups, how far are you willing to go to support equity work? Are you ready to challenge the systemic and organizational structures that have fueled inequities and disparities? There are risks on the professional

and personal fronts that will leave you questioning your decision to take on this work.

- Even adequate planning, preparation, ally development, and DEI competency building may not be enough to transform your institution, division, or unit. Frustration and fatigue will emerge. Are there deal breakers that will force you to seek a new institution or role?

- Throughout your process of leading DEI, remind yourself of the reasons you are pursuing these challenges and why you chose higher education as a profession.

- Don't forget to breathe! As academic leaders, we are tested daily with little to no break from oncoming demands. Due to the nuances manifested in every institution of higher education, there is no magic manual or guide for perfectly executing DEI initiatives. Your humanity, instincts, experiences from personal and professional breakthroughs, and willingness to be a lifelong learner in this space are your fundamental supports to lean on.

NOTES

1. Samantha-Rae Dickenson, "What Is Allyship?" National Institutes of Health Office of Equity, Diversity, and Inclusion, 28 January 2021, https://www.edi.nih.gov/blog/communities/what-allyship.
2. See Dickenson, "What Is Allyship?"
3. See Eduardo Contreras, Maraina Montgomery, and Hernando Sevilla-Garcia, "An Antiracist Framework for Education Abroad" NAFSA (National Association of Foreign Student Advisors), 5 January 2021, https://www.nafsa.org/ie-magazine/2021/1/5/antiracist-framework-education-abroad.
4. Nichole M. Garcia and Oscar J. Mayorga, "The Threat of Unexamined Secondary Data: A Critical Race Transformative Convergent Mixed Methods," *Race Ethnicity and Education* 21, no. 2 (2018), DOI: 10.1080/13613324.2017.1377415.
5. See Eddie Comeaux, "Doin' Work: DEI Implementation Strategies for Leadership Teams," *Forbes*, 24 July 2021, https://www.forbes.com/sites/eddiecomeaux/2021/06/24/doin-work-dei-implementation-strategies-for-leadership-teams/?sh.
6. Lee G. Bolman and Terrence E. Deal, *Reframing Organizations: Artistry, Choice, and Leadership*, 6th ed. (San Francisco: Jossey-Bass, 2017).
7. See Mary-Francis Winters, "Equity and Inclusion: The Roots of Organizational Well-Being," *Stanford Social Innovation Review*, 14 October 2020, https://ssir.org/articles/entry/equity_and_inclusion_the_roots_of_organizational_well_being.

8. See Lily Zheng, "How Diversity, Equity, and Inclusion Changemakers Can Find Balance without Burnout," Berrett-Koehler Publishers (blog), 18 March 2020, https://ideas.bkconnection.com/how-diversity-equity-and-inclusion-changemakers -can-find-balance-without-burnout.

9. See John D. Mayer, Peter Salovey, and David R. Caruso, "Emotional Intelligence: Theory, Findings, and Implications," *Psychological Inquiry* 60 (2004): 197–215.

10. See Daryl Watkins, Matthew Earnhardt, Linda Pittenger, Robin Roberts, Kees Rietsema, and Janet Cosman-Ross, "Thriving in Complexity: A Framework for Leadership Education," *Journal of Leadership Education* 16, no. 14 (2017): 148–63.

CHAPTER 6

Working toward Greater Diversity, Equity, and Inclusion

The Benefits of Wearing Multiple Hats

JAMILA BOOKWALA

"Diversity work is difficult." These are the words of an esteemed colleague that I repeat to myself frequently. Those of us who commit to this work know intimately the truth they contain: the difficulties are innumerable and varied. Far more importantly, however, diversity, equity, and inclusion work is a responsibility, an urgency. DEI efforts are also necessarily multilayered and multidimensional. We must address the needs and concerns of our students, faculty, staff, and community. Focusing exclusively on one constituency or some groups over others creates new inequities. Thus, to make the most impact and bring about structural and systemic change, DEI initiatives on our campuses must in themselves embody diversity, equity, and inclusion. Such efforts must bring together a diverse group of community members, provide equal opportunities for them to engage in discussions to promote change, and welcome their thoughts and concerns regarding DEI advancement with respect and appreciation.

In this chapter, I share my experiences at the intersection of the roles of dean of the faculty within the academic division; chair of the college's council on diversity, equity, and inclusion; and member of the president's cabinet in advancing diversity, equity, and inclusion at the institutional level. This intersectional role offers an uncommon opportunity to propel institutional action and advance structural and systemic transformation. My role has enabled me to raise DEI questions and concerns during discussions and priority-setting sessions of the president's cabinet, the provost's council, and elected faculty committees. In this way, our campus has taken meaningful steps forward in making learning, teaching, and working at Lafayette College in Easton, Pennsylvania, more diverse, equitable, and inclusive.

In the paragraphs that follow, I describe my intersecting roles; share relevant challenges, accomplishments, and opportunities; and offer reflections based on my experiences. My goal for this chapter is that it be of value to deans and other academic leaders whose roles involve making measurable and meaningful contributions toward achieving greater diversity, equity, and inclusion on their campuses. There is no doubt that commitment to DEI takes a campus, and wearing multiple hats can be a plus.

WEARING MORE THAN ONE HAT

If you're like me, a senior administrator at a small liberal arts college, you wear more than one hat. I'm dean of the faculty at Lafayette College, where I report to the provost, whose office is across from mine in a small suite in the campus's main administration building. As dean of the faculty, I'm ultimately responsible for faculty hiring, retention, support, development, and climate. I serve as an advocate for faculty needs and concerns, at the individual and collective level. The dean of faculty is also charged with promoting and protecting diversity, equity, and inclusion in faculty life and, by extension, in student learning experiences and the broader academic life of the college. As dean, I serve on the president's cabinet, along with the provost—an appointment that validates the related but distinct roles and responsibilities of the dean relative to the provost, who is the chief academic officer of the college.

I also chair Lafayette College's Diversity, Equity, and Inclusion Council (DEIC), whose members are appointed by the president. The DEIC is a small group of campus leadership representing students, faculty, staff and administrators, and the broader community. These representatives serve on the DEIC in addition to shouldering full-time positions in which they address the needs of their primary constituents. The council is charged with leading institutional efforts to move the college toward greater diversity, equity, and inclusion through community dialog; building bridges across different offices, committees, and groups on campus that collaborate to advance DEI; and developing and executing plans across campus that advance DEI, at the macro and micro levels, within units, departments, and divisions. In addition, I wear the hat of deputy Title IX coordinator for faculty-related matters and serve ex officio on multiple elected faculty committees.

If you wear multiple hats as an administrator, in all likelihood you find meeting these multiple, often conflicting responsibilities to be a challenge. I certainly do. The demands are obvious: wearing more than one hat means experiencing greater demands on your time and resources, feeling pulled in different directions, and fighting the sense of continued and endless exhaustion. No matter how much you accomplish in a day, a week, or a year, there remains a high pile of work yet to be done to sustain past successes, respond to present needs, and prepare for future endeavors. Nevertheless, I have found that wearing the hats of dean of the faculty, cabinet member, and DEIC chair presents me with opportunities that are rare and ideal for advancing our campus toward greater diversity, equity, and inclusion.

The reasons for this are simple. First, I am able to advance DEI more holistically, as an institutional priority. Not only am I focused on recruiting and retaining a more diverse faculty and dedicated to ensuring greater equity and inclusion among them, but I'm also able to bridge these priorities with parallel efforts for recruiting and retaining more diverse students and staff—all the while advancing initiatives for greater equity and inclusion among these two groups. Second, I am meeting with people at a variety of different tables where DEI discussions are (or should be) conducted. These include discussions involving the president's cabinet; trustees; centers and offices on inclusive teaching, advising, learning, and research; faculty-elected committees; leaders of academic departments and programs; individual members and small groups of the faculty; colleagues on the staff and senior administration; and student representatives. Through these associations, I am in a position to facilitate communication across different individuals, groups, and units about DEI-related matters—keeping the campus's right hand informed about what its left hand is doing in the DEI space.

This doesn't mean that there haven't been bumps in the road—and significant DEI work remains to be done—but I believe there is a sense of interconnectedness on campus in the DEI space. From my intersectional vantage point, it feels that our campus is building momentum, gaining ground against old resistance to DEI efforts, and expanding our community of active allies in the efforts to advance DEI. This is significant. Numerous members of our community are committed to a more diverse, equitable, and inclusive campus, but these colleagues' paths rarely cross. Historically, a sense of working in isolation long persisted in the DEI space. I feel fortunate and honored to have been a part of so many different levels of DEI discussions on campus. They have provided me with the unique opportunity to connect numerous dots, to keep community members better informed about the activities under way in different parts of campus, and to collaborate with colleagues across campus in responding to unexpected circumstances and meeting some long-standing needs related to diversity, equity, and inclusion.

FACILITATING INSTITUTIONAL CHANGE

My unequivocal position is that all segments and sectors of a campus must be included and engaged for DEI efforts to be meaningful and impactful. While the chief diversity officer model is common across the higher-education landscape, it can be a lonely position for that one individual that comes with unimaginable pressures. The person who holds this position ordinarily lacks needed resources and the authority to effect change. Not surprisingly, then, many institutions that adopt the model see high frequent burnout and high turnover in the position and an understandable sense within the campus community of insufficient or even nonexistent institutional commitment to DEI advancement. The DEI Council at Lafayette College offers an alternative. In its current iteration, it can facilitate institutional change precisely because it does not have a single individual on whose shoulders falls the immense responsibility of moving the college and its broader community to become a more diverse, equitable, and inclusive space.

Organizationally, Lafayette's DEI Council is flat. Representation through leaders within the academic division, campus life, human resources, and the president's office has resulted in a consultative and collaborative approach with the singular goal of facilitating institutional change. As council chair, I serve mainly as a convener and as connective tissue between different committees, groups, and offices on campus. I don't intend to imply that the DEI Council has not experienced hiccups, challenges, frustrations, or criticism, or that we could not have done more better and faster. However, it's fair to conclude that DEI conversations are now occurring intentionally at different levels of the college—within groups and committees, offices and centers, and programs, departments, and divisions across Lafayette. There is an unmistakable and collective momentum, and the DEI Council has helped propel it.

Of course, this momentum toward advancing DEI is not unique to Lafayette's campus: colleges and universities across the nation have responded to calls for greater equity and racial justice since the summer of 2020 in the wake of the police killing of Mr. George Floyd. Working in close collaboration with senior leadership and colleagues across campus, we moved forward on a number of initiatives, including:

- Facilitating community conversations and hosting internal and external speakers on racial justice and antiracism
- Holding discussions with colleagues in the campus safety office to discuss the experiences of community members with regard to equity and inclusion
- Conducting a study on the scope of invisible labor carried out by faculty and staff to support students from underrepresented groups, and recommending strategies for recognizing, supporting, and valuing such efforts
- Providing an accounting to the campus community of the college's response to DEI-related needs and concerns expressed by students in recent years
- Making progress toward a required diversity education program for the campus community
- Calling on campus divisions to develop DEI goals as they pertain to education and curriculum, recruitment, retention, and climate

These collaborations were likewise undertaken to educate and rally our community in response to the discrimination and violence targeted at members of Asian, Asian American, and Pacific Islander communities across the nation in the wake of political leadership's irresponsible rhetoric about responsibility and blame for the COVID-19 pandemic.

My intersectional position at the college—bridging faculty affairs, institutional DEI concerns, and cabinet-level discussions and decisions—has offered me the unique opportunity to keep DEI conversations and actions coordinated at multiple levels. As a result, I've served as a source of information, a listening ear for concerns, and an advocate for resources and change. To be clear, I am only one member of the DEIC, and all its members have tirelessly endeavored to advance DEI initiatives at the college. What has been unique for me is that I have been engaged in the entire range of conversations around DEI initiatives, from the cabinet to the individual level.

I am grateful to have played a small role, with my colleagues, in making the wheels turn on a number of new, campus-wide initiatives that have put us on the path of potentially meaningful and measurable DEI progress. These include the planned implementation of a diversity education program for faculty and staff and its expansion to include our students; the modification of annual faculty and staff performance evaluation forms to include hitherto-invisible labor related to supporting and mentoring students from underrepresented groups, so that the light can be shone on such work; the expansion of inclusive practices to embrace both faculty and staff hiring that are designed to build diverse and highly qualified applicant pools and evaluate candidates in a fair and equitable manner; biweekly discussions for the entire campus community to engage in dialog regarding a variety of DEI topics, with an open invitation to share thoughts, concerns, ideas, and recommendations; and the preparation of DEI plans in each division so that DEI goals are articulated not only in the academic (faculty-centric) and campus life (student-centric) divisions but also in the divisions of human resources, finance, development and alumni affairs, investment, information technology, and communications, all of which are integral to the college's mission and success.

REFLECTIONS

In my intersectional role, hurdles are inevitable, but opportunities vast. To help me persist despite—or because of—these hurdles, I've developed a few effective approaches. First, bringing the community together is vital. DEI work is difficult even under the best of circumstances, when resources are in place and efforts are well coordinated. When it is done without wide community input and engagement, however, it feels impossible and is likely to have little positive impact. Listening to concerns, inviting ideas and suggestions, and closing the loop through timely communications are at the core of diversity, equity, and inclusion. Our efforts must embody the best principles and practices of DEI: they must value input and feedback from across the campus community and, in turn, provide updates and follow-up. I strive to do so by remaining accessible and holding myself accountable to the community, building trust through transparency and authenticity.

Second, despite all good intentions, inertia is common. You're likely to receive endorsement for bold new ideas to enhance DEI efforts, and this endorsement is indeed sincere. However, the path to converting ideas to actions, transforming the talk to the walk, is neither speedy nor smooth. Lack of precedence and overcommitted resources sustain the inertia. I have learned to develop a steady persistence in the face of inertia. I do so by raising DEI issues, needs, and concerns and introducing a DEI framework whenever possible during a range of discussions and with a variety of decision-making bodies. This may not always result in the desired outcome; however, I'm certain that my raised hand at in-person and Zoom meetings is a signal that DEI issues should be considered.

Third, disappointment and failure should be taken in stride. As with any leadership position, some efforts won't take off or will fade away. This is more likely when the efforts focus on transforming the institutional-level DEI climate and culture. Initiatives that may seem acceptable to some constituencies may be unpalatable to others. The more ambitious and wide-reaching the initiative, the more likely it is to stall and hit roadblocks. While perseverance is valuable, it's equally important to know when it's time to step back, take stock, or hit pause on a new initiative. I've learned the benefits of emotional detachment from what seems to be an idea filled with great promise. If an idea fails to gain community support or senior administration endorsement, I question its merits and evaluate the criticism with an open mind instead of viewing it as a failure.

Fourth, pushback and protest in response to DEI work are inevitable. I see them as a product of the resistance to change and preference for the status quo—or of the desire for the perfect at the cost of the good. Pushback and protest thus come from both expected and unexpected corners—from resisters and allies alike. The more hats one wears, the more sources of resistance become evident. I've trained myself not to take pushback and protest as personal attacks. I remind myself frequently that DEI initiatives are not about me and therefore resistance, no matter what corner it comes from, is not directed at me personally. Instead, I view pushback and protest as signs that DEI successes are being noted, having impact, and serving as the necessary first steps in the path to change.

CONCLUSION

Diversity work is challenging; so is wearing multiple hats. When these responsibilities come together, feelings of exhaustion are normal. However, the work is deeply meaningful and morally imperative. Reflection and resolve are valuable assets for maintaining focus. The challenges notwithstanding, wearing multiple hats means multiplied potential for positive impact.

— *Takeaways* —

- To be impactful and bring about structural and systemic change, DEI initiatives must in themselves embody diversity, equity, and inclusion.
- There's no doubt that commitment to DEI work takes a campus—wearing multiple hats can be a plus.
- Listening to concerns, inviting ideas and suggestions, and closing the loop through timely communications are at the core of working toward diversity, equity, and inclusion.
- While perseverance is valuable, it's equally important to know when it's time to step back, take stock, or hit pause on a new initiative.

CHAPTER 7

Understanding Higher-Education Policy in Order to Manage Risk and Achieve Equity

MARGARET BROWN MARSDEN

In the dean's office, concerns appear with regularity. A student reports difficulty with their academic program's expectations. Someone from your organization asks a staff member to perform a task, but it's unclear whether the person asking has the authority to make the request. You're copied on an email conversation about an academic dishonesty case and anticipate that it will escalate to your office. Some instances are more consequential and far-reaching: a sexual harassment incident, denial of a student's accommodation, or an injury to a student during an academic activity. Issues that require your involvement call for informed, efficient, and careful use of your campus policies.

The right time to start learning about policy and how it applies is long before a problem arises. This chapter explores engaging with higher-education policy at three levels: identifying, administering, and revising or creating. In practice, deans may work at each level and shift among levels depending on whether they lead or follow policy administration. The final section explores two significant issues: crisis management and diversity, equity, and inclusion (DEI).

IDENTIFYING POLICY

Identifying applicable policies is essential throughout your career—whether you're a newly appointed dean, are moving between institutions, or are continuing in a position affected by policy changes. Policy provides order and structure for the institution, and its creation entails awareness of external and internal policy foundations.

Federal, state, local, and tribal governments enact many external higher-education policies. A complete and expansive list of federal laws and regulations governing colleges and universities is available from the HECA Compliance Matrix, an informational clearinghouse for laws, rules, and regulations.[1] State boards or administrative or service agencies manage higher-education policies differently from state to state.[2] Campus academic, athletic, and social events may fall under local governmental police authority, even as local law enforcement experiences greater scrutiny regarding inequity and social justice in policing.[3] For the thirty-seven tribal colleges and universities in the United States, the relevant policies include, but are not limited to, 25 US Code, Chapter 20, §1801, concerning tribally controlled colleges and universities.[4]

Colleges, universities, and their programs opt in to a set of policies when seeking accreditation. National, regional, and programmatic or disciplinary accreditors are the authorities defining these policies. The Accrediting Commission of Career Schools and Colleges (ACCSC) oversees trade and vocational schools nationally. The Council for Higher Education Accreditation (CHEA) recognizes seven different regional accrediting organizations with broad authority over granting degrees and everything it entails.[5]

Programmatic accreditors are specialized and have standards requiring higher-education institutions to demonstrate that their programs meet benchmarks in a particular field of study.[6] Examples include the Council for the Accreditation of Educator Preparation (CAEP), the Association to Advance Collegiate Schools of Business (AACSB), and the Accreditation Board for Engineering and Technology (ABET). Diverse accreditors oversee licensure for programs in health care and law. Programmatic accreditors can be exacting, and their review cycles more frequent than regional accreditors.

Deans should have heightened awareness of external policies that form the infrastructure for institutions that serve the educational needs of marginalized populations.[7] Historically Black Colleges and Universities (HBCUs) were strengthened by Title III of the Higher Education Act of 1965 (HEA) and Executive Order 12677, signed in 1989 by President George H. W. Bush.[8] Minority-Serving Institutions (MSIs) are also governed under Titles III and V of HEA. Federal law and policy helped establish Gallaudet University, the world's only university specifically designed to educate deaf and hard of hearing students.[9] General knowledge of policy instruments designed to provide open and equal learning opportunities permits all institutions to serve marginalized groups without official HBCU, MSI, or other affiliations.[10]

Ecclesiastical polity may form the guiding principles and policies for private colleges and universities with religious affiliations. Denominations and religious groups originally founded many higher-education institutions. In some, the denomination retains only nominal control; in others, the relationship is highly interconnected. Such variation creates differences between institutions in how strongly religious authority influences local policy development or creates conflict. Some institutions require membership in the church or adherence to its faith heritage by faculty, staff, and students, with resulting challenges to hiring policies and academic freedom guidelines.[11] Other religious-affiliated universities have rejected Title IV federal funding due to conflicts between federal policy and ecclesiastical authority—frequently with regard to Title IX inclusions of lesbian, gay, bisexual, and transgender (LGBT) student protections.[12] Some colleges do not follow federal regulations (such as the Campus Sexual Violence Elimination Act or the Jeanne Clery Act) if they do not accept federal funding. The variation in adherence to ecclesiastical authority may result in significant differences in policy application.

Finally, many external policies that impact colleges and universities are not exclusive to higher education and are less familiar to academic administrators. For example, the Occupational Safety and Health Administration (OSHA) and the Environmental Protection Agency (EPA) together oversee environmental, health, and safety standards that impact employees and the environment. OSHA and EPA oversight guides the operations of higher-education facilities and may regulate academic programs that work with chemicals, radioactive materials, or other potential hazards.

Internal policies are formed by and tailored to the institution. These are approved by the board or other executive leadership and appear in the institutional policies and procedures manual. Human resources (HR) offices may manage those who guide hiring and employment. Others receive oversight through governance organizations such as faculty and staff senates or academic collective bargaining processes.[13]

Embedded in the general institutional policies are those administrated by the registrar, student affairs, or admissions. These units oversee specific areas of university operations. Faculty apply these institutional policies and create procedural guidelines in their syllabi for classroom conduct, deadlines, grading, and appeals. A syllabus, in principle, is "a rule-bound system that attempts to anticipate and induce a set of behaviors in and beyond your classroom."[14] In practice, a syllabus can expand to extraordinary length as it presents information about a course, including administrative policies relevant to a student's enrollment and engagement. Syllabi themselves have been subject to scrutiny because of their function as both pedagogical documents and vehicles of institutional policy. The issue of whether they are legal documents has been challenged in court cases.[15]

As a dean, you need sustained and practical awareness of all applicable external and internal policies, their location, and their connection to the institution's broader infrastructure and identity. Policy knowledge starts by keeping current documents close and periodically reviewing them for refresher information when necessary. Deans should seek opportunities to engage with internal policy through campus committees and with external policy through accreditor-hosted or -sponsored conferences or webinars on specific issues. By actively engaging in policy review, deans can learn more about policy and help to improve it.

Finally, a dean should be capable of differentiating policies from procedures and explaining the distinction to others. Policies typically undergo vetting and approval at several administrative levels, remain relatively stable over time, and form the foundation of your institution. Procedures describe policies in action and provide a set of operational steps or actions for policy implementation. Furthermore, procedures help administrators conduct the ongoing activities of the institution in compliance with policy. As a dean, you must communicate this distinction between policy and procedure to avoid inadvertently creating policy or conflicting with codified procedure.

ADMINISTERING POLICY

Administering policy is a team effort that stretches across the layers of academic administration and includes the act of communicating and enforcing policy and investigating violations when necessary. Deans, including associate and assistant deans, can serve as the "policy police," especially if they're on the front lines of communicating policy to faculty, staff, and students. You may serve as a campus navigator, overseeing an education process to help others seek answers and assistance in policy. Early information about your campus policy landscape can eliminate having to communicate complex policy during a crisis when time is critical. Short educational opportunities can occur during a faculty meeting or through direct, one-on-one reports, allowing focused and timely reminders of essential policies and how they may apply. Examples include a beginning-of-year discussion of your institution's Title IX reporting structure and contact persons or a reminder about the grade appeal policy toward the end of the semester as final exams approach.

HR offices provide guidance and best practices for personnel hiring, management, and training. But for faculty or student issues outside an employment context, HR is not the applicable authority. An institution's general counsel may seem the place for resolving issues, but internal problem solving may require the general counsel to remain in an advisory role rather than take on an adjudicating one. Student affairs offices handle grievance policies and procedures for students. Faculty issues follow a reporting and appeals process informed by the applicable faculty governance structure.

Policy administration for faculty starts with the closest administrator—typically the chair—and then may escalate across levels to deans, directors, or vice presidents and, in some cases, to the president. When the path to policy understanding is complex, a university can create an ombuds-position to provide confidential, third-party assistance. Ombudspersons can guide faculty and staff toward resources or help structure conflict resolution. In pursuing policy-based solutions, clear timelines and de-escalation practices allow due process and set essential boundaries.

Institutions and administrators launch a formal or informal investigation when policy violations are suspected or known to have occurred. The investigation process may involve single offices or administrators, or engage committees (such as those tasked with managing appeals or grievances). A dean may not feel inclined to consider every policy issue review to be an investigation, but employing the term invokes necessary weight and structure. Investigations require a systematic process and culminate in a decision and set of proposed actions. They may require a few short communications or an extensive information-gathering effort with the dean serving as the central administrator. Incidents investigated by a dean's office broadly include student complaints and grade disputes, plagiarism, and faculty grievances. Investigations of discrimination or harassment that threaten an institution's DEI mission should involve dedicated offices with trained and qualified investigators.

Policy investigations require more than just basic knowledge. An investigation starts with historical information and evidence collection. Once complete, an investigation should culminate in a precise decision informed by evidence and accompanied by an accounting of required actions. If the dean delivers the decision, then they must take ownership of it and remain ready to cooperate with the next level in the event of an appeal. Policy is the infrastructure on which a dean's investigative work rests and is scrutinized by those higher in the administrative chain of command.

REVISING OR CREATING POLICY

Throughout policy administration and investigation, academic leaders should identify a policy that is outdated and requires revision. In some instances, a needed policy may not yet exist. Internal policy gaps can result from new external requirements going into effect. Repairing such gaps may mean instituting reform or initiating development.

In revising and creating policy, it is helpful to remember two related ideas: ownership and impact. Administrators, offices, and committees each hold ownership and undertake review and enforcement. "Impact" refers to reach and responsibility with regard to compliance. For example, an institution's administration and finance division may own and oversee travel policies, but everyone traveling on university business or managing travel processes experiences the impact.

Periodic review requires policy owners to ensure that institutional policies are current, appropriate, internally consistent, and aligned with external policies. Institutions should create new policies to address shortcomings when gaps exist, when the policy landscape changes, or when impact is unclear. Policy impact may require human resources (committee, manager, chair); physical resources (record keeping, software, space, equipment); or financial resources. If staffing, space, or budgets do not compensate for the impact, there is a likelihood of weakness or failure and a negative impact on policy management.

New policies require careful review to determine their scope and impact before codification. Approval should involve a range of constituencies broader than that involved with the policy revision process. Diverse constituencies can view a policy from multiple perspectives to determine whether any unintended or undocumented consequences may emerge in practice.

Finally, your institution should have or create a "policy on policies." While sounding redundant, a policy on policies can be a valuable tool for instructing the campus on how policies are defined, formatted, drafted, reviewed, approved, revised, and administered. The colloquial use of the word "policy" can fail to capture the true extent of impact. Encourage others to refrain from using the word "policy" when the term does not apply—or if what they describe refers to a procedure, not a policy.

CRISIS MANAGEMENT AND DIVERSITY, EQUITY, AND INCLUSION

In 2020, changes necessitated by the pandemic and concerns about how campuses serve people of color or the LGBT community amplified the need for policy awareness, administration, and revision. These two areas—crisis management and DEI—are the focus of the rest of this chapter.

Crisis management requires agility and inventiveness. What does this mean for policy? It may mean quickly implementing new policies during the crisis or altering the procedures accompanying them. It also may mean temporarily suspending existing policies while the crisis is in effect.

Some institutions revised student codes of conduct during the pandemic to promote campus and community safety.[16] Others expanded provisions for remote work, and more than 250 institutions altered tenure clocks for pre-tenure faculty.[17] The pandemic is estimated to have cost colleges $183 billion, with a 14 percent average revenue decline for FY21 and unknown impacts on future fiscal years.[18] Responses to the financial challenges and enrollment drops vary and include (in the short-term) freezing tuition, increasing debt, drawing on short-term relief funds, restricting travel, and reducing benefits. Long-term decisions are looming at some institutions, including program closures, increased reliance on contingent faculty, and possible decreases in tenure-track lines.

Colleges and universities can invoke crisis management adaptations of policies when needed. But these crisis-related adaptations might not be permanent. A helpful strategy may be to assemble an ad hoc team or task force comprising individuals already serving on standing committees or in campus offices. Members can carry forward their policy knowledge and experience to task force deliberations. At the end of a crisis, the team may disband and transfer responsibilities back to standing committees and structures. Continuity among task force and standing committee membership aids in implementing any permanent changes that may result from lessons learned during a crisis.

Higher-education institutions had wide-ranging responses following the murder of Mr. George Floyd and subsequent protests against racial injustice.[19] Responses in higher education reflected a more extensive cultural examination of systemic racism in the United States. Some institutions focused on commitments of support and revisions to strengthen their DEI statements. Others worked to address the experience of trauma among students and enhanced training focused on racial justice issues among all campus constituencies. These responses reveal a core concern about policies and procedures that either center or disproportionately enforce systemic racism.

As they did during pandemic-related crisis management, some institutions formed task forces to respond to this moment of DEI reflection. It was only in the latter part of the twentieth century that the Higher Education Act of 1965 desegregated colleges and universities.[20] Qualitative research reports continue to reveal racial stereotyping and unconscious bias in many academic fields, and quantitative data show disparities in student representation within disciplines.[21] Segregation persists in higher education, and problem-solving for DEI disparities must occur on two policy fronts: administration and creation or revision.

Institutions should identify intrinsic bias and systemic racism in their policies. It may be policy administration that causes higher education to fail to meet DEI goals rather than the availability of a diverse pipeline of students, staff, and faculty. Students are subject to numerous internal and external policies, from admissions to graduation. Other policies guide faculty and staff recruitment, employment, promotion, and dismissal.[22] Systemic bias in policy administration can impact admissions and hiring committees, academic leadership, and search committees. Where complaints and adjudication processes occur, controlling interests with implicit bias can and should be eradicated. Centralized reporting built into the policy structure may provide more accessible investigation and data analysis to determine the potential for bias. In creating new policy, diverse constituencies are necessary to ensure that relevant perspectives help draft the language. Historic, antiquated structures may have built-in policies and ownership networks. New systems and ownership are needed to serve equitable pathways.

CONCLUSION

Careful identification, administration, revision, and creation are essential to manage risk and achieve equity in policy. While mission and vision help define an institution's core values and aspirations, policy forms the administrative infrastructure and provides specialized guidance for actions and responses. Policy is the framework for your responsibilities as a dean or academic leader. Ultimately, your campus policies have ramifications for safety, human resources, academic integrity, and other issues that impact risk management and institutional equity practices. Institutional policies must be known and followed to ensure that students, staff, and faculty receive the greatest support for their work.

— *Takeaways* —

- Seek broad knowledge of the ways policy creates order and structure for your institution and higher education.
- Identify both internal and external sources of policy and make sure they're accessible before times of need.
- Engage in regular policy education opportunities with constituents during one-on-one or large-group meetings to provide general knowledge of the campus policy landscape.

- Use task forces and policy modification during crisis management, but commit to a continuity plan to return to normal operations after a crisis.
- Identify intrinsic bias and systemic racism in policies and use diverse workgroups to draft new policies when needed.

NOTES

1. "HECA Compliance Matrix," Higher Education Compliance Alliance, last modified 25 June 2021, https://www.higheredcompliance.org/compliance-matrix/.
2. Mary Fulton, "An Analysis of State Postsecondary Governance Structures," Education Commission of the States, October 2019, https://www.ecs.org/wp-content/uploads/An-Analysis-of-State-Postsecondary-Governance-Structures.pdf.
3. Emma Whitford and Lilah Burke, "Students Demand Campuses Cut Ties with Police," *Inside Higher Ed*, last modified 5 June 2020, https://www.insidehighered.com/news/2020/06/05/students-demand-universities-break-ties-local-police-few-have.
4. United States Code, 2006 Edition, Supplement 5, Title 25—Indians 2011, U.S. Code, last modified 7 January 2011, https://www.govinfo.gov/content/pkg/USCODE-2010-title25/pdf/USCODE-2010-title25.pdf.
5. "2020–2021 Directory of CHEA-Recognized Organizations," Council for Higher Education Accreditation, last modified May 2021, https://www.chea.org/2020-2021-directory-chea-recognized-accrediting-organizations-pdf.
6. Alexandra Hegji, "An Overview of Accreditation of Higher Education in the United States," Congressional Research Service, last modified 16 October 2020, https://crsreports.congress.gov/product/pdf/R/R43826.
7. Hegji, "An Overview of Accreditation of Higher Education in the United States."
8. Gerhard Peters and John T. Wooley, "George Bush, Executive Order 12677—Historically Black Colleges and Universities," *American Presidency Project*, accessed 5 May 2021, https://www.presidency.ucsb.edu/node/269104.
9. David F. Armstrong, *The History of Gallaudet University: 150 Years of a Deaf American Institution* (Washington, DC: Gallaudet University Press, 2014).
10. Marybeth Gasman and Andres Samayoa, "Students at the Margins and the Institutions That Serve Them: A Global Perspective," Center for Minority Serving Institutions, 2015, https://repository.upenn.edu/gse_pubs/343.
11. Becky Supiano, "A Closer Look at Christian Colleges' Statements of Faith," *Chronicle of Higher Education*, 7 January 2016, https://www.chronicle.com/article/a-closer-look-at-christian-colleges-statements-of-faith/.
12. Ibby Caputo and Jon Marcus, "The Controversial Reason Some Religious Colleges Forgo Federal Funding," *Atlantic*, 7 July 2016, https://www.theatlantic.com/education/archive/2016/07/the-controversial-reason-some-religious-colleges-forgo-federal-funding/490253/.

13. Ronald Ehrenberg, Daniel B. Klaff, Adam T. Kezbom, and Matthew P. Nagowski, "Collective Bargaining in American Higher Education," in *Governing Academia*, ed. R. B. Ehrenberg (Ithaca, NY: Cornell University Press, 2004), 209–32.

14. William Germano and Kit Nicholls, *Syllabus: The Remarkable, Unremarkable Document That Changes Everything* (Princeton, NJ: Princeton University Press, 2020), 8.

15. Martha M. Rumore, "The Course Syllabus: Legal Contract or Operator's Manual?" *American Journal of Pharmaceutical Education* 80, no. 10 (2016): 177.

16. Rae Goldsmith, "SIU Updates Student Code to support Campus and Community Safety," Southern Illinois University, 17 August 2020, https://news.siu.edu/2020/08/081720-siu-updates-student-code-to-support-campus-and-community-safety.html.

17. Todd Butler, "Beyond Tenure Clock Management," *Inside Higher Ed*, 9 January 2021, https://www.insidehighered.com/advice/2021/01/19/tenure-clock-extensions-arent-enough-help-support-researchers-and-their-work.

18. Paul N. Friga, "How Much Has Covid Cost Colleges? $183 Billion," *Chronicle of Higher Education*, 5 February 2021, https://www.chronicle.com/article/how-to-fight-covids-financial-crush?cid2=gen_login_refresh&cid=gen_sign_in.

19. Joy Gaston Gayles and Alyssa N Rockenbach, "The Transformative Power of Student Voices in the Midst of Racial Injustice," *Inside Higher Ed*, 17 May 2021, https://www.insidehighered.com/views/2021/05/17/engaging-students-about-racial-injustice.

20. Peter Hinrichs, "An Empirical Analysis of Racial Segregation in Higher Education," Working Paper 21831 (Cambridge, MA: National Bureau of Economic Research, 2015), https://www.nber.org/system/files/working_papers/w21831/w21831.pdf.

21. Tomas Monarrez and Celia Washington, *Racial and Ethnic Segregation within Colleges* (Washington, DC: Urban Institute, December 2020), https://www.urban.org/sites/default/files/publication/103279/racial-and-ethnic-segregation-within-colleges_1.pdf.

22. Colleen Flaherty, "A Bad Fit?" *Inside Higher Ed*, 14 July 2020, https://www.insidehighered.com/news/2020/07/14/study-concept-faculty-fit-hiring-vague-and-potentially-detrimental-diversity-efforts.

PART III

Leadership and Partnerships

CHAPTER 8

Educational Ecosystems for Equity

MARGARET HUNTER

What is an educational ecosystem? For decades, many universities viewed themselves as islands of intellectual activity or ivory towers, isolated from other people and institutions in the community. The expression "town and gown" captures this sense of distinction or separation. Today, people are moving more frequently in and out of educational experiences and institutions over their lifetime. High school students take college classes throughout their secondary educational experience. College graduates come back to universities and get specialized certificates paid for by their employers. And adults with established careers come back to finish incomplete degrees so they can advance. People from many walks of life in the community are coming to a variety of institutions for education in many different modalities over the course of their careers—and not in a linear way. The "swirling" behavior of today's transfer students now applies to most people over the course of their educational experiences.[1] So-called nontraditional students are the new traditional students.[2] For all of these reasons, educational institutions are interacting with one another in more and different ways that require new relationships for student success. This is the foundation of the educational ecosystem.[3]

When we view colleges and universities as parts of a larger educational ecosystem, we are better able to make interventions in patterns of inequality and structural discrimination. For example, when we examine the relationship between the college attendance rates of local high school students and our own institution's admissions policies, we reveal an opportunity to partner

with our local public schools to better meet the needs of high school graduates. Similarly, when community colleges work closely with local governments to offer a free year of community college tuition, we're building new
pathways toward degrees by intervening in systemic inequality.

An educational ecosystem for equity is a web of relationships across multiple institutions designed to create more opportunities for educational access
and student success for larger numbers of people and to close racial and class-
based equity gaps, especially for regional communities. The ivory tower separation of the past is no longer desirable for most higher-education institutions.
Increasingly, our colleges are tightly woven into the educational ecosystem of
their regions. And if they aren't, they will need to be in order to survive.

THE CHANGING LANDSCAPE OF HIGHER EDUCATION

Financial pressures, shrinking state funding, fewer high school students, a
doubting public, a crowded higher-education marketplace, less tolerance for
debt, more practical student attitudes toward degree completion, and a changing economy are all compelling reasons why partnerships are crucial for the
stability and future of our institutions.

We have all witnessed the rapid and profound changes in higher education
over recent decades. One of the most vivid is the large number of institutions
that have been closing annually. Competing for fewer students and increasingly
tuition dependent, many smaller institutions can no longer stay afloat on their
own, and partnerships within their educational ecosystems are crucial for survival. For large public institutions, closure is not usually on the table, but with
diminished state funding, budget cuts are the new lingua franca. While flagship
publics tend to get the lion's share of major gifts to public universities,[4] many
public master's comprehensive universities have addressed their budget gaps
through creative collaborations with their local public TK–12 school districts,
community colleges, large local employers, and city or county governments.

If you couple the revenue challenges mentioned above with students'
growing unwillingness to take on loan debt, fueled in large part by the public's loss of confidence in higher education, you have a perfect storm. Our
institutions are struggling to demonstrate that the tuition costs are "worth it"

relative to the resultant debt. Colleges and universities are increasingly stressing this value proposition in a crowded higher-education marketplace.

The crisis over value has led to a more widely held strategic or practical orientation toward college degrees. Understandably, most of us still market our universities as offering "life-changing," "transformative" experiences in which students can "change themselves and the world." And while this still appeals to some students, many have adopted a more pragmatic approach to earning a bachelor's degree that begins in high school with "dual enrollment" or Advanced Placement (AP) credits. More and more high school students are entering their first year of college with 30, 40, or even 60 hours of college credit, thereby saving them thousands and sometimes tens of thousands of dollars. Needless to say, the push toward dual-enrollment programs has added significant financial pressures on universities—as well as registration complexities and record-keeping difficulties.

Finally, the changing economy and creeping credentialism have made bachelor's degrees more necessary for people to be competitive in landing well-paying jobs.[5] The competition for good jobs is fierce as more and more positions become part-time, contingent, contract based, or part of the gig economy. These economic changes have pushed more adults with significant labor market experience back into college to complete degrees they began decades ago so they can be more competitive and have more economic stability.

MEMBERS OF THE ECOSYSTEM

Public school districts are important partners for local universities. Depending on the selectivity of your institution, these partnerships can be either complicated or straightforward. Many public school districts serve disproportionate numbers of low-income students and those who would be the first in their families to attend college. For this reason alone, many university leaders feel a mission-driven or ethical obligation to partner with public schools in order to ensure that young people in the local community have a pathway to college. Promise, dual enrollment, precollegiate, and summer bridge are all popular types of programs for university partnerships with TK-12 school districts. If you lead a highly selective university, partnering with local public schools can be fraught with the politics of race and class and the myths of meritocracy. Despite these challenges, many institutions have cocreated thriving programs for local public school students to help admit them to their own university or even to their competitors.

Once seen as starting points for the unprepared or as destinations only for associate's degrees and technical education, community colleges are finally understood to be a practical starting point for students who want to save money, stay near home, and take advantage of smaller class sizes, more flexible schedules, or any number of other strengths the community college system offers. "Guided pathways" and articulation agreements with bachelor degree–granting institutions that smooth the transition and minimize "wasted" or duplicated units are top priorities nationally. Although articulation agreements seem straightforward in theory, they are always harder to implement in reality. One significant challenge is that some four-year institutions assume that their version of any given course is superior and, therefore, must be taken at their institution. At the same time, there are constraints in some community colleges that limit course offerings and related lab, performance, or practicum work necessary for transfer.

Another common challenge is the lack of curricular integration for private or independent universities where the curriculum may reflect the mission or history of the school, and may not align well with public institutions in the state. Despite these challenges, partnerships between community colleges and private institutions are not just strategically important but also ethically necessary given the high cost of higher education and the fact that about five million students are enrolled in community colleges in any given semester. Moreover, underrepresented students of color and low-income students are much more likely to begin their higher-education careers in community colleges, with Latinx students having the highest proportional levels of community college enrollment, at about 55 percent.[6]

Many universities want to partner with public school districts or community colleges to build pipelines of students and increase enrollment. Growing in popularity, dual-degree programs allow small liberal arts colleges to partner with larger universities on undergraduate engineering programs, for example, or to create 4 + 1 pathways that lead to graduate degrees in only one year after the bachelor's is earned. Large publics may also partner with one another on doctoral programs or specialized programs connected to medical or law schools. In addition, financial pressures have led some institutions to try shared services such as library consortiums, housing opportunities for students and faculty, and transportation programs.

Finally, as many universities compete for adult degree completers, they're creating exclusive partnerships with local government agencies and large employers to provide classes needed to complete a set of bachelor's or master's degrees. Examples include partnerships with county social service offices that enable employees to complete degrees in public policy, social work, or public administration, and partnerships with large local employers that offer computer science or human resources certificates or badges to help upskill their workforce.

Many of these partnerships are built on unique online or hybrid programs designed to be accessible for working adults. Partnership programs with government agencies and large employers succeed because they offer evening and weekend schedules, online courses, classes taught at the worksite, and personalized attention from professional academic advisors and faculty. These are the hallmarks of successful adult degree completion programs, but they're also the ingredients for success in traditional degree tracks, especially because they're increasingly composed of students with similar demographic profiles: older, low income, first generation, working, transfer, students of color, and students with dependents.

LESSONS FOR SUSTAINABLE
AND SUCCESSFUL PARTNERSHIPS

The following seven ideas will assist you in building sustainable and successful partnerships. First, partnerships should be mutually beneficial. Be sure that there are significant advantages for both partners. If there aren't, or if they aren't obvious, it will be hard for people at the participating institutions and in the larger community to support them. Leaders of a joint steering committee will need to be frank with one another so that advantages and disadvantages can be addressed openly. The shared benefits should also be addressed in the memorandum of understanding (MOU) so that negotiations can be adjusted when they fall out of line with the MOU's requirement of dual benefit.

Reintroduce your institution to your partners. It's likely that leaders from other institutions have outdated or inaccurate perceptions about who your university is, who your students are, and what your strengths are. Most institutions have changed significantly in the past ten to twenty years, and many of us are not fully aware of those changes in our educational ecosystem partners. Does your institution serve a much higher proportion of low-income students than it used to? Have you opened a successful new academic program recently? Does your local community college have more PhDs on its faculty than in the past? Dispelling myths about the identity and values of your university and its students is crucial. This is especially important if your institution may have caused community harm in the past through exploitative research relationships or exclusionary admissions policies. Be open to learning new things about your community partners, too.

Meet as equals. It's almost never the case that partnerships are entered into by coequal entities. Differences in factors such as prestige or wealth and size can influence the perception of which organization has more status in the relationship. The representatives from each school will need to develop strong relationships with their colleagues in the partner institution. When everyone feels appreciated, understood, and valued as equals (for example, the superintendent of a struggling public school district and the provost of an R1 research university), then the partnership can flourish. Building this level of trust and mutual appreciation will require some intentional relationship building.

Envision new things together. Many attempted partnerships begin with one institution creating a new program and asking the other school to send students to it. This benefits the receiving institution but is not necessarily a big win for the feeder institution. Rather than unilaterally created programs, try an authentic collaboration instead. Work together and build something new from the ground up that has tangible benefits for both partners. Bringing faculty from each institution together when building a new academic program is crucial for shared governance. Although the process may take longer, it's much more likely to succeed and endure.

Nurture the relationship. Like a garden, institutional partnerships must be tended to regularly. Many partnerships are quickly lost, broken, or fade away when key people leave their positions (and that happens frequently). In addition to establishing personal relationships, look for ways to institutionalize collaborations so they have a built-in structure. Is there an enrollment meeting every fall with all educational partners? Is there an annual lunch with the university president, community college provost, and their teams to set the agenda for the coming year? Work on both the institutional structure and the interpersonal aspects of the relationship.

Predicting near-term needs is a crucial skill. What educational requirements do you see emerging in the next five years? Build programs with your new partners to meet those needs rather than reacting to trends from the past. Do you have increasing numbers of adult students returning to college to complete their degrees? If so, consider building an adult degree completion program rather than a shiny new, first-year program for eighteen-year-olds. Partner with your colleagues in institutional research to learn what your campus-wide needs are likely to be.

Finally, advertise to build public support. Sharing news about your partnership is critical to its success and will likely build feelings of goodwill toward your university, especially if the program is shared jointly and involves students. You can help build public trust in higher education and in your institution in particular when you're seen as collaborating with other important educational institutions to meet the community's educational needs. Large public universities will likely need governmental, political, or legislative support for any major partnerships; therefore, intentionally cultivating community buy-in is crucial.

CONCLUSION

Understanding your institution as one part of a larger educational ecosystem is key to building successful partnerships in your region. The landscape of higher education is changing drastically and quickly, and successful partnerships are required to thrive in the new economy of higher education. Partnerships are good not only for universities but also for students. Students are increasingly swirling in and out of educational institutions throughout your region. The more institutions work together, the more successful our students will be. Operating as an ecosystem for equity allows educational institutions to cooperate through strategic partnerships to pool resources, share specialized knowledge for student success, and build a holistic educational experience for community members over the course of their lives.

— *Takeaways* —

- The changing financial context of higher education has elevated educational partnerships as a key tool in addressing regional equity gaps for community members and prospective students in higher education.
- Dispelling myths about your university and repairing harm to the community that may have been done in the past are central to building trusting and productive relationships with ecosystem partners.
- Equity is best addressed holistically with multiple educational institutions cooperating and leveraging their resources for and expertise with student success.

NOTES

1. American Association of Collegiate Registrars and Admissions Officers (AACRAO), "Who are You Calling a Swirler? 4 Transfer Populations to Know," *AACRAO Connect*, 13 December 2013, https://www.aacrao.org/resources/newsletters-blogs/aacrao-connect/article/who-are-you-calling-a-swirler--4-transfer-populations-to-know.

2. Blythe Bernhard, "As Nontraditional Students Become the New Norm, Colleges Must Support Generational Diversity," *Insight into Diversity*, 11 February 2020, https://www.insightintodiversity.com/as-nontraditional-students-become-the-new-norm-colleges-must-support-generational-diversity/.

3. Steven Mintz, "Creating a More Collaborative Higher Education Ecosystem: Why Well-Resourced Institutions Need to Contribute More to Higher Education as a Whole," *Inside Higher Ed*, 17 January 2019, https://www.insidehighered.com/blogs/higher-ed-gamma/creating-more-collaborative-higher-education-ecosystem.

4. Laura Hamilton and Kelly Nielsen, "Our Broke Public Universities," *Chronicle of Higher Education*, 1 June 2021, https://www.chronicle.com/article/our-broke-public-universities?cid2=gen_login_refresh&cid=gen_sign_in.

5. Randall Collins, "The Dirty Little Secret of Credential Inflation," *Chronicle of Higher Education*, 27 September 2002, https://www.chronicle.com/article/the-dirty-little-secret-of-credential-inflation/?cid2=gen_login_refresh&cid=gen_sign_in.

6. "Community College FAQs: Community College Enrollment and Completion." Community College Research Center, Teachers College, Columbia University, accessed 14 November 2021, https://ccrc.tc.columbia.edu/Community-College-FAQs.html.

CHAPTER 9

Searching for the Butterfly

The Dean's Engagement with Internal and External Partners

DEL DOUGHTY

I

Right now, somewhere in Silicon Valley, there's a man (and, for the purpose of this story, we'll say it's a man) who is well on his way to becoming a tech billionaire. When he makes it, he'll discover in himself strong opinions regarding education, and in particular higher education. To be even more particular, he's got the eye of the tiger for environmental education (it could be any cause—childhood literacy, public history, women in STEM—but for the purpose of this story, we'll say it's environmental education). This is not a bad thing. With wildfires burning every summer, the guy is concerned about the effects of climate change, and goodness knows, the planet can always use more advocates. His opinion gradually shapes itself into an idea, and the idea a plan. With all his money, he establishes a foundation to improve the state of environmental studies in high schools and colleges. It's ambitious, and when he casts his vision on Facebook and Twitter, it garners attention in traditional media. Some say it's genius, a few think it foolish. In any case, there's ample funding available, so people listen.

A few weeks later, you're going about your business in the office one afternoon when a biology professor knocks on your door and asks if you have a moment. She's holding a few sheets of paper in her hand and seems animated. "I wanted you to look at this opportunity," she says, sliding the papers across your desk. "It's a grant." Your eyes scan the page as she explains the details. She's so excited, she's practically tripping over the information. However, you catch the key words and phrases—collaborative, three years, carbon recapture, public and private, mentored undergraduate research, $150,000—and grasp the gist. "What do you think?" she asks at last. "Is this something we should pursue?"

You lean back in your chair, remove your glasses, and place the tip of a stem in your mouth, allowing it to dangle for a moment, as though deep in thought. What's really happening is that you're watching your future flash before your eyes: long chains of emails going back and forth at all hours of the day, meetings, budget spreadsheets, dreary PowerPoint slides, a picture of you and a few others from the university holding a big check and posing for a photo. Damn, you think. You already have initiative fatigue, and just when you were hoping things were slowing down and you could catch your breath, there's this. But there's no obvious good reason to say no, and so you find yourself shrugging and answering, "Sure. Why not?"

The professor fist pumps and says she'll get right on it. She says she's excited. She asks if you're excited. You say that you are. Grants are exciting.

II

You work at a small private institution. Down the road, about a seventy-five-mile ride on the interstate, there's Regional State U. The dean there is writing a book on clean energy. As you drive home that evening, you think of her. Both of your institutions belong to a regional consortium that promotes distance education in schools, museums, and libraries, and you sat next to her at a couple of meetings in years past and chatted over coffee and scones on a couple of occasions. You remember that she is passionate about the potential of wind and solar, that she can wax eloquent about the continued reliance upon fossil fuels. She would be perfect for this grant opportunity. You decide to email her to arrange a phone call.

III

In your role as dean, you are called upon to engage with a wide variety of partners and players, both inside and outside the institution. Within the university, there's the registrar's office, enrollment management, advising, student life, human resources, the business office, advancement, and athletics. Depending on the issue at hand, any combination of these units may appear on your daily schedule. You may share a common institutional mission with them, but each unit has its own agenda and perhaps its own professional society and standards. For the sake of cooperation, it's good to remind yourself of this simple fact from time to time. There will be occasions when it feels as though a particular unit's agenda runs crosswise to yours in academic affairs—when, for example, human resources asks faculty during the first week of classes to join with them in redesigning the annual performance review process. Bad timing.

The main thing to remember about these units of the university is that they're not part of the academic core; that is, they're not teaching or research faculty. That should be obvious to everyone, but it's not. It can be astonishing that staffers in, say, enrollment management or student life sometimes know very little about the rigor and stress of academic life and work. This knowledge gap often manifests itself in the form of resentments. Staff members who don't understand faculty life may think that professors work only half the week, get summers off, attend junket conferences in San Francisco or New Orleans, and flaunt the dress code by wearing shorts and Crocs to work. The CFO might have great financial acumen, but if he was hired straight from the health care industry, he probably won't know beans about the struggles of a young assistant history professor. As dean, and therefore as a link between these groups, it's your job to educate staff members about faculty life. Invite them to events. Build bridges.

Off campus, the cast of characters is even broader. You find yourself dealing with government agencies, accreditors, nonprofits, private foundations, the media, and other secondary and postsecondary institutions, all with their own argot and sets of clever acronyms. Broadly speaking, these players fall into one of three groups: governmental, nongovernmental, and professional.

In the first category, the chief player is the federal government, which takes many forms. It may seem odd to think of the federal government as a partner, and perhaps it's a stretch to do so, but it certainly is an external player and one you cannot get along without—see the file labeled "Too Big to Ignore." (In fact, the federal government may be more like the air, the medium in which you move and have your being.) If you're at a land-grant or a Historically Black College or University, for example, the Morrill Acts have shaped your mission and your priorities. If you're at an R1 university, you likely receive significant research funding from an agency such as the Department of Agriculture or the National Institutes of Health. At such an institution, you're likely to be highly involved in grant acquisition and administration. In addition, the federal government makes its presence felt at almost all institutions through initiatives such as the CARES Act, veterans' benefits, TRIO programs, the Fulbright program, entitlement programs stemming from legislation (e.g., Title III, Title V, Title IX), and, of course, student financial aid. Further, the feds provide policy guidance on research involving human subjects and—crucially—issues related to civil rights and discrimination in all of its various forms.

Depending on your type of institution and the particulars of your job description, your dealings with the federal government in any of its aspects may be only indirect and occasional. In most interactions, you'll rely on the aforementioned internal partners. The key here is to develop a basic knowledge of how these federal programs and policies work. During the COVID-19 pandemic, for example, academic administrators needed to know which kinds of instructional expenses were eligible for funding and which were not. As another example, how classes are designated may have had an impact on a student's financial aid. Remember: your primary concern is the core of the academic enterprise, but in order to keep that going, you need to understand how that flywheel meshes with the gears of the federal flywheel. To do that, you need to work well with your internal partners.

The state government is another key player that doesn't always look or feel like a partner; but again, your understanding of the people who embody it is critical to your success. State governments obviously exert a gravitational force on community colleges and four-year publics, but in some states they also engage directly with privates or at least have a bearing on them as licensors. The key parties here are the state legislature and its chief tributary, the coordinating board or board of regents. When it comes to legislatures, you'll want to know two groups of people: your local representatives and senators, and the chair and members of the higher-education oversight committee in each house. The ship of state is big, and no one person can steer it, so it's at this granular level that you can have the most influence on the ship's direction. A course correction of one degree can change your destination over a long time frame. Attend town halls and receptions. Subscribe to and read legislative updates. Log in to public hearings. You'll also want to huddle with your institutional leadership to discuss advocacy efforts. Much of that work falls to the president. But it pays to reach out to house and senate subcommittees ahead of a legislative session to let representatives know that you're willing to offer comments on any pending bills.

Among nongovernmental actors, you'll most often find yourself in the company of the media, private foundations, nonprofits, and vendors. With regard to the media, your instinct will be to pump them full of good news, to promote new initiatives, and to celebrate achievements. You should embrace that instinct. But remember that the very same media will be quick to pick up and amplify scandal and outrage. Therefore, learn how to give a statement, and learn what not to say. In times of crisis, make sure you know who is authorized to speak on issues. Usually, that means the president and communications director. Private foundations and nonprofits vary greatly in size, mission, and regional interest. Like our Silicon Valley billionaire's passion for environmental education, foundations can magnify or extend the reach of your mission when their priorities align with yours. But grants can be as challenging to administer as they are to get. As for vendors—those people who bomb your inbox with endless offers to help you—I'll have more to say about them in a moment.

Finally, there are professional organizations. Everyone who holds a leadership role in higher education must deal with an evaluative organization, that is, an accrediting body. These come in two flavors: regional and program specific. Either way, there's always a lot of pressure when accreditors announce that they're coming for a site visit. In that case, the first order of business is to have someone on your team compose a self-study. These reports (which can run up to three volumes of tables, charts, graphics, and text) require long hours and lots of collaboration if they're to be successful.

Good assessment is vital to the cause, and here is where vendors and specialists from the corporate sector may present themselves to "help" you. If you have the time and resources on your side, the right software may indeed be useful. But if you can afford no more than a down-market product, and if not everyone on your team sees its value, you might be better off going it alone.

Beware of vendors—the solutions industry. Solutions drive up costs, which are absorbed by the institution or passed on to the student. Either way, this affects the bottom line, which affects how you can conduct the core business of the enterprise. Accredited programs provide a seal of approval; but, in practice, they'll sometimes madden you with their demands for what they perceive as continuous improvement and perfection. Remind yourself that excellence, not perfection, is the goal. One of the best things I ever heard on the topic of accreditation was: "If you discover something is broken, fix it. If you can't fix it, make a plan to fix it." At first, I thought about writing it down on a sticky note and putting it on my computer; then I thought I might have the saying framed and hung on the wall. But then I realized that I would never forget it, and I never have.

There are more things in heaven and earth than are dreamt of in your job description. To succeed in such a complex world requires a certain combination of skills. Communication is foremost, especially listening. You need a sharp memory, an ability to recall conversations and keep track of updates, corrections, and revisions. You need to enjoy meetings. If ever you catch yourself saying "I am all about collaboration" and then, thirty minutes later, you find yourself groaning internally as you trudge toward your third meeting of the day, you probably aren't "all about collaboration" as much as you'd like to think you are. And if you really want to excel, you need wit, a facility for making connections between ideas, practices, and people. Working with so many different groups and kinds of people is either one of the hardest things about being a dean or one of the most exhilarating.

IV

A few weeks after the excited fist pump, the autumn leaves are falling as midsemester nears. The grant deadline is approaching, too, and it feels as if everything is happening at once. You stare out your office window, watching a small army of men with blowers slung across their backs, moving in unison against the leaves. You're waiting for your institutional data management team to provide you with some figures, and you're hoping to get them so that you can plug them in and route the proposal to the provost, CFO, and president, as well as their counterparts at Regional State U and the partnering high school.

You consider briefly what the president will think of the project. It calls for the development of new content in science courses for STEM and education majors, which briefly caused a point of contention when the education professor at Regional objected that the new content would distract students from the information that they need to know for their certification exams. This riled up your education faculty and started them bickering with some of your arts and sciences professors. Fortunately, after some negotiation, you were able to allay the concerns of the education faculty enough to move ahead. The centerpiece of the grant would enable select upper-division science majors and high school seniors to take paid summer internships with a carbon recapture plant in the state.

To put all of these pieces together was no small task. You worked with administrators and faculty in science, business, and education at two different universities; a high school assistant principal; a staff member from your career development office, who walked you through the internship agreement; your registrar and institutional effectiveness officer, who supplied a lot of data; the contract administrator in the business office, who helped you draft the MOUs; your compliance officer, who reviewed the proposal from a risk management perspective; and, of course, executives at the carbon recapture plant, who defined the scope of work that the interns would undertake. No wonder your neck is a little sore.

Will the plan work? Will you get the grant and, if you do, will students be interested? Will the internships have an impact that will give your environmental studies program a needed enrollment boost? Could carbon recapture be a pivotal technology in the battle against climate change?

A few weeks ago you barely listened to the proposal, but now you find yourself fairly fluent on the issue. You've heard the billionaire talk on YouTube videos, and you think that you would enjoy having a conversation with him about it.

V

Six months later. You got the grant, and for a few minutes you and the biology professor were campus celebrities. Within the first hour of the news breaking, you received a half-dozen congratulatory emails from colleagues. But then your calendar began to fill with invitations. The communications officer emailed to ask for notes and a quote. The marketing director and the recruiting coordinator wanted to get together to learn how they might pitch the program to prospective students and families. The grants administrator followed in short order with a slew of questions about account numbers. Finally, there was an email from the billionaire himself—or, rather, one of his deputies—who "invited" you and your team to a convening later in the spring. The billionaire wanted all grant recipients to assemble for a two-day implementation session, and he wanted someone at the dean's level to be there. In fact, you learned that your presence would be required at monthly update meetings as well. The mere thought of those extra Zoom meetings was enervating. Suddenly, that $150,000 didn't sound like a lot of money. You wondered: Would this endeavor be worth it?

A few weeks after getting the grant, you hosted a joint meeting with all the key stakeholders: representatives from Regional State U, the local high school, the carbon recapture plant—about a dozen people. Since it occurred around lunchtime, you sprang for some catering. The bill came to around $100, which was not a lot, but when your budget director told you that the grant didn't pay for food and that the money to cover lunch would need to come from your operating budget, the amount felt about ten times that size.

VI

The academic enterprise is about the dynamic between the professor and the student. The former is a scholar, possessing deep knowledge in an academic discipline with perhaps two or three areas of specialization and a well-developed talent for sharing what she knows. The latter is curious, eager to learn as much as he can for the purpose of understanding or doing something or becoming something. Higher education is work, but when it's going well, it hardly feels like it. At its best, it's a beautiful, joyful, cooperative arrangement, and it has been going on that way for centuries. If you could travel back and forth in time and visit colleges or universities all over the earth, you would recognize this dynamic wherever you landed.

That's the heart of it. That's what you believe. It's a sustaining myth.

Now that you're a year-and-a-half into the billionaire's carbon recapture grant, you find yourself holding to your credo tightly, dearly, and often with an abiding sense of melancholy. The project has been a modest success at best. After the initial burst of excitement, only four students from your institution have signed on to participate, and one of those dropped the internship halfway through. The team from the carbon recapture plant has had some turnover and seems to have lost interest. The tension that erupted between the science and the education faculty has continued to fester in other spots of the curriculum. Would it have happened anyhow? Finally, as you approach the end of the fiscal year, you have to find a way to spend $15,000 of grant money lest you are forced to return it. There's a report due to the billionaire's foundation, and you think about how to frame the year's activity so that it doesn't sound cynical or smell like failure.

One afternoon near the end of the semester you attend your institution's annual experiential learning fair. It's a poster session, and as you walk among the trifold displays and chat with students, you feel refreshed by their creativity and energy. At one of the displays, you encounter one of the students who interned at the carbon plant. Her poster has engaging graphics that quickly explain how recapture works, and there's a photo of her in a lab coat at the plant. As you talk with her about her experience, you can see that she has a joy and a genuine interest in the subject. But surprisingly, it's not the scientific part of the work that she liked most about the internship, she says, but rather the opportunity to be part of a high-functioning team. That, she says, was a thrill, and one she hopes to discover again.

You converse with her a little while longer and, eventually, must move on. As you do, you take with you a renewed sense of purpose. It strikes you that you have experienced the butterfly effect in reverse: many months ago, far away in Silicon Valley, an inspired vision manifested itself into a project that involved thousands of hours of labor and hundreds of thousands of dollars to produce this brief encounter at a student poster session. By a strictly accounting logic, it would seem that the game hasn't been worth the candle, so to speak. And at times throughout the project, you might have agreed. But a butterfly flapping its wings anywhere is cool, miraculous even. At this moment, you feel lucky to have witnessed it and played some part.

— *Takeaways* —

- As a dean, you'll have numerous internal and external partners. Get to know them all—their incentives, their processes, and their idioms. Insofar as you can, try to build bridges of understanding between them and your faculty.
- Collaborative projects and initiatives among internal and external partners are demanding. As best you can, weigh the costs and benefits before committing. Time and money are certainly factors to consider, but so is meaning. In any given venture, expect there to be ebbs and flows of emotion, doubt, passion.
- What is the core of the academic enterprise? How can you advance it? When do you need to defend it? Those are questions that you must be able to answer.

CHAPTER 10

Higher Education and Community Collaborations in Times of Crisis

Josephine Mendoza Kershaw

Times of crisis bring out the best and the worst in humanity. As Martin Luther King Jr. noted, "The ultimate measure of a man is not where he stands in moments of comfort and convenience but where he stands at times of challenge and controversy."[1] In their academic leadership roles, deans are called upon to be at their best during difficult times, drawing on experience to muster expertise and optimism to rally faculty, staff, and students to step forward past the uncertainty. The skill set needed in a crisis goes further than technical or academic knowledge, extending into all that has been learned from experience to manage the challenges at hand.

CONTEXT

The COVID-19 pandemic brought enormous uncertainty for schools, colleges, and universities. This crisis exacerbated the challenges facing higher-education institutions, particularly regional public universities and smaller colleges with fewer resources. Singular to COVID-19, this was foremost a public health crisis, but with substantial economic and social consequences. For deans and educational leaders, navigating through the COVID-19 pandemic demanded unprecedented initiative in order to restructure systems, preserve student and employee safety, and ensure instructional quality while operating with constrained resources. Among the lessons that colleges and universities learned in building partnerships to bolster the community's response, the following five stand out:[2]

- **There is no manual.** The reassuring words "We'll figure things out" became a familiar phrase as faculty and deans adjusted to situations as they arose and attempted to respond in the best way they could with the available information that sometimes changed almost daily.

- **Leaders act.** During times of adversity, people rely on calm and decisive leaders: those in leadership positions need to acknowledge the crisis situation and, at the same time, respond without overreacting. Leaders will be making decisions with uncertain outcomes and without comprehensive information available to them. Just as making decisions and acting with courage are imperative, planning for a range of possible outcomes—and potentially changing course as new data come to light—is vitally important to steer proactively past difficulties.

- **Communication is essential.** Transparency, clarity, and consistency in communication are important to overcome the fear, concerns, and demands faced by the college workforce and the stakeholder communities they serve. Messaging must be tailored to the audience, and various modes of delivery may be selected for effective outreach. Aligning urgent communication for the most vulnerable populations and conveying frequent, iterative information disseminated to all stakeholder audiences through daily podcasts, emails, and the like provide a sense of psychological safety.

- **Take care of your team.** Taking care of your team is key: consider safety first, foster mental health, and provide support and hope. Fiscally responsible decisions and efforts to avoid furloughing employees allay workforce anxiety. Meeting challenges and hardships together can strengthen relationship bonds. To this end, it has been shown that a critical element of managing challenging situations is resilience—the idea that together the team will persevere and be stronger after the crisis as individuals, as departments, and as an institution.

- **Innovation will be necessary**. Difficult times can inspire innovation and promote change at unprecedented levels. Investments in technology to strengthen distance learning, telehealth, and web connectivity were accelerated during the social distancing brought on by the COVID-19 pandemic, all of which hastened the shift to new, "hyflex" modes of course and service delivery. To effectively move forward during the COVID-19 crisis, educational leaders also needed to look for new channels for collaboration and cooperation, both on campus and across institutions, as well as with community partners.

To weather a crisis—particularly when the way things used to work don't work anymore, or when change becomes a necessity—leaders who have effectively met challenges have undertaken four actions: (a) creating a culture of honesty and support, (b) distributing leadership, (c) communicating effectively, and (d) focusing on factors that can be managed or controlled.[3]

During large-scale disasters or public health emergencies, the landscape can rapidly evolve for higher-education leaders who are initially charged with making quick decisions while attending to the health and safety of students, faculty, and staff. Over the first year of the pandemic, events could be characterized as occurring in three waves:[4]

Wave 1. At the start of the pandemic in early spring 2020, decision making first involved canceling classes and events, sending residential students home, pivoting to online instruction, and altering policies and procedures to adjust to the changes.

Wave 2. Higher-education leaders then engaged in significant budget reductions, adjusted for reduced summer enrollments, planned for alternative fall scenarios, and continued to monitor and adapt policies while considering the long-term impacts on their student and employee populations.

Wave 3. With the fast-tracked emergency use approval of COVID-19 vaccines in spring 2021, planning for a return to "normalcy" commenced.

Many educational institutions, health professions schools, and community colleges (particularly those in rural areas) served as key hubs for vaccine clinics. In case similar crises arise in the future, it would be valuable to document the lessons learned about how these unprecedented partnerships can be facilitated and established between higher-education institutions, community agencies, and health systems. The remainder of this chapter focuses on partnerships and collaborations that facilitated coordination of COVID-19 vaccine clinics.

COLLABORATION MODELS

In the face of public health emergencies such as COVID-19—or any community disaster—proactive efforts to build meaningful relationships with community organizations and public safety partners *before* the crisis can significantly help educational leaders navigate a smooth, collaborative response. Such relationships facilitate use of established processes to communicate needs, request resources, and synchronize efforts. Building bridges and emergency management partnerships contributes to more effectively addressing the challenges of future crises.

Collaborating effectively to maximize resources during widespread calamities is important for communities and educational institutions. The coronavirus pandemic created a unique public health situation that may, at its best, become cyclical in nature like the flu or, at worst, persist in deadly resurgences that require continued restrictions. Three models of community health planning have been used that encompass partnerships and collaborations on various levels.[5] These models provide flexible frameworks to better meet current needs and trends in community health improvement and have proven useful for potential and continuing collaborations between higher-education institutions and the community.

The first model, Mobilizing for Action through Planning and Partnerships (MAPP), has underlying principles that include systems thinking, dialogue, shared vision, data, partnership, and strategic thinking.[6] Developed by the National Association of County and City Health Officials (NACCHO) in collaboration with the Centers for Disease Control and Prevention (CDC), the MAPP process promotes community organizing and partnership development. It involves assessments of the local public health system, community themes and strengths, community health status, and the forces of change. These assessments are designed to help communities identify strategic issues and formulate goals and strategies that flow in a recurring cycle of planning, implementing, and evaluating.

In the second model, the Planned Approach to Community Health (PATCH; also developed by the CDC), collaboration occurs vertically between public agencies at the federal, state, and local levels, as well as with voluntary organizations, educational institutions, and other private partners.[7] Key elements of the PATCH model include (a) community member participation, (b) data-based program development, (c) collaborative development of a comprehensive health promotion strategy, (d) evaluation for feedback and improvement, and (e) enhancement of community capacity for health promotion.

The third model, the Community Health Improvement Process (CHIP), facilitates health planning efforts through taking inventory of community assets and resources and tracking performance to address health problems and needs.[8] Its two interacting cycles—problem identification and prioritization—provide for community organizing and assessing and selecting priority areas. Moreover, the analysis and implementation cycle in the CHIP model encompasses seven phases that flow from planning, through implementation, to evaluation with benchmarks, and to key health indicators.

Adding to the complexity of partnerships and planning models, the types of relationships that are formed reflect the diversity among the communities and organizations involved. Relationships range from informal collaborative agreements sealed by a handshake to formal contracts with merging of assets and organizational structures. Accordingly, the collaborations can be short-lived or have longer-term commitments that evolve over time. In organizational relations literature, cooperative relationships may be referred to interchangeably as partnerships, networks, collaboratives, or strategic alliances. For higher education specifically, three types of partnerships have been identified: community relationships, collaborations with other educational institutions, and public-private partnerships.[9] Research has revealed that successful collaborative arrangements have certain common characteristics. Having a shared commitment to collaborative leadership, partnership purpose, coordination, and progress constituted four common strategic attributes among institutions that have had greater success through alliance.[10]

COMMUNITY PARTNERSHIPS TO IMPLEMENT
COVID-19 VACCINE CLINICS

Often, collaborative partnerships are established to address a common problem or issue. In the case of the COVID-19 public health crisis, safeguarding
the health of students, employees, and vulnerable community members was
the common priority. Once the fast-tracked COVID-19 vaccines became
available for emergency use and distribution, many institutions worked with
area health systems to provide facilities and sites for mass vaccination clinics,
particularly in rural regions of the country. At North Arkansas College, the
college president, the dean of health professions, and the HR director coordinated with the local hospital, federal emergency management officials, and
the county health department to provide facilities and volunteers to administer vaccines for community members in the surrounding areas.

On a much larger scale, the Oregon Health and Science University
formed a partnership with three health care systems to operate a mass-
vaccination clinic.[11] The partners combined their vaccine allocations and
clinical staff with a community venue that enabled one of the highest through-
puts in the country, vaccinating more than 5,200 people per day at the Oregon
Convention Center. To disseminate lessons learned, both of these collaborations developed templates to facilitate replication and adaptations in other
types of settings.

In contrast to the on-the-ground, on-site collaborations, other institutions
of higher education contributed virtual technology expertise to community
alliances to combat COVID-19.[12] For example, in West Virginia, the School
of Osteopathic Medicine's Center for Rural and Community Health partnered with the community's COVID-19 task force to provide a vaccine registration system, database management, and online map data integration to
bring vaccinations to the county's homebound residents.

In North Carolina, the East Carolina University (ECU) Brody School of
Medicine and the Vidant Health System collaborated to build a website with
updated COVID-19 vaccine information for the communities in its forty-one-
county service area. ECU also used its geographic information systems capabilities to construct a vaccine priority index tool that helped identify high-risk
populations and facilities such as nursing homes that urgently needed vac-

cination. The CDC compiled useful summaries of vaccine clinic implementation, tool kits, and strategies.

Higher education's involvement in the COVID-19 vaccine distribution effort reached new heights when the US Department of Education and the Biden administration launched the COVID-19 College Challenge in June 2021. Partnerships had previously formed between federal retail pharmacies and high-enrollment community colleges that aimed to provide on-site clinics for their communities. Institutions participating in the 2021 challenge pledged to reach out to their campus communities and actively promote COVID-19 vaccinations. Working from the top executive levels, postsecondary institution presidents committed to three key actions: engaging all students, faculty, and staff members; organizing their college communities; and delivering vaccine access to every student and employee.[13] Close to six hundred colleges and universities from forty-eight states signed up to participate on a page listed on the White House website.

Besides offering direct cash incentives to overcome COVID-19 vaccine resistance, some higher-education institutions partnered with community organizations to reach younger students in middle and high schools to encourage vaccination.[14] For example, a partnership in Michigan with Albion College, the Albion Health Care Alliance, the Battle Creek Family YMCA, the Calhoun County Public Health Department, and Marshall Public Schools organized vaccine clinics with a raffle prize of one year of free tuition at Albion College to middle and high school students who received vaccinations at these clinics. Additional incentives included free books, a one-year YMCA family membership, and campus-dining gift cards.

FUTURE CONSIDERATIONS

Depending on how it is viewed, a crisis can evoke danger or produce exciting opportunities to question assumptions about why we do what we do and then to find new and innovative ways to do things in the future. The new practices adopted during the COVID pandemic may become normal or at least fundamentally change how things are viewed. In the words of Peter Drucker, "The greatest danger in times of turbulence is not the turbulence; it is to act with yesterday's logic."[15] As educational leaders move into the post-crisis environment, they would be prudent to question institutional mind-sets, program rationales, and program delivery. An exploration of future directions, which may involve dealing with possible recurring epidemics, may benefit from a systemic resilience approach to crises that involves the following key steps:[16]

- Explore the system, define its boundaries and dynamics.
- Develop scenarios assuming alternative ongoing and future transitions.
- Determine goals and the level of tolerance for risk and uncertainty.
- Codevelop management strategies dealing with each scenario.
- Address unanticipated barriers and sudden critical shifts.
- Decide, test, and implement strategies.
- Monitor, learn from, review, and adapt.

Proactive flexibility is key as educational institutions pivot in response to new virus variants. We might again be entering a state of "VUCA," the US military's acronym for a volatile, uncertain, complex, and ambiguous situation. Preparation for alternative paths in an institution's strategic directions will be essential to successful leadership in an uncertain future. The past will serve us best if we learn from the experience and put that learning toward greater preparation for the next crisis. Deans and educational leaders would do well to convert unexpected adversities into opportunities for moving from best practices of the past to innovative *next* practices of the future.

— *Takeaways* —

- In the face of public health emergencies, such as COVID-19, or any community disaster, proactive efforts to build meaningful relationships with community organizations and public safety partners *before* the crisis can significantly help educational leaders navigate a smooth, collaborative response.
- Navigating through the COVID-19 pandemic demanded unprecedented initiative to restructure systems, preserve student and employee safety, establish transparent communication channels, and ensure instructional quality while operating with constrained resources.
- Just as making decisions and acting with courage are imperative, planning for a range of possible outcomes—and potentially chang-

ing course as new data come to light—is vitally important to steering proactively through difficulties.

- Deans and educational leaders would do well to consider alternative paths to achieving the institution's mission and converting unexpected adversities into opportunities to transition from historic best practices of the past to innovative *next* practices of the future.

NOTES

1. According to the *Detroit Free Press* (16 March 1963) these words appeared in a Lenten sermon that Dr. King delivered the previous day at Central Methodist Church in Detroit.
2. Paul Hofmann, "Lessons for Leading in National Emergencies: A Review and Preview of Best Practices," *Journal of Healthcare Management* 65, no. 6 (2020): 387–88, https://doi.org/10.1097/jhm-d-20-00255; Jenny Darroch, "Transitioning to a New Deanship in Unprecedented Times," *AACSB International* (blog), 13 April 2020, https://www.aacsb.edu/insights/2020/april/transitioning-to-a-new-deanship-in-unprecedented-times. https://www.aacsb.edu/insights/2020/april/transitioning-to-a-new-deanship-in-unprecedented-times.
3. Jenny Darroch, "Transitioning to a New Deanship in Unprecedented Times," *AACSB International* (blog), 13 April 2020, https://www.aacsb.edu/insights/2020/april/transitioning-to-a-new-deanship-in-unprecedented-times.
4. Sharon Kruse, Donald Hackmann, and Jane Clark Lindle, "Academic Leadership during a Pandemic: Department Heads Leading with a Focus on Equity," *Frontiers in Education* 5 (2020): 272, https://doi.org/10.3389/feduc.2020.614641.
5. See Institute of Medicine Committee on Assuring the Health of the Public in the 21st Century, "Models for Collaborative Planning in Communities," in *The Future of the Public's Health in the 21st Century* (Washington, DC: National Academies Press, 2002), https://www.ncbi.nlm.nih.gov/books/NBK221247/.
6. Institute of Medicine Committee, "Models for Collaborative Planning in Communities," 406–7.
7. Institute of Medicine Committee, "Models for Collaborative Planning in Communities," 407–8.
8. Institute of Medicine Committee, "Models for Collaborative Planning in Communities," 409–10.
9. Stephen Pelletier, *Making Partnerships Work: Principles, Guidelines, and Advice for Public University Leaders*, Task Force Report (Washington, DC: American Association of State Colleges and Universities, 2018). https://www.aascu.org/policy/publications/Partnerships.pdf
10. David Sarcone and Chad Kimmel, "Characteristics of Successful Health Alliance Strategies: Evidence from Rural Healthcare Experiences," *Journal of Healthcare Management* 66, no. 2 (2021): 146–47, https://doi.org/10.1097/jhm-d-19-00245.

11. Kimberlee Ables, "All4Oregon Healthcare Partnership Quietly Operating Nation-Leading Vaccination Clinic at Oregon Convention Center," *Metro News*, 4 March 2021, https://www.oregonmetro.gov/news/all4oregon-healthcare-partnership-quietly-operating-nation-leading-vaccination-clinic-oregon.

12. Courtney Hereford and Greg Kearney, "Rural COVID-19 Innovations: COVID-19 Vaccination," *Rural Health Information Hub*, 8 July 2021, https://www.ruralhealthinfo.org/topics/covid19/innovations/vaccination.

13. US Department of Education, "Biden Administration Launches COVID-19 College Challenge to Get More Young People Vaccinated," press release, 3 June 2021, https://www.ed.gov/news/press-releases/biden-administration-launches-covid-19-college-challenge-get-more-young-people-vaccinated.

14. Trisha McCauley, "Albion College Offering Year of Free Tuition to a Student Who Gets COVID-19 Vaccine," *News Channel 3* (Kalamazoo, MI), 18 June 2021, https://wwmt.com/news/local/albion-college-offering-year-of-free-tuition-to-a-student-who-gets-covid-19-vaccine.

15. Peter Drucker, *Managing in Turbulent Times* (New York: Harper Collins, 1980), 226.

16. Gabriela Ramos and William Hynes, "A Systemic Resilience Approach to Dealing with COVID-19 and Future Shocks," *OECD Policy Responses to Coronavirus (COVID-19)*, 28 April 2020, https://doi.org/10.1787/36a5bdfb-en.

CHAPTER 11

Using Institutional Expertise to Foster Connections through Local Leadership Development Programs

ROSS PETERSON-VEATCH

Presidents and boards are encouraging academic leaders to engage their local communities on deeper levels. Civic and institutional leaders understand that antiquated "town-gown" relations that have become "town versus gown" antagonism are an obstacle to raising the quality of life in cities across the country. I believe that involving students in local service projects and on-campus service-learning programs helps break down barriers and provides participants with leadership opportunities. But sometimes our goals are not directly related to the student experience. Institutional leaders may just as likely ask deans to lend a hand with fund-raising, or "friend-raising," in the community, or to represent the institution to the community as part of a larger effort to enhance the institution's reputation.

Developing relationships with community leaders who can generate any one of these outcomes is often a daunting task. Because many of us come from the faculty, our own disciplines may or may not provide any context for this kind of work. Distrust stemming from past failed efforts may present unique and insurmountable obstacles to an easy conversation about community engagement. We may need advice or encouragement from our advancement office, or even coaching and direct support. One approach to fostering connections with a built-in context is to support leadership development programs.

This chapter presents ways academic leaders can foster community connections by engaging in local leadership development programs. In addition to advocating for leadership studies on our own campus, this essay explores projects based in Goshen, Indiana, and Cowley County, Kansas.

LEADERSHIP EXPERTISE AS A FOUNDATION FOR MAKING CONNECTIONS

As faculty members, we begin our academic careers in the classroom, lab, or library, and remain deeply committed to exchanging ideas and engaging in conversations that advance our disciplines. As we make our way to and through the dean's office—as associate deans, deans, and vice presidents—it sometimes feels as though we have abandoned the academic life for a more action-oriented professional career. In the hallways between sessions at the annual meeting of the American Conference of Academic Deans (ACAD), for example, we lament the loss of time for research or for the kinds of interactions with students that originally brought us into this profession. Many of us, though, eventually acknowledge that we have a new discipline: leadership.

Through this new discipline we discover many colleagues who have perspectives different from ours—ones shaped by their own disciplines and professions. Our daily work demands multiple points of view, and interdisciplinarity is the prevailing framework for addressing the complex problems we face. In solving many of our professional dilemmas, we can tailor resources for a more general audience. These tools provide a foundation for conversation with management professionals in other fields and can be the basis for establishing community connections through volunteering in support of local leadership development.

Leadership studies offers a rich array of frameworks for problem solving. Foundational texts that focus on the academic realm include *Reframing Organizations*, by Lee G. Bolman and Terrence E. Deal (Jossey-Bass, 2013); *Reframing Academic Leadership*, by Joan V. Gallos and Lee G. Bolman (Jossey-Bass, 2011); *Field Guide to Academic Leadership*, by Robert M. Diamond (Jossey-Bass, 2002);

and *How Academic Leadership Works,* by Robert Birnbaum (Jossey-Bass, 1992). In addition, James McGregor Burns's classic *Leadership* (Harper Colophon Books, 1979) and Edwin Freidman's *Failure of Nerve* (Church, 2017) are not about higher education per se but provide perspectives from historical, political, and organizational contexts that illuminate issues related to leading our colleges and universities. Aligning administrative structures and resource flows with institutional strategy is explored in Robert L. Morrill's *Strategic Leadership* (Rowman and Littlefield, 2007), Robert S. Kaplan and David P. Norton's *The Balanced Scorecard* (Harvard Business Review Press, 1996), Michael K. Townsley's *Small College Guide* (NACUBO, 2009), Margaret J. Barr and George S. McClellan's *Budgets and Financial Management* (Jossey-Bass, 2011), and Robert C. Dickeson's *Prioritizing Academic Programs and Services* (Jossey-Bass, 2010).

In addition, many deans have found it useful to incorporate leadership perspectives from outside academia in dealing with personnel issues. Helpful sources include Edward M. Hallowell's *Shine: Using Brain Science to Get the Best from Your People* (Harvard Business Review Press, 2011), Jeremy Hope and Steve Player's *Beyond Performance Management* (Harvard Business Review Press, 2012), and especially Robert Kegan and Lisa Laskow Lahey's *How the Way We Talk Can Change the Way We Work* (San Jossey-Bass, 2001). On the importance of personal and emotional development for improving our work and ability to deal with complexity in our professional and personal lives, see Kegan and Lahey's *Immunity to Change* (Harvard Business Review Press, 2009).[1]

As we build expertise in these areas and gain experience facilitating decision making among faculty and students, we develop the capacity to support existing or establish new leadership development programs in our communities. Eventually, we may even have the necessary tools to build and write curricula for these programs. This capacity can open avenues for us to participate in various local efforts, leading to authentic connections with civic leaders. Local chambers of commerce and community foundations often provide their communities with leadership development opportunities in the form of short workshops, daylong seminars, and institutes that can last a week or more. Because these programs are educational and adopt materials that we may already be using in our own work, they can serve as entry points into fruitful relationships.

SUPPORTING LEADERSHIP DEVELOPMENT
PROGRAMS IN TWO COMMUNITIES

The previous two institutions I worked for are small, residential colleges in rural cities under thirty-five thousand people. Both campuses are among the largest employers in their communities and are located in counties with active community foundations. Just as service was a part of my work when my primary role was in the classroom, I intentionally include service in my work as an academic leader. In order to align service with my administrative responsibilities, I volunteered in local leadership development programs at the chamber of commerce in one city and at the community foundation in the other. Each community offered multisession "courses" that extended over weeks or months and included a group project and culminating case presentation.

Goshen College and Goshen, Indiana

From the early 1990s to the mid-2000s, the population of Elkhart County, Indiana, shifted from about 5 percent to about 35 percent Hispanic. A boom in the county's main industry—the production of recreational vehicles (RVs)—propelled that demographic shift. Migrant workers who had picked various regional crops secured jobs in factories instead of moving on after the harvest season. The surge in jobs attracted their friends and family members to the area.

In 2015, Goshen College was in the final year of a major grant focused on intercultural understanding through which the college established its Center for Intercultural Teaching and Learning (CITL). Over the previous eight years, the community had recognized CITL for sponsoring efforts to support dialog across a potential racial-ethnic divide. The Goshen Chamber of Commerce had intended to offer a program for the growing Latinx segment of business leaders, but had engaged instead in a far-reaching community development initiative. The center approached the chamber as a partner and agreed to sponsor and help launch the leadership program. With the combined resources of the college and the chamber, we were able to construct an academy focused on leading in a diverse community.

The Intercultural Leadership Academy (ILA) lasted thirteen weeks and involved weekly sessions, two weekend retreats, and a set of group projects on which participants presented at a final case competition luncheon with local business leaders as invited guests. At that event, the guests judged the participants' projects and awarded a small seed grant to fund the ideas. I worked directly with the chamber president and a small group of community leaders (the Curriculum Task Force) to develop three key tools: learning outcomes for the whole institute and for each session; the projects' parameters and the rubric for judging them; and resource materials such as books, articles, and videos. Young to mid-career professionals were the intended members for this program, though we also had participants who were closer to retirement.

The overall learning outcome of the program was that participants would "improve communication, collaboration and confidence" in the service of developing their capacity to lead teams of people from very different backgrounds. Learning outcomes focused on *knowledge, skills,* and *dispositions,* each of which was elaborated as follows:

Knowledge
   A. Build knowledge of Goshen's diversity
   B. Build knowledge of a leader's role as a steward
   C. Work with facts

Skills
   A. Communication skills
   B. Collaboration skills

Dispositions
   A. Increase confidence
   B. Inclusive leadership
   C. Collaborative leadership

When the Curriculum Task Force finished its work, we were confident that we had designed a coherent set of experiences and projects that would lead to the learning outcomes identified above. The work was satisfying because we believed it would have a major impact on the participants and on the employers who sponsored their attendance.

After working with the group on this project, I continued to volunteer for the rest of the event, serving as host for many of the weekly sessions, leading the weekend retreats, and facilitating the case competition at the end. Since we invited many community leaders to present on a variety of topics, I was also able to connect with political, business, and civic leaders with whom

I had had no previous interaction—there had been no context for us to cross paths before the academy.

My involvement in the ILA provided connections that I could now use to develop relationships for a variety of purposes. For example, one of the participants in the academy worked in the office of the city engineer and expressed interest in our college students becoming summer interns. We engaged two local attorneys to present their perspectives on immigration law, and they agreed to give their talks to classes at the college. In general, working with the ILA gave me a much better understanding of how our college students could engage with local businesses in ways that were both sustainable and valuable for the employers and the students. In addition, some of the guests invited each week asked me if I would present to their business or civic group on a leadership topic. Volunteering with ILA created authentic ways to foster meaningful connections.

Southwestern College and Cowley County, Kansas

As a part of my own leadership development, in 2010 I participated in a summer institute in which I encountered Kegan and Lahey's Immunity to Change (ITC) exercise.[2] This approach helps participants examine a basic assumption they hold, typically one that may be unconscious and that constrains their choices. The exercise helps identify where and how an assumption is blocking progress toward a personal or professional improvement goal. It also guides participants in becoming "released" from the constraint that the assumption exerts over their choices. This training had a significant impact on me. As I was developing curriculum to launch a master's degree program in intercultural leadership, I secured a seat at a forthcoming training so that I could learn to lead the program.

By the time I moved to Southwestern College in Winfield, Kansas, to assume the role of vice-president for academic affairs, I had been actively using the ITC exercise for seven years as part of leadership courses I taught and faculty retreats I led for my own and other schools. I approached the Winfield Chamber of Commerce to see if it had plans for any leadership programs. The staff directed me to the Legacy Community Foundation—the sponsor of a county-wide program called Leadership Cowley that gathers business and civic leaders from all ages into a cohort for a six-session program.

The Legacy Community Foundation directs a board of Leadership Cowley alumni that develops and delivers the sessions, based on a curriculum from the Kansas Leadership Center (KLC).[3] The foundation's executive director had recently been to a KLC seminar in which she participated in the ITC process and found it as meaningful as I had. This gave us an opportunity to consider using it in the county's program.

Currently, I am once again working with a small board in developing a leadership curriculum for its specific audience. The focus of my work with them is to help decide where the ITC exercise best fits in their curriculum and whether it should be part of the initial six-session leadership program, or something offered as "advanced work" to graduates of Leadership Cowley. The board consists of management professionals from businesses and organizations as diverse as a local bank, a music festival with an international reach, and the regional economic development corporation.

The Leadership Cowley project has given me an opportunity to engage in meaningful relationship building with a diverse group of community leaders. Since I had success using this approach to fostering community connections at a previous institution, I made another attempt that proved successful in less time than it took before and with no extra resources—only my desire to make those connections.

CONCLUSION

Many academic leaders face invisible barriers to fostering connections with the community. Some may have nothing to do with us personally but much to do with the history of our institutions, the work of our predecessors, or local social or political conditions. It's easier to establish and sustain meaningful and productive ties with the towns and cities in which our institutions are located when we can offer something concrete in service to our communities. Our students can provide community service, but those experiences should be enriched by stronger ties between our communities and institutions. Creating meaningful opportunities for students often requires us first to establish connections with civic organizations that can help us understand specific ways the community can benefit from our institution and vice versa.

As academic leaders we are most successful when we commit to learning new things. The resources and expertise we use to resolve complex problems in our own work on campus can serve as the context for fostering connections with professionals in our communities. Leadership development programs offer one avenue through which the effort we put into learning new ways of managing our professional dilemmas can be useful to others.

— *Takeaways* —

- Because it's sometimes daunting to foster meaningful connections between our institution and community, deans need an authentic way to enter those kinds of relationships.
- Leadership studies provides a wealth of material on which to draw in supporting leadership development programs in your community; the more you study and develop yourself, the more you will have to offer.
- Volunteering in support of local leadership development efforts, especially programming organized through local business and civic organizations like chambers of commerce and community foundations, can be fruitful for all involved.
- Your work can benefit not only your community but also your institution, its students, and, of course, you.

NOTES

1. Kegan, the longtime educational director of the Harvard Summer Institute for Management and Leadership in Higher Education (informally known as the MLE), incorporated the Immunity to Change exercise into that institute to great effect.
2. See Robert Kegan and Lisa Laskow Lahey, *Immunity to Change: How to Overcome It and Unlock the Potential in Yourself and Your Organization* (Cambridge, MA: Harvard Business Review Press, 2009).
3. More information about the Kansas Leadership Center is available at https://kansasleadershipcenter.org/.

CHAPTER 12

Building Reciprocal Relationships for Careers and Lifelong Learning

CHERYL BAILEY AND WENDY A. WEAVER

A little work in forming valuable relationships in a college's region goes a long way. If members of the public see higher education as aloof or irrelevant and disconnected from commerce and the community, building synergetic bridges is the antidote. We are the pipeline for what they need: knowledgeable and insightful employees. But where do we start? To create a mutually beneficial relationship between an institution and its region, researching the region's needs and strengths is a first and essential step. Effective research includes conversations and information gathering. These conversations establish a rapport that prevents the "ivory tower" effect that isolates a college from its environment. Groundwork of this kind unlocks a number of doors for students, including input into the curriculum that gives graduates an edge in the marketplace and real-world connections as they search for internships or jobs.

Our experiences as deans, one already embedded in the community and the other an incoming dean, provide insight into how and why these connections are truly reciprocal.

RESEARCH BY AN EMBEDDED DEAN

For the dean who has been in the community for some time, less research may be needed. It would take little research to determine that Milwaukee, the city in which both authors live and work at Mount Mary University, has a high poverty rate and many social needs. As a consequence of its mission, Mount Mary has a long history of teaching and advocating for social justice. On-campus posters and discussions focus on the disparity of both social and actual capital evidenced in our community. Eighty-five percent of our undergraduates come from the greater Milwaukee area, and they reflect its demographics. In the past five years, 64 percent of our students were low-income and 58 percent of undergraduate, degree-seeking students are from traditionally underserved populations. Seventy-one percent come from homes at or below the Milwaukee-area median income; 24 percent have a reported family income below $15,000. The University Factbook and institutional research department provide this information yearly.

For Mount Mary's first-year seminar Leadership for Social Justice, there are plenty of facts about Milwaukee that serve as a springboard for class discussions. Milwaukee is the largest city in Wisconsin and the thirtieth most populous city in the United States. Twenty-seven percent of people live below the poverty level—double the national rate of 12 percent. Hundreds of nonprofit organizations operate near campus to address the Milwaukee community's many concerns. Mount Mary already had some connection to many of them. The university's mission, situation, and demographic provides a strong foundation for strengthening the relationship between nonprofit organizations and our students and curricula.

RESEARCH BY AN INCOMING DEAN

An incoming dean, particularly one moving into a new area, has more research to do. Having relocated to Milwaukee and hearing that it's in a food corridor (a geographic region with a significant number of food industries), this new dean began research with basic Google searches that led to newspaper articles, state-level programs, and federal government initiatives. News reports discussed food companies trying to find people to employ; other stories focused on residents in parts of Milwaukee who don't have access to fresh food.

These themes seemed a good fit for Mount Mary students, since they are often first generation, are concerned about getting a job after graduation, and are keenly aware of social justice. A professional career would lead to social mobility and meaningful contributions to the community. Searching the Bureau of Labor Statistics revealed that the state of Wisconsin is one of the five highest employers in food science in the nation. Further research led to the Wisconsin Food and Beverage Center, with its focus on teaching high school students about careers in "Farm to Factory to Fork." The center has lists of area food companies with common household names such as Kikkoman and Ocean Spray.

Upon meeting representatives from companies, we learned that many food processors in Milwaukee and Wisconsin are not household names but nevertheless make spices or other ingredients that go into products we recognize in the grocery store. For example, in Kenosha, Wisconsin, a company makes the familiar flavor that coats Doritos chips. Other companies create packaging for food. Conversations with Palermo Pizza led to the understanding that packaging of frozen pizzas needs to block certain wavelengths of light for pepperoni to retain its coloring. Simple research that started with Google yielded a great deal of information that proved valuable in creating a program to meet the needs of students and industry partners.

Two outcomes of our research were curricular improvements and strong networking opportunities for students. At the course level, the research by the embedded dean led to connecting first-year students to nonprofit organizations in a more holistic way. At the programmatic level, the research by the new dean led to a new major.

COURSE-LEVEL CURRICULA

The coursework for Mount Mary's first-year seminar Leadership for Social Justice had traditionally been bifurcated into social issues (race, class, and gender) and a service-learning component. When General Electric invited the campus to be trained in "design thinking" at its Menlo studio, we were introduced to this method of innovation and a new way for our service learners to interact with nonprofit organizations. Rather than taking only ten hours over the course of a semester, work with nonprofit organizations became the focus of the class.

Because faculty from across the campus teach this interdisciplinary course and curriculum is under their purview, the dean facilitates conversations among the faculty who determine common elements for their syllabi. Faculty guide students to collaborate with a nonprofit organization in a design-thinking project. As a class, the students go to the site; company representatives, in turn, visit the class. The community partner assesses the students' project, and the faculty member combines the assessment with their own evaluation to produce the final grade for the project. This collaboration has been so successful that one organization has continued to work with the same professor and new batches of first-year students four years in a row.

Students now study relevant social issues in the authentic context of the community partner and the people it serves rather than as theoretical constructs. Through the lens of the nonprofit, students see how issues of social justice play out in our community and imagine how our community can better respond. Since we actually know individuals at the partnerships, it's easier to reconnect with them about topics other than the class. Once the nonprofit organizations get to know our students, faculty, and mission through this course, their perception of Mount Mary is no longer governed by the antiquated notion of white privilege and uninvolved, theory-focused academics. These interactions have led to meaningful relationships. When another division of Mount Mary—the development office, for example—contacts them, they are far more receptive.

CURRICULA AT THE PROGRAM LEVEL

Because initial research showed a demand for careers in food science, additional research looked at the types of institutions that offer degrees in this discipline. Typically, programs were offered by research-intensive institutions, and, surprisingly, the Milwaukee area did not have a food science degree offering. A draft curriculum was created by reviewing curricula from institutions around the country.

With this draft in hand, the dean and director of corporate and foundation relations visited food science companies for their feedback and input. Companies often commented how they appreciated being able to influence the preparation of future employees. For example, they emphasized the need for courses in the robust preparation of statistics instead of calculus, and the importance of sensory testing of food. Companies test their food on large numbers of people, and statistical analysis is crucial to deriving meaning from the data. Conversations with industry about the curriculum led to the development of an advisory board. The board identified the professional certifications expected of graduates, emphasized the need for a master's degree for working professionals, and identified the need for a sensory lab.

At this point, the dean developed a program proposal for faculty and administration to consider. An adjunct with food science experience came forward and was hired full-time to lead the new food science program. The dean, the director of corporate and foundation relations, and the faculty member continued their conversations with industry. Because the professor had food science experience, she was able to have deeper conversations with industry. She and the development office continue to work very closely together to respond to industry needs. Mount Mary embedded certifications in the curriculum, created a master's degree with extensive feedback on scheduling, and built a sensory lab as part of a new Mount Mary food lab.

Having these conversations produced unexpected insights. For example, employees encounter a barrier in earning an advanced degree. Working professionals want to perform thesis research at their company, but this usually involves proprietary information. Publication expectations at research-intensive institutions prevent the use of such confidential information. Mount Mary is a teaching-intensive institution, and faculty are not under the same pressure to publish high numbers of papers derived from their students' work. Therefore, master's students in food science at Mount Mary can perform research for their theses at a company on condition that proprietary information is shared only with the thesis committee. This enhanced the program's ability to serve professionals seeking to attain higher credentials and furthered the companies' interest in supporting their professional employees' education. Our competitive edge was discovered only through building a relationship with these companies.

NETWORKING AT THE COURSE LEVEL

Students hear that they need to network, but they don't know what that means. Many Mount Mary students are first generation and often don't have family members with the connections necessary for job opportunities in their desired fields. During their first-year seminar, our students interact with a variety of professionals in a guided and solution-oriented manner. This experience takes the pressure off of their first foray into networking. Students don't realize they're "networking" until they've already done it.

Networking also serves as a foundation for professional communication and conduct. Students often care so much for the organization and what it's doing for the community that they want to make a good impression and be helpful. As they are guided in these introductory professional connections, their first steps are active listening and keen observation. Both of these skills are characteristic of advanced professionalism, and their practice promotes goodwill with the organization because its representatives feel heard and valued.

Developing relationships with nonprofit organizations opens a number of doors for students through service learning or internships, or both. For some students, these connections serve as a catalyst for the type of work they want to do. Students also recognize analogous careers in the for-profit sector. Either way, it's a win-win situation for both the student and the organization.

NETWORKING AT THE PROGRAM LEVEL

Industry connections forged through conversations about the food science curriculum led to corporate interest in helping Mount Mary recruit students and integrate industry expertise into the student experience. This integration took the form of panel discussions with industry professionals for prospective and current students, student visits to companies to meet food scientists in the environment in which they work, and internships and employment. All Mount Mary food science majors have secured jobs by the time they graduate.

Building partnerships with industry through collaboration among academics led to reciprocal relationships in which connections and workload are shared. These partnerships have given Mount Mary's development office a foot in the door and compelling reasons for continued contact. Our colleagues in development enthusiastically organize industry panels for admissions, scholarship programs, and individual courses. They also plan speed-networking events with industry professionals. One company hosted its food sensory experiments on the Mount Mary campus and paid our undergraduates for their work as researchers. Another funded a science course to investigate a research question for which the company didn't have the time or personnel to pursue. Students presented their findings at a poster session where industry professionals asked questions. From all these interactions, students have learned that careers are not linear but take many different pathways, and that there will be pathways not even yet imagined.

CONCLUSION

Research about an institution's region does not need to be onerous. Nightly news, local papers, Google searches, and data from the Bureau of Labor Statistics gave both of us the information we needed to get started. Then, it simply took the courage to call or email organizations in the community. Partnering with the development office, whose staff do this work frequently, greatly facilitated the process. Once these businesses realized we wanted to help the community and provide even better preparation for our students, they were very receptive. Not only were they willing to meet and talk, but they also wanted to learn more about our college and students. Relationships soon formed. They confided their needs, and we worked together to launch students into careers and lifelong learning.

— *Takeaways* —

- Relationships are relatively easy to develop and are deeply rewarding.
- Research begins with looking up information and engaging in active listening.
- Working with on-campus departments and off-campus partners spreads the workload and opens up more opportunities.
- Employers value being asked to help shape curriculum.
- Employers get emotionally invested in the program and students.

CHAPTER 13

Narratives That Connect Our Collective Communities

Integrated Learning at St. Catherine University

TARSHIA L. STANLEY

The Integrated Learning Series (ILS) at St. Catherine University in St. Paul, Minnesota, is one of the places I've found to do work that brings me joy as an administrator and educator. My colleagues, our students, and I began the program in the fall of 2018 by curating a series of events, courses, and performances and linking them to a theme that supports our mission. This theme then allowed us to connect across campus silos while providing a place for the local community to engage more deliberately with the university's mission to educate women to lead and influence in just and equitable ways. To create a more interconnected community, we crafted a narrative around what is important to us as a university and built on that consensus. The Integrated Learning Series is currently described in this way:

> For more than a century St. Kate's has been educating women to lead and influence. One of the ways we embody that mission is through the Integrated Learning series. Located at the intersection of creative energy and critical reflection, the Series is one way we partner academics with activism, the paper with the performance, and the campus with the

community. It is the array of courses, activities, speakers, events, performances, and exhibitions that coalesce into our ways of knowing.[1]

The ILS, as I lead it, really began when I was interviewing for the dean's position at St. Kate's in the spring of 2018. There was a pivotal moment when I learned that the director of the performing arts center had been working on a grant to bring the opera based on Octavia E. Butler's novel *Parable of the Sower* to St. Catherine University.[2] It was significant that my most recent scholarly work had led me not only to teach and write about Octavia E. Butler but also to found the Butler Literary Society. It was auspicious that I'd hosted the creator of the *Parable* opera at my previous institution just one week before. As I interacted with St. Kate's faculty, students, and staff many of them seemed excited to bring the opera to campus. I hoped it meant that they were aware of what was happening around speculative fiction in general and Black speculative fiction in particular. These genres are important new sources of sociopolitical critique that many theorists have only just begun to acknowledge.[3] Their excitement meant that here was a place actively trying to embody its mission, a place where students were poised to embrace new directions in theoretical approaches. If I needed a deciding factor to join St. Kate's, this possibility of introducing a new audience to Butler's work—and integrating it into the curriculum and the culture—was it.

I'm sure I received one of the warmest welcomes of any new administrator when I arrived on campus. Having an onboarding committee to introduce me to the history and culture of the university was extremely important to my being able to do the work that laid the foundation for the Integrated Learning Series. The committee introduced me not only to key people and programs on campus but also to the history of the institution and the local community. I met staff at the Minnesota Humanities Center and participated in their programming called the Bdote.[4]

The Bdote experience was important because it acknowledged the indigenous peoples upon whose land we were all working and provided another narrative around which the campus could build solidarity with the community. In addition, my interactions with community artists, writers, and activists helped lay a foundation for the ILS that set a precedent for community input. Being

invited to share my work on Octavia Butler as a way for the campus and community to get to know me allowed me to listen for ways we could all connect.
Soon I began meeting with a committee of faculty, staff, and students to think
of strategies for linking my scholarly knowledge with the impending opera.
This is how the ILS committee was born.

When the committee began its work, the opera was scheduled to premiere
on campus in April 2019. This created a sense of urgency as we began to
think of the performance as a culminating event in a year of interactions with
Butler's work. We soon realized that, although the opera was coming that
spring, it didn't have to be the end of our engagement with Butler. In fact, it
shouldn't be. It would really take two years of intentional programming to
give interested faculty time to include her in their curriculum and to sufficiently involve alumni, local artists, and community members in what we were
doing. I suggested the biennial Octavia E. Butler Literary Society Conference,
to be held in 2020 as the final event for our series. We then began to plan in
earnest the ways we could infuse Butler's work into the curriculum.

It was important from the beginning that integrated learning include the
community. My work as a teacher and scholar has always focused on making
sure that what I do is relevant to people who don't normally have access to
the academy. In addition to all the things in the job description, my responsibility as an administrator was to put support structures in place to ensure
that this kind of interconnected work was featured as a benefit of living near
and partnering with an academic institution.

As I began to build out the Integrated Learning Series, it was important
to reiterate St. Kate's mission—to educate women to lead and influence.
Whenever there was a challenge or cross-purpose in our programming or
planning, I reminded stakeholders of our guiding mission and vision. The
next step in the process was to be sure faculty understood what I hoped we
could do and the potential for them to amplify the work in their classrooms.
At an all-school meeting, I made a formal presentation on the series and continually stressed that it would make more visible the work faculty were already doing. I started with the mission and defined what I meant by integrated
learning. I reiterated the possibilities of involving the community and helping them see the campus and our programming as an asset they may not have
accessed previously. Next, I laid out the ways the faculty, staff, students, and

alumni might engage our theme and stressed the fact that it would take two to three years for us to do justice to the series. We could not have an Integrated Learning Series that lasted one semester or even one academic year. It would take prolonged and sustained engagement for the theme to truly resonate.

As our theme, we adopted Butler's Earthseed tenet from *Parable of the Sower*: "All that you touch You Change. All that you Change, Changes you."[5] After presenting the concept to the faculty, I invited the committee members and the superconnectors to get to work. The superconnectors were faculty and staff who I knew could germinate an idea and influence the curriculum and culture with their insights for programming. As a result, our Butler-themed series included reading her work in classrooms, at community book clubs, at alumni book discussion dinners, and in faculty and staff reading groups. Faculty and staff were invited to lead some of those discussions, and I led the others. The Catherine G. Murphy Gallery and the O'Shaughnessy Performing Arts Center used their programming to join us in this work. A highlight was when a group of art students read *Parable* in their class and then created visual images around the text. One of those images became the flyer for printed and digital marketing materials for the 2021 conference of the Octavia E. Butler (OEB) Literary Society.[6] The Butler Society paid the student to use her work, and now she has that distinction in her portfolio. It was a valuable opportunity to show students how their classroom work could be directly connected to careers they were interested in after graduation. My favorite event was when I read *Parable of the Sower* with student leaders on campus.[7] It gave me an opportunity to bond with them and to understand their leadership styles.

As ILS planning progressed, I realized that I needed to expand my definition of superconnectors. We needed alumni affairs, marketing and communications, the St. Catherine University library, the mission chairs, and the Sisters of St. Joseph of Carondolet (the founders of St. Kate's) to support our efforts.[8] One of the superconnectors even shepherded the creation of a short documentary based on our journey that first year.[9] Another key element of truly integrating a theme across the campus and the community was leveraging established community connections with our primary artist. Toshi Reagon— who created *Parable* the opera in partnership with her mother, Bernice Johnson Reagon—visited the campus several times prior to the opera's performance in

April 2019. Reagon's process as an artist-activist is to visit the performance site ahead of time and get involved in the community. This has become a pillar of Integrated Learning at St. Kate's: we invite the primary artist, lecturer, or speaker to meet the campus and community in an abbreviated "artist in residence" format. We may not be able to host a guest the entire semester, but we can have them do several brief visits.

As a result of the Reagons' interactions with the local community, we leveraged their contacts by asking these community connectors to get the word out about what was happening on campus. They helped us sell out the eighteen-hundred-seat O'Shaughnessy Performing Arts Center. We reciprocated by hosting their corresponding community events on campus. It was during these events that I met several lifelong residents of the Twin Cities who had never set foot on St. Kate's campus. These same people and others came back for the actual event. I wish I had words to describe the electricity on campus the night of the *Parable* opera. Students, faculty, staff, alumni, administrators, and people from every part of the community became members of St. Kate's. It is a memory we hold on to and try to reproduce in all that we do.[10]

Due to the pandemic, the two-year series based on the work of Octavia Butler was extended an additional year. It was fortunate that change itself was at the heart of the work we'd been doing for two years. Originally scheduled for June 2020, the OEB Literary Society's conference was pushed back to March 2021 and held in a virtual format. As we planned the conference, we discussed what we had learned from our engagement with the opera, as well as the premise of the OEB Society's residing at the intersection of academic and nonacademic readers of Butler's works. We went back to our community activists and invited them to be what I titled community curators. They worked alongside me, as the founding president of the Butler Society, and the conference organizers to convene an event that featured both academic and community panels. As a result, more than seventeen hundred people registered and participated at some point throughout the two-day conference.[11]

The pandemic transformed the series in other ways as well. Shortly after the murder of Mr. George Floyd, our campus was looking for a new way to connect. We couldn't do so physically, but we had the connective tissue created by the series. Both the campus and the community knew that they could come together at any physical event designated ILS—cyberspace should be no different. I worked quickly to create a summer series that could in some way speak to the questions with which Mr. Floyd's death was demanding we grapple. "The St. Catherine University Integrated Learning Summer Series: At the Confluence of the Liberal Arts and Social Justice—Race in the Machine" met each Tuesday evening for one hour. We featured both St. Kate's faculty experts and scholars from around the country. We sought to provide insights into how our nation had ended up on that street corner in Minneapolis on May 25, 2020, for nine minutes and twenty-nine seconds. The sessions were recorded and made available on *YouTube*.[12] During the fall 2020 series, we continued with the theme of systemic racism and dedicated the month of October to women's suffrage, especially women voters in Minnesota. Then in the spring of 2021, in the wake of the election and the insurrection at the US Capitol, our theme was "When Women Lead: Courage, Confidence, Collaboration." As I looked back on the 2020–21 academic year, I realized I'd spent one evening a week for a year helping spin a web between the campus and the community and worked to remind us how much we have to offer one another.

We have already begun to plan the next series and the broad theme in which all our stakeholders can engage. We'll spend the next two to three years partnering with Native Minnesotans to explore "Indigenous Thought Leadership." Native women alumni of St. Kate's are acting as the external steering committee for this endeavor. I have never forgotten the encounter I had at the Minnesota Humanities Center during my first months on campus. I've moved as much of my programming budget as I could to make sure students, faculty, and staff have participated in Bdote in preparation for what we will learn and do over the next few years. This series will require intensive research, empower and enlighten students, yield publications, raise money for Native scholarships, honor the Native community, and produce many partnerships. We hope to create space for recompense and healing with the Native community as well as all the other communities damaged by systemic inequities perpetuated by higher education.

In these tumultuous times I've learned to stay engaged in projects that restore my energy and my soul as an educator. The Integrated Learning Series has provided me with the balance that I need to do the very difficult parts of my job. It has also provided a place of connection between myself and the faculty and between the campus and our local community. This point of connection is the place where we have created narratives that bind us together. We recognize that we're not doing new work, but we seek to work in new ways. We want to connect the classroom more directly to our mission and use the museum, the performing arts center, and our community resources as extensions of the classroom. The ILS is an invitation to become and remain a member of St. Kate's whether one is a student, employee, or community member.

I've learned that building partnerships across campus and within the community requires:

- Defining and communicating a vision for all stakeholders
- Creating a team of people who have reached across the university and out into the community
- Leveraging partnerships with important units on campus (marketing, communications, trustees, development, museum, performing arts center, etc.)[13]
- Leveraging partnerships with artists, activists, community members, and champions on campus
- Allocating time and resources to support the growth and development of partnerships

The path to scripting narratives that connect our collective communities may begin organically but can only grow with focused intent. We have succeeded because we have expanded the walls of the classrooms, inviting those on campus as well as alumni, community members, and community activists to join us in our work. Building trust strengthens relationships. When we need to chart new directions or to correct the course, we return to this shared understanding of what connects us. Building community means situating the university as an important part of and partner in the local and, ultimately, global story.

— *Takeaways* —

- Amplify the power of the liberal arts by helping make visible for students the connections between content, skill sets, and lived experiences.
- When faced with a challenge or cross-purpose, return stakeholders to the institution's mission and vision.

- Keep engaged in projects that restore your energy and soul as an educator.
- If you're not doing new work, seek to do work in new ways.

NOTES

1. "Integrated Learning Series," St. Catherine University, accessed 21 November 2021, https://www.stkate.edu/events/integrated-learning-series.
2. Octavia E. Butler, *Parable of the Sower* (New York: Four Walls Eight Windows, 1993). See also the website *Octavia E. Butler's Parable of the Sower*, https://www.parableopera.com.
3. "Introduction," in *Approaches to Teaching the Works of Octavia E. Butler*, ed. Tarshia L. Stanley (New York: Modern Language Association Press, 2019), 9–16. In the introduction I further explain how Black speculative fiction has become a site of sociopolitical protest.
4. "Learning from Place: Bdote," Minnesota Humanities Center, accessed 21 November 2021, https://mnhum.org/k12/professional-development-educators/learning -from-place-bdote/. The Bdote is a daylong interactive excursion sponsored by the Minnesota Humanities Center and led by Native Dakota people. They explain to participants the Dakotas' relationship with the land in the Twin Cities. This is particularly important because St. Kate's sits on traditional Dakota land.
5. Butler, *Parable of the Sower*, 13.
6. The Octavia E. Butler Society, https://oebsociety.wordpress.com/.
7. I remember a snowy Sunday in February 2019 when I was due to meet the book club and I thought the inclement weather would stop us. However, the students were excited to discuss the book and wanted to meet nonetheless.
8. I am forever grateful to Dr. Amy Hamlin, who was the Neufeld Mission Chair for the Liberal Arts. Dr. Hamlin shepherded my onboarding committee and the making of the ILS documentary. See "Endowed Mission Chairs," St. Catherine University, accessed 21 November 2021, https://www.stkate.edu/about/mission-and-vision/endowed-chairs.
9. "*Parable of the Sower* Integrated Learning Series at St. Catherine University," *YouTube*, 27 February 2020, https://youtu.be/eBCjcoq9GdE.
10. For ticketed events, it's important for the Integrated Learning Series to create equitable access and pricing.
11. "March 2021 Conference Program and Registration," Octavia E. Butler Society, accessed 21 November 2021, https://oebsociety.wordpress.com/2021-conference-registration -the-confluence-octavia-e-butler-at-the-intersection-of-cultural-critique-and-climate -collapse-march-7-8-2021/.
12. "Integrated Learning Series 2020" (seven videos), *YouTube*, updated 14 August 2020, https://www.youtube.com/playlist?list=PLX9r_vcNwGgrzXusfMUSX_dM5VaCglhPg.
13. Partnerships with trustees require moving through the requisite channels.

PART IV

Leadership and the Institution

CHAPTER 14

Working with the Upper Administration and Leadership Team

GREGOR THUSWALDNER

Years ago, when I was on a search committee to hire an academic dean, a candidate we interviewed mentioned the importance for him of academic publishing. Staying active in his field gave him street credibility with the faculty in his administrative role at a state college. What helps deans with their credibility and rapport when it comes to working with the institution's upper administration? How can academic deans establish and maintain a productive working relationship with the upper leadership team? How can deans win their trust and successfully "manage up?"

As a former dean and current provost, I have found that besides being fiscally responsible, an effective dean has to have strong communication, interpersonal, and mediation skills. In addition, deans have to see themselves as the chief academic leaders, strategists, and advocates in their area.

THE DEAN AS ADVOCATE AND STRATEGIST

Deans need to recognize that they are the prime representatives of and advocates for their unit, school, or college. Roper and Deal go a step further when they remind deans of the significance of their role: "You need to view your iconic position symbolically to appreciate that you are not just the leader, spokesperson, or representative for your college. You are the college. If you have a good relationship with your provost, faculty members and students in your college will benefit."[1] Personifying your academic unit should imply knowing it intimately; successful deans have to distinguish between various needs and wants that department and program leaders may bring to them. In meetings with their supervising vice-president, deans should be able to discuss the most pressing needs and concerns. Because upper administrators have several direct reports with large portfolios, it's in the best interest of a dean to offer potential solutions to the issues a unit or school faces. A dean who expects a senior administrator to solve a problem on their behalf may be incompetent.

Advocating for one's school or college entails not only requesting additional resources but also communicating the successes in one's area. In a way, a dean should see themselves as the chief marketing officer, which is particularly important in times of scarcity and potential budget cuts. Leaders should communicate the vitality and viability of the unit they oversee. Furthermore, advocacy requires educating the provost or other upper administrators about the school or college's complexities. As Roper and Deal point out, "One of the dean's most important jobs is to 'educate' the provost. This job is especially crucial when a new provost comes on board."[2]

The "education of the provost" should not be relegated to regularly scheduled meetings but needs to continue in other venues. Roper and Deal recommend inviting the provost to attend and speak at school events. Providing a platform for the chief academic officer to meet and connect with various constituents gives the dean's unit more clout. In other words, a dean should see themselves as bridge builders between their world and the world of the upper administration. In Hanley's words:

> The dean is the "bridge," ensuring that communication from *above* (up) is shared *below* (down) and that from *below* (down) is shared *above* (up). Moreover, she is simultaneously responsible for being the bridge that maintains strong and clear communication with peers (across). In this role a dean must remember that bridges take thought and vision to create and trust to cross. This means she needs to craft information that not only informs others but also engages them and secures their confidence and support.

In addition, she needs to recognize that bridges can be approached from different directions and be open minded in accepting the ideas of others and offering her respect and support for their contributions.[3]

The original meaning of "translate" is "to carry over." A translator's task is to carry information from one language to another. This responsibility is also crucial for deans, as is speaking the same language, to use a similar metaphorical expression. As Buller points out:

> Never assume that, simply because you and the upper administration are using similar language, you have precisely the same object in mind. To you "strengthening the academic program" may involve expanding the number of majors and reducing your overall student-to-faculty ratio. To your president, it may mean fewer majors to create a more focused curriculum and redirecting funds to the largest and most popular majors. Until you have a clear conversation about how you intend to implement the institution's strategic goals, you'll never know whether your priorities are in line with your president's.[4]

Successful deans recognize the tension between the needs of their units and those of the wider institution. They also realize that having good relationships with fellow deans in other areas enhances their working relationship with senior administrators. Deans who can work effectively with other deans are seen as team players who have the well-being of the institution, not just their unit, in mind. When deans mutually support one another's causes, it's more likely that the upper administration will take their recommendations and requests more seriously. For example, a dean in health sciences may support the appeal by the dean of arts and sciences to hire additional faculty in chemistry and biology. As Roper and Deal write, "When deans of professional schools harness their collective power, few provosts or presidents can safely ignore them."[5]

Leaders can form alliances in order to reach their shared goals. At the same time, deans should use their collective power and influence wisely. Nobody likes to be manipulated and bullied, and this is no less true for upper administrators. Instead, deans should always choose a diplomatic approach when discussing collective interests. Olson and Simerson note:

> The best collaborative leaders focus on what are commonly called win-win situations. While they are achievement oriented, they don't view success through a strictly competetive lens. Faced with a dilemma, they are prone to seek out a "third way" that can avoid creating winners and losers in a situation. This is often for the longer-term benefit of the team or organization, as the collaborative leader pays attention to issues of organizational culture, seeking out ways to create an inclusive team environment where stakeholders feel that they have a say in decisions and ownership of collective outcomes.[6]

Deans can become more effective strategists when they draw on and apply systems thinking in their interactions with the upper administration. They realize the fact that everything is interconnected and, as Olson and Simerson observed, they "recognize . . . relationships and interdependencies in a complex system or situation, including the ability to anticipate the intended and unintended consequences of a given action."[7] A systems-thinking approach helps deans see the bigger picture, which informs the way they think about planning for the future of their academic unit. Problems and goals are no longer seen in isolation but rather, as Peter Senge wrote, as "components of larger but less visible structures that affect each other. To understand a system is to understand those interrelationships and how they recur and change over time."[8]

POSITIVE WORKING RELATIONSHIPS

For academic deans to thrive, they need to develop positive working relationships with the president's leadership team, particularly, but certainly not exclusively, with their direct supervisor as well as their assistants and staff. It's prudent to plan and prepare for one-on-one meetings by creating an agenda. As middle managers, deans support the senior administration. Mautz calls this "purposeful support," which he differentiates from blind support: "The support you offer should be intentional about the why and how to make your spirit of servitude more meaningful. It's not about impressing your boss (although that's certainly a great side effect), it's about performing well in your duty to support your boss."[9] Effective provosts also see the need to support their deans, and they can become mentors and coaches helping deans grow professionally.

Collaborating with and offering one's support to a senior administrator builds trust and can go a long way. For example, developing a close relationship with the VP for enrollment management is mutually beneficial: it can positively impact enrollment numbers in one's unit, making the VP look good when they report back to both the president and the board. Deans can create other opportunities to develop a closer relationship with the president and their cabinet by shadowing them for a day or two. In programs such as the Senior Leadership Academy, co-organized by the Council of Independent Colleges and the American Academic Leadership Institute, deans create professional development plans that usually include shadowing senior administrators, learning more about their portfolios, and getting to know them better on a personal level.

Different senior administrators have different personalities, working styles, quirks, and the like. But there's one thing they all have in common: they don't like to be caught off guard. Deans should make every effort to keep their supervisors informed. As a general rule, it's advisable to be vigilant and to give the provost a heads-up about brewing conflicts and concerns that could quickly spin out of control and negatively impact the institution.

Disagreements with upper administrators should be dealt with diplomatically in one-on-one meetings—never publicly. Buller uses the term "collegial disagreements," which he defines as "pointing out to your supervisors why your perspective on a matter differs from theirs (perhaps a policy that will be seen in one light by the governing board will be viewed quite differently by your college's faculty or students, or a new initiative will have repercussions that are more immediately noticeable at your level than elsewhere) and exploring with them alternative approaches."[10]

Deans are appointed by and serve at the pleasure of the provost. Challenging the provost in a public setting automatically undermines their authority, and it's very likely that such an unruly dean will be removed. Time and again, the *Chronicle of Higher Education* and similar publications run stories about academic leaders who have derailed. Self-sabotage—in the form of arrogance or perhaps subpar interpersonal or communication skills—is often named as a reason why administrators lose their jobs.[11]

What if senior administrators themselves are difficult to work with? Kets de Vries recommends approaching a less-than-stellar boss with empathy, because "most bad bosses are not inherently bad people; they're good people with weaknesses that can be exacerbated by the pressure to lead and deliver results."[12] Empathy enables deans to see the real reasons for their supervisor's questionable behavior. Asking fellow deans for advice in dealing with a difficult provost or other challenging senior leader often yields positive results. Resist the temptation to bad-mouth a callous boss: sarcasm and negativity always backfire. Kets de Vries also underlines the importance of "framing your questions in a positive way: 'How can I better achieve your goals?' rather than 'What am I doing wrong?'"[13]

For good reason, deans find it problematic when faculty circumvent them and approach the provost instead. Likewise, provosts are disconcerted by deans who go straight to the president with their grievances. If a seemingly insurmountable problem in the relationship between dean and provost occurs, the dean should follow the institution's policies and procedures that address this type of conflict, rather than immediately sharing it with the president and other constituents.

THE DEAN AS MEDIATOR

Because part of their role is to manage up and down, academic deans sometimes find themselves between a rock and a hard place. Thus, mediating between two or more sides is an essential function of a dean. Buller is right when he says that deans should not see themselves "simply as the upper administration's yes-man." Instead, he compares an effective dean to "a sage counselor who provides . . . supervisors with the information and insight they need to do *their* jobs effectively."[14] Or, as Jaser writes, "the most effective [middle managers] are in possession of humane, sophisticated communication skills and the knack to mediate and find common grounds between actors at different levels in the organization."[15] Similarly, Gunsalus contends that "much of your administrative life is one negotiation after another, and negotiation requires effective listening, speaking, and influencing skills."[16]

Fisher, Ury, and Patton's classic *Getting to Yes: Negotiating Agreement without Giving In* provides a framework that can help deans in their day-to-day work with upper administration. Their method called "principled negotiation" consists of the following four factors:

People: Separate people from the problem.

Interests: Focus on interests, not positions.

Options: Invent multiple options, looking for mutual gains before deciding what to do.

Criteria: Insist that the result be based on some objective standard.[17]

Deans can increase their efficiency if they internalize these four aspects of the principled negotiation process. In particular, separating the people from the problem at hand makes discussions more professional and less personal.

Focusing on people, not their problems, involves asking open-ended questions. This strategy helps deans identify the needs and interests that provosts and other senior administrators may have. Questions such as "Could you help me understand . . . ?" "How could we fix . . . ?" and "How could I be of help?" can unearth interests and needs that lie behind an upper administrator's position. According to Fisher, Ury, and Patton, "Interests motivate people; they are the silent movers behind the hubbub of positions. Your position is something you have decided upon. Your interests are what caused you to so decide."[18]

When people take a firm position, they imply that a specific problem can be solved in only one particular way. Let's assume the provost dislikes decisions the biology chair has made and wants the dean to fire this person. An open-ended question like "In what ways will a different department chair do a better job?" can bring the provost's motivations behind their position to the fore. Once that position is known, a dean may be able to shed a different light on the problems and work with the provost on potential solutions. Keeping an objective standard in mind while proposing alternative options for mutual gain is also important. This discussion might include pointing out that the chair's decisions were sound because they were based on solid information, such as enrollment data or reports from the College and University Professional Association (CUPA).

CONCLUSION

As important as mediation skills are, not every interaction between deans and senior leadership is a form of negotiation. Upper administrators rely on the effectiveness of their deans; they trust that deans manage the day-to-day operation of their unit well and lead their departments and programs in the right direction. Likewise, deans trust that the upper administration makes reasonable decisions based on the input the deans provide. For their reciprocal relationship to work well, deans and the senior administrators above them should have a healthy dose of self-confidence and self-awareness. Ideally, this relationship is defined by mutual respect and trust, a positive outlook, and a good sense of humor.

— *Takeaways* —

- Effective deans see themselves as the primary advocates for and strategists of their unit and know how to best collaborate with upper administrators to strengthen their units.
- Effective deans know how important it is to have a positive and trusting working relationship with the upper administration.
- Effective deans focus on needs and interests rather than positions. As middle managers, they know how important it is to mediate between the faculty and the upper administration.

NOTES

1. Susan Stavert Roper and Terrence E. Deal, *Peak Performance for Deans and Chairs: Reforming Higher Education's Middle* (Plymouth: Rowman & Littlefield Education, 2010), 62.
2. Roper and Deal, 59.
3. Darla S. Hanley, "The Administrative Dance: Managing Up, Down, and Across," in *The Resource Handbook for Academic Deans*, 3rd ed., ed. Laura L. Behling (San Francisco: Jossey-Bass, 2014), 147.
4. Jeffrey L. Buller, *The Essential Academic Dean: A Practical Guide to College Leadership* (San Francisco: Jossey-Bass, 2007), 112.

5. Roper and Deal, *Peak Performance for Deans and Chairs*, 60.
6. Aaron K. Olson and B. Keith Simerson, *Leading with Strategic Thinking: Four Ways Effective Leaders Gain Insight, Drive Change, and Get Results* (Hoboken, NJ: Wiley, 2015), 103.
7. Olson and Simerson, 216.
8. Peter Senge et al., *Schools That Learn: A Fifth Discipline Fieldbook for Educators, Parents, and Everyone Who Cares about Education* (New York: Crown Business, 2012), 124.
9. Scott Mautz, *Leading from the Middle: A Playbook for Managers to Influence Up, Down, and Across the Organization* (Hoboken, NJ: Wiley, 2021), 39.
10. Buller, *The Essential Academic Dean*, 111.
11. See Patrick Sanaghan and Jillian Lohndorf, *How Higher-Ed Leaders Derail: A Survival Guide for Leaders* (Denver: Academic Impressions, 2018).
12. Manfred F. R. Kets de Vries, "Do You Hate Your Boss?" in *Dealing with Difficult People* (Cambridge, MA: Harvard Business Review Press, 2018), 122–23.
13. Kets de Vries, 129.
14. Buller, *The Essential Academic Dean*, 111.
15. Zahira Jaser, "The Real Value of Middle Managers," *Harvard Business Review*, 7 June 2021, https://hbr.org/2021/06/the-real-value-of-middle-managers.
16. C. K. Gunsalus, *The College Administrator's Survival Guide* (Cambridge MA: Harvard University Press, 2006), 68.
17. Roger Fisher, William Ury, and Bruce Patton, *Getting to Yes: Negotiating Agreement Without Giving In* (New York: Penguin, 2011), 11.
18. Fisher, Ury, and Patton, 43.

CHAPTER 15

Key Components of a Successful Relationship with the Advancement Office

MICHELE YAPSUGA EWING AND ELAINE MEYER-LEE

Deans and chief academic officers play a principal role in fund-raising. Institutions now seek to increase their philanthropic support in order to take the pressure off student revenues in an age of declining populations of young adults and growing income inequality. In addition to the more traditional championing of governmental or foundation funding, savvy deans are more active in pursuing institutional grant writing, private gift solicitation, and corporate sponsorship and other types of partnerships. Leadership of academic units, whether to fund special projects and new strategic initiatives or, better yet, to provide crucial budget relief to sustain our missions, requires creativity in diversifying revenue streams.

Given these financial challenges, it's more essential than ever for chief academic officers to work closely and effectively with their counterparts in the advancement or development office. This chapter provides an overview of the key components of a successful relationship and focuses on the types of communication and trust building necessary to create synergy between units. It includes warnings about potential minefields and examples of how to make the magic happen.

COMMUNICATION AND TRUST

Somewhere along the way in your higher-education career, you'll discover that the academic enterprise intertwines with advancement. It may seem that advancement officers entertain at dinner parties or special events and emerge with opportunities for funding a project, professorship, or scholarship. But fund-raising is both an art and a science—a delicate balance of data mining, building a case for support, and fostering connections with donors who share similar interests with the institution or are motivated to contribute to resolving a societal or personal issue. In the best partnerships, communication and trust are critical components in building a relationship between academic officers and advancement. Therefore, as you launch into this partnership, it's incumbent on you to understand this symbiotic role, establish priorities, and share information.

Academic officers must communicate key information to advancement about the educational enterprise, current programs, and short- and long-term priorities. Without this communication, advancement efforts may simply fund the status quo. Relying on habit could result in missed opportunities to involve donors in burgeoning initiatives or to connect them to details that pique their interest beyond immediate projects. Conversely, advancement professionals bring understanding of prospective donors' interests and are able to suggest creative and compelling ways to enhance and share a vision for academic priorities. By pairing information from academic officers with the knowledge and savvy of advancement professionals, many academic projects or programs could receive funding that they otherwise would not. For this reason, colleagues in advancement should be seen as academic advocates, an extension of the academic leadership team.

Beyond expressing a desire to partner with the vice-president of advancement, to actually achieve this objective, academic leaders must determine what such a partnership means. How much time are you willing to devote every month to donor cultivation and engagement? Which role (visionary, storyteller, solicitor, closer) are you most comfortable assuming when you're on a donor visit with advancement? What is your comfort level in asking for financial support? What is your background or experience with academic or program-related grants offered by private or family foundations? Despite the wide variation in individual approaches, personal relationship building and fund-raising are the most essential development skills for academic leaders.

Deans who consistently raise money are those who prioritize fund-raising and carve out significant time for honing their skills in this area. If fund-raising is new to you, some aspects of development may come easily (such as stewardship, letter writing, or early engagement), while others (such as solicitation or negotiation) could take a great deal of effort or practice. Developing fund-raising skills goes beyond "hitting the road." While building personal relationships is an important component of the job, it makes up only 20 percent of the overall responsibility for fund-raising. The other 80 percent of advancement efforts takes place before and after the visits. Academic leaders must make time for frequent (ideally, weekly or biweekly) internal meetings with advancement to convey updates and keep each other appraised of programming, priorities, faculty initiatives, donor interests and recent interactions with the institution, and funding opportunities.

Prior to scheduling a visit with a prospective donor, there is much work to do. Academic leaders and advancement professionals must take time to collaborate in defining the visit's anticipated outcomes and the participants' roles. Do not shortchange yourself or your staff in this step. In this preparation, among other things, you'll want to become clear about your institution's brand and its defined areas of distinction, and to have ready a concise and *practiced* elevator pitch on both the institution and your key priorities. Being able to succinctly articulate your vision to the prospect is critical: Identify the strategy for and goal of the conversation. Run through the general order of who will say what in anticipation of getting the team to the point of the visit, the solicitation, or the closing of the gift. Do not assume that the development professional will make the ask. Many donors, especially those giving six figures or more, will want *and expect* the academic leader to ask them directly. This is more personal and compelling. Frankly, some donors won't commit unless you ask them personally, since they're investing in the vision that you articulate. A well-crafted strategic visit will cultivate both the relationship and the solicitation, while a poorly executed visit can delay a commitment, frustrate a donor, and potentially sideline the project from receiving funding. If pressed for time, touching base with your advancement colleague for just fifteen minutes before a visit can make the difference between establishing a connection with the donor and spending the next three months doing damage control for having squandered the visit.

Upon assuming leadership and, at a minimum, during every quarter thereafter, academic leaders should assess their landscape and clarify what falls under their advancement purview. Know which are the top twenty-five donors to your institution (individuals, corporations, private or family foundations). Become familiar with all endowed, quasi-endowed, and current-use funds and build a working knowledge of your institution's financial structures and budgets as they relate to donor funds. Review recent stewardship communications before meeting with donors to understand whether the funded programs have been successful, especially so that you can thank them for their current or recurring investment. If a program wasn't successful, seek to understand why and what happened. Note the expected frequency of communication with your top donors and discuss what role or opportunity you'll have for facilitating communication in the future. Be cognizant of each donor's current relationship with the institution and key faculty members. Don't neglect to connect with staff members who have a long legacy: they may be the ones who provided continuity to the relationship before you arrived.

The more you know about a donor's background, motivation, interests, and ongoing relationship with your institution, the better. One of advancement's main roles in this collaboration is to ensure that no surprises arise in your visit. Therefore, rely on advancement to provide strategies, donor profiles, and background research. In addition, when your visit is complete, spend time to debrief the exchange, discuss and capture action items, determine next steps, and clarify who will follow through with each. Timely follow-up is critical and could be as simple as an email thank-you, a phone call, or a well-crafted proposal. This documentation will further your future relationship with and understanding of the donor.

In addition to meeting regularly or sharing information, another effective way to initiate strong collaboration is to include an advancement representative in strategic academic conversations, department meetings, and retreats. An understanding of your shared goals and resources benefits both units. In turn, advancement should include academic leaders annually in its planning retreats or invite them as a guest speaker at a monthly staff meeting—especially to present on new projects or initiatives so that advancement can fully understand the academic terminology, concepts, financial need, and desired outcomes.

As the content experts, academic leaders should anticipate requests from advancement for contributions to talking points, proposals, and letters of inquiry, and make the most of them. Donor meetings are spaces for collaboration with advancement that are essential to building the case for support; introducing, reinforcing, or demonstrating educational needs; and clarifying how funds will be administered for stewardship. Chief academic officers need to ensure that development professionals are knowledgeable about the institution's operational and academic mission, as well as the interests and priorities of the academic enterprise so they can appropriately represent the institution to donors. If, after the initial gift, academic leadership and advancement together build the donor's confidence in leadership via a unified vision and well-executed implementation, the donor often funds the institution more than once and usually at growing levels of support.

When engaging with donors, fellow academics, or administrators about funding opportunities and financial support, inevitably leaders have challenging discussions. As trust is built, each unit's success is enhanced, and the proven collaboration serves as the bridge during difficult conversations, misunderstandings, and disagreements.

A few noteworthy don'ts include don't assume; don't play politics; don't withhold information; and don't change the conditions, metrics, or outcomes of projects without conveying it to your colleagues. Like any relationship, academic leaders and advancement professionals must commit to respecting each other's expertise through an investment of time, attention, and inquiry. Establishing expectations is critical, but don't discount the importance of informal connections: a quick email can provide context and mitigate disaster. Speaking candidly and frequently prevents surprising colleagues and allows adaptation and solution-oriented conversations. Your shared goals are funding a project, assuring happy donors, and creating a positive experience for everyone throughout the process.

BUILDING THE WORKING RELATIONSHIP
TO YIELD RESULTS

Advancement can assist you in choosing which projects, programs, and priorities should receive fund-raising attention. Colleges and universities will always wrestle with operational costs, seeking more unrestricted dollars to meet growing needs. It might seem easy for the chief academic officer simply to provide advancement with an annual list of needs and be on their way; however, it's not that simple. Donors today are sophisticated and demanding. At the touch of a button, they have access to articles, blogs, vlogs, and webinars that provide insight into higher education, the mechanics of giving, and the impact of philanthropy worldwide. They expect—in some cases demand—access to information and high-level leaders to understand the inner workings of the institution and know who is making investment decisions *before* they will commit to a six-figure gift. This is why the partnership and trust between academic leadership and advancement is so critical. Advancement will help you assess potential roadblocks and challenges, prepare materials (emails, proposals, and stewardship), strengthen your case for support, and provide honest feedback regarding the feasibility of funding initiatives. All of these will build capacity and trust with donors.

As transparency regarding donor expectations and intent becomes increasingly important, universities are investing in research, prior to accepting gifts, into donor backgrounds and connections to funding. Vetting who is giving the money is as important and complex today as identifying a likely donor, securing the gift, accepting it, and stewarding it to the donor's satisfaction. Scandals like Varsity Blues, headlines highlighting corrupt corporate leadership (such as the once-revered Sackler family, the Purdue Pharma owners largely blamed for the US opioid crisis), and devious billionaires (like Jeffrey Epstein, a convicted sex offender who gave millions of dollars to MIT and Harvard) have brought attention to fund acceptance policies, donor naming rights, and gift-counting transactions. College campuses are grappling with student and alumni scrutiny of gift acceptance based on social and moral issues, at times pressuring the administration to forgo a transformational gift, regardless of impact, to avoid unfavorable press. Chief academic officers must rely on advancement professionals for in-depth research about the donor to protect the institution from reputational risk. These efforts start at the beginning of the donor relationship, continue over the donor's lifetime, and extend into perpetuity.

As your relationship evolves with the advancement professionals at your institution, the fund-raising process will grow more creative and enjoyable. More important, you'll get beyond focusing on menial tasks and move on to collaborating on transformative funding ideas, establishing long-term objectives, and refining priorities to meet the needs of your institution. This is what puts the fun in fund-raising. Some academic leaders may think they are solely responsible for providing the priorities and funding ideas, for which advancement should then deliver the donors. Advancement, however, is not an ATM. This relationship should not be transactional, communicating, in essence, "I need $50,000, thank you very much!" The relationship is a symbiotic one: academics generate fundable and exciting programs (curriculum, internships, cocurricular initiatives, special projects), and advancement generates funding for them. Together they take part in an iterative and collaborative process.

Not all necessities are fundable by donors, and advancement can flag those that are not. Basic institutional or operational needs are not compelling. Donors rarely want to pay to keep the lights on or support faculty salaries on an annual basis. They may do so in emergencies, such as during the COVID-19 pandemic; however, even the most loyal donors will tire of funding costs they consider to be part of operating expenses. While not every faculty position or new initiative can be supported or will become an endowed fund, with creativity it is possible to build considerable budget relief into requests. In such cases, relying on advancement expertise will be helpful. When defining priorities, consider how you'll tell the donor the story of the impact of the gift beyond just what the institution wants. Who benefits from the position or program? How does this priority align with donor interests? A transformative gift is built on a solid premise. Even for fundable ideas, feedback from advancement on sculpting the project and defining the right donor engagement can enhance the initiative beyond the original scope.

CHALLENGES OR MINEFIELDS TO AVOID

For donors, the timeliness of academic initiatives is critical, as are the initiative's relevance, value alignment, and potential synergy with their own work. Conversely, it's important not to let the fund-raising tail wag the academic dog. Just because a generous grant or gift is available for a particular project doesn't mean your institution should pursue it. Much institutional energy and momentum can be wasted trying to reinvent initiatives to fit the flavor of the month in chasing funds, which can lead to faculty skepticism and burnout. Instead, deans and provosts need to stay focused on well-articulated strategic initiatives with broad internal buy-in. To build better credibility on all sides and secure results over the long term, pursue donors who are aligned with the institution's mission for projects with high potential for return on investment.

All academic processes need to be protected from inappropriate external donor influence. The well-covered case of Nikole Hannah-Smith's tenure at the University of North Carolina (UNC) at Chapel Hill is a prime example of the dangers. Reports of donor interference in academic processes were extremely damaging not only with Chapel Hill's internal constituencies but also to its external reputation, including limiting access to other grant-giving foundations. Integrity is important at all levels of academic-advancement interactions. New curricular programs need to go through the appropriate phases of shared governance review, even if they could be fully endowed. Sometimes, a substantial gift must be declined if it doesn't meet faculty approval. Even in situations that don't involve external political motivations or explicit conflicts of interest, it's essential to stay grounded in sound academic governance principles.

Once a gift has been accepted, it's equally important to honor the donor's intent throughout the duration of the funding, even in perpetuity, as with endowments. Honoring that intent can be challenging, given evolving academic program needs and administrative transitions over time. It may be tempting to sweep the proceeds of some older funds toward the overall bottom line in tight budget times. However, doing so is not only unethical, but such violations of intent could also alienate the donor's heirs and other potential donors. Pay attention to the structure of gift agreements or memoranda of understanding in order to allow as much flexibility as possible. Collect gifts into larger, broader funds rather than creating narrowly restricted funds that can be difficult to award long term.

URGENCY AND OPPORTUNITY

Public disinvestment in higher education, the perception of a degree as a private good rather than a common one, and the large increase in the number of first-generation and high-need students have created immense pressures on institutional budgets. It's imperative for those of us in academic leadership to partner closely with our colleagues in development leadership to engage external donors, rather than trying to balance our budgets on the backs of our students. By diversifying our fund-raising streams, we can connect with people, foundations, corporations, and agencies that are dedicated to issues we're addressing, such as social mobility, women's entrepreneurship, clean energy, and historic preservation.

Consumer pressure for corporate social responsibility has greatly increased the opportunities for engaging major business entities, which in some ways have taken over from political leadership in addressing key issues. If we partner with such organizations more broadly (for internships, job placement, and mentoring), we can develop multifaceted reciprocal relationships that lead naturally to financial sponsorships or programmatic support. An academic initiative that attracts the attention of a major donor can lead to larger opportunities for the whole college. This benefits advancement's larger goals, and advancement's successes can, in turn, open up major new possibilities for the academic division. Close collaboration between academic and development leadership can, therefore, build momentum toward a transformative cycle for the whole institution.

— *Takeaways* —

- Growing budgetary challenges mean that constant mindfulness and creative integration of fund-raising are increasingly important priorities for deans and chief academic officers. Effective collaboration with advancement colleagues is essential in this regard.

- Communication and trust are key elements of a positive two-way relationship. Academics need to discuss priorities with their advancement colleagues, learn from them, and rely on their expertise in discerning and pursuing fund-raising opportunities.
- Mutually beneficial partnerships help to avoid potential minefields such as distraction from priorities, compromise of the integrity of academic processes, association with entities that are not aligned with institutional values, and donor alienation.

CHAPTER 16

There Is No Known Limit to the Capacity of the Human Mind to Learn, Grow, Develop, and Change

J. HERMAN BLAKE AND EMILY L. MOORE

Any observer of the contemporary landscape of higher education would conclude that academic deans have never been as challenged as they are today. Within the presumptive frameworks of institutional missions, values, and goals, deans are faced with a rapidly changing social environment that is also shaped by extraordinary technological changes. The conditions make leadership, transparency, and trust more necessary than ever but also more difficult. Almost daily, deans are challenged to maintain institutional stability while simultaneously incorporating new programs within the academy—often with tight financial restrictions. However, through their strategic location, intellectual acuity, and personal qualities, deans can determine the direction of an institution and its ultimate success.

In this chapter, we reflect on our personal involvement with academic leadership through individual and joint experiences. After separate administrative careers, twenty-five years ago we married and unified our lives while continuing paths of academic leadership. We also established a consulting firm to advise academic institutions and associations as well as philanthropic and governmental agencies.[1] While reflecting many values, central to our achievements were emphases on (1) liberal arts, (2) high expectations, (3) mutual respect, (4) leadership, and (5) diversity.

Our combined ninety years of experience included service in almost every type of academic institution, including faith-based private liberal arts colleges; elite, private liberal arts institutions; Historically Black Colleges and Universities; research universities; an urban university; a land-grant university; and a medical university. Together, we served at various times as a program director, department and division chairs, deans, provosts, vice-presidents, and president, all while holding regular faculty appointments. We maintained combined and individual research programs centered on issues of student academic achievement, independent study of Black militants in urban communities, HIV/AIDS prevention in rural southern American communities, and the devastation of HIV/AIDS among women and children in sub-Saharan Africa.

While mentored and guided by senior colleagues, we also had serendipitous opportunities for counsel from national leaders in higher education, religion, government, and philanthropy. Our decisions were often made with this wisdom and guidance.

THE FOUNDING OF OAKES COLLEGE

The University of California, Santa Cruz (UCSC), was established in 1965. J. Herman Blake was appointed acting assistant professor of sociology in 1966. Three years later he was selected to lead a coalition of faculty, staff, and students in establishing a completely new undergraduate college on the campus.

Blake partnered with Ralph Guzman, a newly appointed political scientist. They envisioned the creation of an undergraduate college that would enroll minority as well as majority students in an academic community focused on liberal education, high academic achievement, and strong social bonds. Two separate groups of faculty and students were assembled to formulate plans to implement this vision. The groups advised campus architects on the design of student residences and academic facilities. Blake and Guzman worked with the disciplines to recruit faculty able not only to meet University of California expectations for research and scholarship but also teach undergraduate courses to a much more diverse student body than UCSC had enrolled up to that time. They also worked with university administrators to raise funds for special programs, facilities, and an endowment.

Oakes College was officially launched in 1972. Upon the recommendation of the UCSC chancellor, the university's Board of Regents appointed Blake as provost. Within five years the new college reached its zenith with a faculty that was approximately 50 percent minority and 35 percent female. The liberal arts curriculum included a strong emphasis on the natural and physical sciences. The 650 students were 35 percent minority—Asian, Black, Latino, and Native American; the remaining white students included a significant number from working-class families. An emphasis on high academic achievement through active involvement in the learning process was supported with supplementary educational programs as well as social activities and student life programs. Administrative staff—including custodians—were sensitively included in the life of the college.

The outstanding performance of students, faculty, and staff led Blake to formulate his philosophy of education: "There is no known limit to the capacity of the human mind to learn, grow, develop, and change." This philosophy became an intellectual guide in all of our work.

HURRICANE KATRINA

The devastation of Hurricane Katrina in 2005 killed hundreds and left millions homeless in New Orleans and Gulf Coast communities. In its treacherous path, Katrina breached levees and significantly impacted, among other institutions of higher education, New Orleans' Historically Black Colleges and Universities: Dillard University, Xavier University, and Southern University.[2]

For Dillard University the issues were immediate and substantial, including damage to campus buildings that required renovation or demolition, a decrease in student enrollment, and loss of faculty and staff that caused financial concerns as well as curricular disruptions and accreditation issues. The need to secure outside resources to rebuild every aspect of the campus was compounded by historical issues facing most small, private higher-education institutions. To continue its mission, Dillard sought to use its past experiences to forge a successful future. Previous administrations had planted the seeds of preparation for an unimaginable natural disaster. Decisive leadership and actions by the administration following the hurricane worked to get ahead of an unknown challenge in a new setting.

Seventeen months after Katrina, in 2007, Emily Moore, professor emerita at Iowa State University and an experienced senior academic administrator, was offered the position of provost and vice-president for academic affairs at Dillard. Her responsibilities included working with faculty, staff, and administrators in sustaining and improving the academic program offerings, developing the curriculum, and maintaining accreditation. These were normal issues in academe, but the natural disaster of Katrina left the campus in constant distress. Dillard needed time to heal.

Moore used all of her leadership skills—communication, transparency in decision making, clear direction, and well-articulated expectations for oneself and others. In this case, Langston Hughes's assertion in his *Simple Stories* about "listening eloquently" was most germane.[3]

Dillard's committed, hardworking faculty, chairs, and deans were determined to hold their institution to high expectations and support their students' goals and achievements. While many had experienced hurricanes and knew what to do before leaving campus and what to expect on their return, Katrina was different: the levees broke and created indescribable havoc. This disaster disrupted professional and personal lives in ways that impacted people's entire well-being. This was a stress that created a framework of turmoil surrounding a hole that the storm tore in the heart and soul.

Moore had not personally lived through the hurricane, but every day she saw and experienced its aftermath in the eyes of faculty, staff, administrators, and students. Afterward, when the weather changed to cloudy with strong winds and heavy rain, it seemed that the eyes of some on campus reflected the fear of Katrina. It was a fear that did not end when the storm left. They told Moore their stories and she listened.

Some lived in FEMA trailers, while others stood in long lines just to get a trailer. Some lived on one side of their homes with the other side opened, damaged, and in need of repair. When allowed to return to their offices, classrooms, and labs, members of the faculty, staff, and administration worked to clean storm debris while teaching and attending to course preparation, curricular matters, and administrative concerns. Moore worked with deans, program chairs, and faculty on the academic calendar and class scheduling, all the while considering state requirements, regional association policies, and professional guidelines. They sought to relieve the stress on the entire system. It was a total commitment to students, the institution, and its survival.

For Moore, revitalization of the library was a major concern. Floodwater devastated the library and released asbestos. Every item in the collection had to be rehabilitated and stored off campus. With her help, the dean of the library, its staff, and senior leadership obtained funding and other resources to rebuild a state-of-the-art library. By that time, three years of Dillard students had never used the collection.[4]

In celebration of the newly renovated library, a rededication procession of students, accompanied by the music of a traditional New Orleans "second line" band, crossed the campus for a book placement and ribbon-cutting ceremony to show the successful transition.

Part of an institution's success is independent perseverance. But the ongoing assistance from numerous academic institutions, foundations, associations, government agencies, and individuals helped Dillard University to bridge the unknown and, in some cases, made the difference for success. To acknowledge institutions that accepted and hosted students during the academic years away from Dillard, each returning graduating student carried a pennant during commencement naming their host school as a visual appreciation.

IOWA STATE UNIVERSITY

Iowa State University (ISU) was the first US institution designated a land-grant college. The authors of this chapter were appointed to the faculty at ISU in different colleges in 1998 and taught graduate and undergraduate courses there until 2005. Many of the undergraduate Black students were admitted with full academic scholarships and financial support. Nonetheless, for twenty years their graduation rates had been below the national average for Black students at public universities.

When we asked senior administrators about this pattern of underachievement by fully qualified Black students, we were advised to "stay in our own lanes" and leave the issues of Black students' academic achievement to other administrators. However, we could not ignore the loss signified by two decades of underperformance. Under Blake's leadership, we started student-led academic discussion groups that emphasized high expectations for all students and were guided by our philosophy of education: "There is no known limit to the capacity of the human mind to learn, grow, develop, and change."

The three different peer-led academic discussion groups welcomed students from all racial and ethnic backgrounds. The lead group (The A-Team) was coeducational and multiracial. The two other multiracial groups were for females (The Circle of Trust) and males (The Band of Brothers). There were six student leaders: three Black, one white, one Latino, and one Asian—three were female and three were males. Students focused the discussions on problems in their courses, strategies to improve academic achievement, and activities that impeded their progress. In their separate groups men and women would also include personal issues.

Meetings always included sandwiches and beverages provided by the Black Studies Program, and always involved faculty members, graduate students, and student affairs staff. Occasionally, a department chair or dean would be invited to comment and answer questions—they always left impressed by the students' seriousness.

These academically focused groups actively involved students in collective strategies designed to increase their time on task, intensify their learning skills, and build their self-confidence. A group of nineteen Black men was asked to sign a covenant promising to devote more time to their studies and pursue a semester GPA of 3.0 or higher. In the first effort, twelve of the nineteen students reached the 3.0 GPA goal, with four of them reaching a 3.5 GPA and making the Dean's List. Subsequent group discussions among the students were revealing and enhanced their insights into effective academic strategies.

We also established a research project that involved undergraduate and graduate students interviewing faculty members about their own transitions from student to scholar. In preparation for the interviews, students reviewed the relevant literature, designed questionnaires, and applied for institutional review board (IRB) approval. They reported on their research to the student discussion groups.

As a result of this comprehensive and inclusive approach, the six-year graduation rate for Black students at Iowa State University increased from 34 to 44 percent—well above the rate for Black students in public universities. It continued at that level and higher for seven consecutive years.[5]

ACADEMIC LEADERSHIP IN HIGHER EDUCATION: A WORD TO OUR COLLEAGUES

Increasingly complex issues of higher education come in many forms to all of us serving in academic administrative positions. They challenge our readiness. If we aren't prepared, insecurities can show in our decisions and actions. We don't have to know all the answers. We do need to have a team whose members know and act with integrity in their responsibilities. More important, those of us in leadership roles must be guided by values and integrity, acknowledge our own strengths as well as weaknesses, take responsibility, listen eloquently, analyze the issues to be addressed, and then lead.

Leadership is a relentlessly complex undertaking. Eloquent slogans and shibboleths belie the profound knowledge and intuitive understandings of successful leaders. We have sought to include such knowledge and understandings in every aspect of our leadership—exhibiting our commitments through example as well as exhortation. If not always successful, our actions always echoed our convictions. Reflecting on our history and experiences, we illuminate the primary values that guided us as our responsibilities increased and circumstances changed.

Our leadership challenged us to reach beyond our perceived limits while simultaneously reaffirming the essence of our character. The parameters of our work as administrators continued to expand and transform within a vortex of constantly changing issues. We let the values that emerged from our backgrounds and experiences guide us with a vision of hope rather than despair.

It is our conviction that, standing on foundations of history, experience, and wisdom, academic deans are the influential leaders who will meet the challenges and guide higher education through the twenty-first century.

— *Takeaways* —

- Through their strategic location, intellectual acuity, and personal qualities, deans can determine the direction of an institution and its ultimate success.
- Understand the value of communication and transparency in decision making.
- Provide clear directions and expectations for yourself and others.

- Be guided by your values and integrity, acknowledge strengths as well as weaknesses, take responsibility, listen eloquently, analyze the issues to be addressed, and lead.
- Let the values that emerge from your background and experience guide you with a vision of hope rather than despair.

NOTES

1. Scholars for Educational Excellence and Diversity, Inc., was active from 1996 to 2020.
2. Glenn S. Johnson and Shirley A. Rainey, "Hurricane Katrina Impact on Three Historically Black Colleges and Universities (HBCUs): Voices from Displaced Students," *Race, Gender and Class* 14, nos. 1–2 (2007): 100–119, http://www.jstor.org/stable/41675199.
3. "Listen eloquently" is attributed to Langston Hughes. See Herman Beavers, "Dead Rocks and Sleeping Men: Aurality in the Aesthetic of Langston Hughes," *Langston Hughes Review* 10, no. 1 (1992): 3. A similar phrase, to "listen fluently," is also attributed to Hughes. See Donna A. S. Harper, ed., *The Collected Works of Langston Hughes*, vol. 7 (Columbia: University of Missouri Press, 2002), 50.
4. See John Pope, "Dillard U. Library Makeover Revitalizes School, Students," *New Orleans Times-Picayune*, March 17, 2008.
5. See J. Herman Blake and Emily L. Moore, "Retention and Graduation of Black Students: A Comprehensive Strategy," in *Best Practices for Access and Retention in Higher Education*, ed. Irene M. Duranczyk, Jeanne L. Higbee, and Dana Britt Lundell (Minneapolis: Center for Research on Developmental Education and Urban Literacy, University of Minnesota, 2004), 63–71, https://files.eric.ed.gov/fulltext/ED491508.pdf. See also Emily L. Moore and J. Herman Blake, "Inherent Philanthropy in Multicultural Faculty Work at a Research University," in *Faculty Work and the Public Good: Philanthropy, Engagement and Academic Professionalism*, ed. Genevieve G. Shaker (New York: Teachers College Press, 2015), 97–108.

CHAPTER 17

Leadership in the Transition from a College to a University

CLAUDINE KEENAN

To: President's Cabinet, Academic Deans, Administrative Directors,
    Union Leaders, Faculty and Student Senate Presidents
Re: University Status

Dear Colleagues,

Our regional visiting team, in its decision to reaccredit us with no mandatory follow-up requirements, asked why we are still called "the college." Indeed, the visitors pointed out, our state regulations governing "college" versus "university" status allow for two main types of universities: research or teaching.

While we were founded as a liberal arts college more than forty years ago, we have always offered professional degrees, which have outnumbered our liberal arts degrees over the past decade or so. What's more, we've been growing in overall enrollment, and we're adding small satellite campus locations to better reach our students where they live.

The time has come to consider petitioning the state for university status. Our dedication to the centrality of teaching means that we will apply under the category of teaching university.

Any questions?

Sincerely,

4th President of a Liberal Arts College, 2012

For those of us who are deans, reading a message like this one immediately generates many questions—namely, those we anticipate hearing from our students, faculty, and staff constituencies:

- Will tuition go up?
- Will class sizes increase?
- Will research expectations increase?
- Will our jobs be outsourced?
- Will we have to pay to rebrand everything in one fiscal year?
- Will parking get even worse?

We thought, as we read the president's email a decade ago, that everyone would be asking questions such as these. We knew that this was the perfect time for us to lead, because deans are skilled at bridging the divides that are likely to arise between administrators, faculty, staff, and students, especially during a change process.

Leading change is a complex responsibility that relies heavily on our ability to operate within the norms of an organizational culture and in keeping with the current institutional climate.[1] Unlike many of our upper-level administrative colleagues and supervisors, most academic deans maintain dual membership in both faculty and administrative cultures. In these roles, we forge identities that enable us to shift our perspectives and our language, communicating with different constituencies as needed.[2]

This chapter demonstrates how academic leaders can cast a major change process as a learning experience that provides faculty, staff, and students with opportunities to collaborate from their differing perspectives and roles within the institution.[3]

LEADING FROM THE MIDDLE AND MANAGING RESOURCES

Our position as academic deans in the center of the institution allows us to manage the two vital resources that impact change processes: time and human interactions.

Whether we personally agree or disagree with the president's inclination is almost irrelevant. From our middle space in the institution, we can see both the aspirational advantages of a change like this and the real obstacles that our constituents will likely encounter. Consequently, rather than advocate for a position, our first goal is to recognize this process as a learning opportunity that fuses the practical with the analytical tendencies of our staff, students, and faculty members.

Several chapters in the third edition of ACAD's *Resource Handbook for Academic Deans* note that successful deans approach change by respecting the institution's culture and context, the symbolic frame of Bolman and Deal's well-known four-part paradigm (the other three frames being structural, human resource, and political).[4] Whether or not we've had previous success identifying change as a learning opportunity in the human resource frame, most academic cultures value learning above all other pursuits. Overlaying the learning aspects of the human resource frame with the procedural tasks of the structural frame offers strong possibilities for managing a successful change process. Nimbly combining elements of these two frames, deans can showcase their abilities to communicate fluently with students, faculty, and staff in the language of learning: posing questions, researching answers, and discussing findings and potential impacts with constituents throughout the institutional community.

Having identified this approach, the academic deans who studied the president's message also recognize that the learning process takes time. Thus, time became the first resource we need in order to manage effectively.

MANAGING UP

Depending on the size of your institution, deans may have varying access and influence on the president—in this case, the administrator who is driving the change. Immediately after sending his initial message, the president met with the provost to review the state regulations for university status. Together, they determined that the institution's number of graduate programs, students, and resources already meet the state's regulations, and concluded that the status change could be accomplished with a simple petition that inventoried these resources—a structural change.

While presidents and provosts might be tempted to move quickly under what appear to be such straightforward conditions, deans understand that the pace of change itself can sometimes pose a threat to success.[5] Unlike some other major changes (such as a time-sensitive mandatory follow-up requirement from a regional accreditor, a financial crisis, or a scandal), a voluntary change like seeking university status faces little time pressure.[6]

In our case, eight academic deans worked primarily through our provost—a typical communication hierarchy for many institutions—to identify this change as a collaborative learning process. Provosts rely on deans to gather preliminary faculty, student, and staff responses to a proposed change through two basic mechanisms: formal (school, department, or college meetings) and informal (closed-door or casual hallway conversations). Deans immediately communicated both types of preliminary responses to the provost in their weekly deans' council meetings, noting that there was widespread misinformation about the definition of the word "university" itself, let alone the implications that might accompany the proposed change to institutional status. For example, deans sensed movement in the political frame among some departments, which saw the change as an opportunity to garner more resources, ostensibly in order to meet what some faculty mistakenly perceived would be an increase in research expectations.

Accordingly, we made a clear case to the provost in favor of articulating status change as a learning process in both the human resource and structural frames. Having presented these initial conversations in this way, the deans ultimately recommended that the provost suggest a faculty senate task force to the president—a typical example of how deans "manage up."[7]

In making this recommendation, all eight of the deans acknowledged the trade-off between slowing down decision making and allowing faculty who were leading the learning process to dispel misinformation, a necessity before any constituency group could take a defensible position on the president's proposed status change. Acting on this recommendation, the president and provost called for a broadly participative process that included a prominent role for faculty leaders to collaborate on designing their own approach to this work.[8]

SHARED GOVERNANCE AND MANAGING COMMUNICATION

The college president and provost asked the faculty senate president to convene a representative task force on university status. They empowered that body to generate a charge, appoint a representative membership that included three deans along with faculty members from each of their eight schools, and produce a timeline for completing their work. At our institution, the senate typically formed at least two task forces every year, most of which generated reports with recommendations that the institution then endorsed or adopted. One key strength of this tradition has been that academic deans or administrative directors serve in an ex officio capacity on these committees. As Kezar emphasizes, managing change in higher education requires that leaders embrace and convey an explicit approach.[9] The task force included three of our eight deans, whose roles were to maintain clear, consistent communication between faculty leaders, top-tier administrators, staff, and students.

Deans communicate with multiple constituencies and engage with them in a variety of formats. Utilizing these skills, the three academic deans who attended every task force meeting recommended that the faculty leaders set up a website that could publish the task force's membership, their charge, and updates on their progress. Members began by generating an extended list of questions like those our deans anticipated at the start of this chapter. These became the draft research questions that guided the first stage of the learning process. In turn, the three academic deans brought these questions back to the provost, president, fellow deans, and other administrators. Deans also conveyed the research questions to their office staff, as well as to students and families who attended their open house and other events where academic deans typically play a leadership role. In this way, the deans communicated clearly with all constituents during the early part of the process. The campus community was engaged in a series of learning activities, beginning with the draft research questions that many constituents were invited to refine.

At each task force meeting, deans continued to lead from the middle by carrying back to faculty leaders any additional questions or nuances they heard from staff, students, other administrators, and faculty members who were not on the task force. Deans also helped to facilitate the research process, providing technical support to members who designed surveys and also recommending ways to customize the questions for faculty, staff, and student audiences. The deans also helped faculty members who sought information from peer institutions in the state and assisted in collecting and labeling articles from scholarly journals and the popular press in order to publish a reference list on the website. Thus, we fulfilled our roles in managing support for the structural aspects of this faculty-led learning process, and in doing so became reliable reporters of the group's progress through the research stage of its work.

The deans also provided logistical support to the task force by arranging a series of town hall meetings with groups of students, faculty, and staff members. We promoted these meetings "up, down, and across" our constituency groups as forums for sharing the initial findings from the surveys and preliminary answers to the research questions as documented by interviews with our peer institutions and in the published articles.[10] The initial findings became an important mechanism for placing this next stage of the learning experience in the context of the overall endeavor. Many students, faculty, and staff still conveyed misperceptions about the status change. While the institution already met the regulations for petitioning to become "a comprehensive or teaching university," most respondents to the student, faculty, and staff survey erroneously believed that the petition would require substantial change. Their survey responses reflected ongoing confusion between a research university versus a teaching or comprehensive university. Deans and faculty task force leaders recognized that the next round of learning activities should be aimed at helping to clear away misunderstanding by using the information that the task force members had compiled.

At these meetings and in all formal and informal conversations during this time, deans reinforced the neutral position that faculty leaders on the task force had agreed to take in facilitating public conversations. Refraining from politicking for or against the change, deans and faculty prepared carefully balanced "pro and con" responses to many of the questions that stakeholders asked during the public forums. The collaborative-change approach was strengthened by a persistent openness to listening to, discussing, and debating each of the questions, informed by the research that members had compiled. In addition, rather than seeing change as a linear process, deans understood that the iterative nature of learning was shaping our shared approach to managing this change. After recognizing the persistence of misinformation across larger group meetings, the task force worked with all the academic deans and their counterparts in other administrative divisions to schedule a round of smaller meetings in schools, departments, and centers.

LEADING THE RESOLUTION

The task force resurveyed each audience, asking whether the respondents had attended one or more town hall or other meetings. The findings from these surveys identified clear learning impacts that the public conversations had on respondents. Notably, across all constituent groups, those who attended one or more of the events were more likely to favor a status change than those who had not attended any. More important, the misperception that additional changes would be required before petitioning the state for a change in status had decreased significantly. The college's constituencies had learned the difference between a research and a teaching or comprehensive university.

In keeping with its commitment to maintaining transparency, the task force updated its website regularly during the two years of its work. As of this writing, nearly ten years later, all survey instruments, summary results, references, regulatory code provisions, slide presentations, and meeting minutes continue to appear on this website. These artifacts and those of similar task forces serve as touchstones in both the structural and symbolic frames and make the products of our institutional culture tangible.

The summary report by the university status task force recommended to the provost and president that the then-college engage in a follow-up task force to include students, families, administrators, and staff members from other divisions of the college, in addition to faculty and academic deans. While the faculty senate group had completed its charge to lead a learning process about what the status change would mean to the institution, our conclusions were just as well balanced as our pro-and-con responses during the public conversations. Ultimately, the president and provost read the report, consulted with additional members of the campus community, and then drafted a petition for university status.

As most scholars of higher-education management note, leading during a time of change doesn't end with the decision to implement that change. Deans continued to play a leadership role during the implementation, assisting in drafting and revising the petition, continuing to talk with constituency groups about preparing for the change, and, finally, promoting attendance at a symbolic celebration. At this event, the new university banner was unfurled, spotlighting aspects of the new logo that preserved some of the founding imagery associated with the college's first forty years in operation.

CONCLUSION

In hindsight, deans who read the president's email quoted above understood that as an institution we could have implemented a unilateral structural change. However, our understanding of the institutional culture and climate gave us good reason to pause before endorsing a top-down approach. We realized very early in our daily informal communications that this change offered us an opportunity to showcase learning, a key component of managing change through an overlay of the human resource and structural frames. Having experienced success with senate task forces at our institution years before, and for many years since the events recounted in this chapter, we have adapted this approach to several other university-wide changes.

Throughout these experiences, we have recognized the importance that Bolman and Deal place on being able to nimbly shift or to skillfully overlay frames as needed. For example, in 2021, the university wordmark was updated, featuring a symbolic "50" to celebrate our fiftieth year of teaching. As with the first official university logo, the 50 also contains a sketch of trees that has been part of our institutional iconography since our founding. With this symbol in our signature files, web pages, and Zoom screens, deans are once again building bridges among our constituents as we prepare for regional reaccreditation. We're sharing drafts of the self-study report with our constituents and embedding their feedback in revisions, highlighting this part of the process as the learning opportunity that we've come to embrace as a foundation of our university culture, especially as we celebrate this symbolic fifty-year milestone. For university leaders—faculty, chairs, deans, directors, provosts, presidents, and board members—recognizing what works best for a specific type of change at a particular time can lead not only to an effective process but also to a stronger culture of learning across the institution.

— *Takeaways* —

- While we are near the top of our institution's administration, deans thrive as leaders in the middle, with access to constituency groups that include students, staff, and faculty members.

- In leading from the middle, we are well positioned to influence the two key resources in change management: time and human interactions.
- Our most effective tools for managing change are our strong understanding of our institution's culture and our ability to articulate that understanding in a clear, customizable approach to collaborative decision making.
- Tying these three strategies together fosters a customized yet reproducible approach to change that we can adapt for most noncrisis related situations.

NOTES

1. Three valuable sources on leading change are Katie Conboy, "Managing Change Successfully," in *The Resource Handbook for Academic Deans*, 3rd ed., ed. Laura L. Behling (San Francisco: Jossey-Bass, 2014), 93–98; Edgar H. Schein and Peter Schein, *Organizational Culture and Leadership*, 5th ed. (Hoboken, NJ: Wiley, 2017); and Frank Eyetsemitan, "Understanding Institutional Climate," in *The Resource Handbook for Academic Deans*, 3rd ed., 57–60.
2. See Mary Bucholtz and Kira Hall, "Identity and Interaction: A Sociocultural Linguistic Approach," *Discourse Studies* 7, nos. 4–5 (October 2005): 585–614, https://doi.org/10.1177/1461445605054407.
3. For foundational explorations, see Donald A. Schön, *Educating the Reflective Practitioner* (San Francisco: Jossey-Bass, 1990); and Donald A. Schön and Martin Rein, *Frame Reflection: Toward the Resolution of Intractable Policy Controversies* (New York: Basic Books, 1994).
4. See Lee G. Bolman and Terrence E. Deal, *Reframing Organizations: Artistry, Choice, and Leadership* (New Jersey: John Wiley & Sons, 2017). References are made throughout this chapter to Bolman and Deal's four frames, which are well known among academic leaders: structural, human resource, political, and symbolic.
5. See Adrianna J. Kezar, *How Colleges Change: Understanding, Leading, and Enacting Change* (New York: Routledge, 2014). This chapter is informed by Kezar's work.
6. See Susan R. Pierce, *Governance Reconsidered: How Boards, Presidents, Administrators, and Faculty Can Help Their Colleges Thrive* (Hoboken, NJ: John Wiley & Sons, 2014).
7. See Darla Hanley, "The Administrative Dance: Managing Up, Down, and Across," in *Resource Handbook for Academic Deans*, 3rd ed., 143–48.
8. See Kezar, *How Colleges Change*.
9. Kezar, *How Colleges Change*.
10. See Hanley, "The Administrative Dance."

CHAPTER 18

Leadership and Effective Use of Institutional Structures to Advance Strategic Initiatives

KELLY H. BALL AND LILIA CUESTA HARVEY

Ongoing curricular and cocurricular transformations are the new normal in higher education as leaders propose strategic initiatives to address emerging trends—specifically, the need to innovate in an increasingly complex and competitive market and the imperative to provide students with an education that fuels their social mobility. Success is predicated on institutional and organizational structures that shape the development, implementation, and sustainability of these initiatives. Academic and administrative leaders can effectively leverage these organizational structures to innovate and accelerate change that benefits students and the institution, ensuring the success of both.

Agnes Scott College, located in Atlanta, Georgia, is a private liberal arts college for women that also offers coeducational graduate and postbaccalaureate programs. In the 2020–21 academic year, 48.7 percent of the undergraduate population of 1,014 students were underrepresented minorities. Between 2017 and 2020, *U.S. News and World Report* ranked Agnes Scott College as the number-one "Most Innovative" liberal arts college in the nation. These rankings reflect the college's significant work in developing and implementing three major curricular and cocurricular transformations since 2015 with the goal of better serving students while also sustaining the institution's long-term financial health.

Agnes Scott faces the same challenges as most other colleges and universities in the United States: the impending 2024–25 enrollment cliff for traditional-aged undergraduates; the need to increase institutional aid to support low-income students; the need to communicate the value of a liberal arts degree to prospective students; and other, institution-specific challenges affecting tuition revenue, such as the changing appeal of a women's college to seventeen-year-old applicants.

In response to these challenges, Agnes Scott College embarked on a series of strategic changes to ensure the institution will continue to educate students for decades to come. Each initiative has an explicit focus on the needs of the college's diverse population of undergraduate and graduate students, including lower-income and first-generation. These initiatives include a transformative redesign of the general-education program, the development of graduate programs, and a comprehensive plan to incorporate career readiness (for undergraduate students) and professional development (for graduate and postbaccalaureate students) throughout the curriculum and cocurriculum. The college launched these three initiatives in steady succession, beginning with the overhaul of its general-education program in 2015.

Institutional leaders, and especially academic deans, led these changes by leveraging key structures to catalyze the successful implementation of each initiative. As leaders of higher-education institutions know well, meaningful change requires many types of catalysts. Structural catalysts are formally established committees, working groups, offices, or persons who are empowered with decision-making authority to accelerate the initiative. Alternatively, structural antagonists, if not anticipated, navigated, and avoided, create barriers to the initiative's development or pose significant obstacles to its implementation and sustainability.

Like most institutions, Agnes Scott has a traditional shared-governance structure with a faculty senate, faculty committees, administrative leadership, and staff working groups. These structures act as both catalysts and antagonists in the change process, necessitating an intentional approach from leadership to navigate them. The successful development and implementation of each initiative was directly supported by these established structures, which in turn rely on the strategic appointment of ad hoc committees.

This chapter addresses how institutional structures and leadership shaped the success of these transformative initiatives—from initial conception to implementation—and offers lessons and insights that academic leaders can apply to other institutions. Each section summarizes one initiative, highlights the institutional structures that either supported or hindered its development and success, and concludes with a key leadership insight gleaned from the process.

GENERAL-EDUCATION REVISION: LEVERAGING AD HOC AND ESTABLISHED STRUCTURES

Agnes Scott transformed its general-education curriculum, branded as SUMMIT, as a proactive response to the increasing financial pressures on small liberal arts colleges. The college sought to rethink its approach to the liberal arts while staying true to its mission "to educate women to think deeply, live honorably, and engage the intellectual and social challenges of their time." The development of SUMMIT included a strategic positioning study conducted in the 2012–13 academic year and, as a presidential initiative, required the participation of the entire campus community to achieve the program's curricular and cocurricular goals. The result was an expansive overhaul of the undergraduate curriculum with a focus on global learning and leadership development. Fully launched in 2015, SUMMIT led Agnes Scott College to achieve record-breaking first-year enrollment, increased student satisfaction with academic advising, and widespread faculty and staff engagement.

Key catalysts of SUMMIT's development included presidential championing and a robust system of shared governance motivated by an engaged faculty senate led by the elected officers of the Faculty Executive Committee (FEC), including the president, vice-president, and parliamentarian. During the development of SUMMIT, FEC officers also identified and appointed faculty and staff to evolving pop-up task forces, which they convened as needed. The function of the pop-up task forces was to provide faculty leadership on significant but relatively discrete curricular decisions, such as a specific policy or development of new student requirements. Throughout the development process, academic leadership organized multiple opportunities for communication of proposed ideas among the faculty via lunch-and-learn sessions and regular or specially called faculty meetings.

Administrative leadership further catalyzed the implementation of SUMMIT by creating a new administrative position with faculty status to lead the initiative: the associate vice-president for global learning and leadership development. The assistant vice president established a new standing committee—the Faculty SUMMIT Committee (FSC)—to assist with development and implementation of the evolving initiative.

As a standing committee, the FSC serves several key functions, including advising on the general-education curriculum and cocurriculum, introducing new elements, and making changes to improve the initiative over time. Since its inception, two structural questions about the FSC have emerged: What degree of autonomy does it have relative to other academic committees and departments? What limits does the committee's structure impose on the initiative's continuing evolution? Given the significant allocation of institutional resources and SUMMIT's strategic importance to the college, the committee must have the capacity to assess and revise the initiative over time without becoming overly invested in maintaining the status quo. The faculty senate, which includes the chair of the FSC, continues to deliberate these structural questions.

In addition to the FSC, the new associate vice-president created three faculty leadership roles, each with course releases, to steward the various aspects of SUMMIT. These colleagues worked with the FSC to champion SUMMIT, recruit faculty to teach in the innovative general-education program, advise on needs for faculty professional development, propose revisions to the curriculum, and, ultimately, to serve as a de facto department.

Key leadership insight: the structures, whether catalysts or antagonists, that contribute to the development of an initiative will not necessarily be the same or the optimal ones to support the initiative's implementation and ongoing sustainability. As you lead, consider taking the following actions: determine the benefits and limits of various structures for different points in the initiative's existence; avoid overuse of any one kind of structure; plan for periodic changes to the supporting structures and prepare to shift the implementation timeline as needed; and ensure regular communication among all parties responsible for implementation.

GRADUATE PROGRAMS: DEVELOPING NEW, MISSION-DRIVEN STRUCTURES

One year after the launch of SUMMIT, Agnes Scott began a multiphase process to determine what new kinds of academic programs it might offer in addition to its residential baccalaureate programs. As a small liberal arts college, the institution's motivation was clear: it needed to expand its footprint and grow its student body in order to achieve its enrollment goals by serving new populations other than traditional undergraduates. But how would it accomplish these ambitious goals?

As the first structural catalyst, key members of the college's leadership met with the Faculty Strategic Planning Committee to discuss the parameters for market research. What kinds of academic programs would the college explore? How would these programs complement its current liberal arts college offerings that lead to the bachelor of arts and bachelor of science degrees?

The iterative process based on these questions took several months, during which administrators and faculty deliberated about what kinds of programs it could best offer. The results of the market research were clear: the college needed to let go of some of its exciting ideas in order to embrace plans that would best meet the needs of prospective students. The president led this difficult process by being the first to acknowledge that several of the most popular ideas had little supporting data to indicate future enrollment success. Reminding the campus of the goal to serve a broader population of students and increase enrollment, she became a champion of the ideas backed by strong market research, and she hosted events for faculty to deliberate the results. This process allowed faculty leadership, with the support of the president and chief academic officer, to assess the new programs' feasibility.

This assessment became the second structural catalyst that advanced the development of new graduate programs. Now that the college was developing graduate programs and pursuing institutional-level change through its regional accreditor in order to issue master's degrees and certificates, the administrative and faculty leadership had to consider what it would take to implement these programs successfully. In a series of meetings, these leaders determined what resources would be needed, with an explicit charge to look beyond the operating budget and to think about faculty and staff hiring needs.

Market research and the feasibility assessment resulted in a comprehensive plan that administrative and faculty leaders presented to the entire faculty for a formal resolution, as well as to the staff for an informal vote of support. Following these votes, the leaders presented the plan to the Board of Trustees, which unanimously voted to approve it.

Soon after the approval of the graduate program, structural antagonists began to surface. One of these centered on resource allocation. Because the initiative was at first supported through operating funds, a fear emerged: if resources went to the graduate programs, would there be enough for others? One example of this concern related to faculty hiring. Department chairs expressed misgivings about employing faculty to teach at the graduate level when they simultaneously needed to employ instructors to teach undergraduate courses in established programs.

Concerns about resource allocation have continued to be an obstacle, even as the graduate programs now produce substantial revenue. Structural antagonists risk limiting an institution's capacity to nimbly develop new programs.

As the graduate programs got under way, additional structural tensions on campus affected the college's ability to implement the programs successfully. First, the graduate programs represented a shift in institutional identity. Could Agnes Scott become an institution that educates both full-time, residential undergraduate students and full- and part-time graduate students? As the weight of this question bore structurally across offices, the college created a graduate programs office to serve the academic functions of those programs. Stakeholders across campus assumed that the new office would have the capacity to absorb all functions related to graduate programs and students, thus allowing other offices to retain their focus on established workflows and what was perceived as the institution's core work of educating undergraduate women. This tendency slowed the implementation because more resources had to be allocated to stop-gap operations than to program development and growth.

Second, the president who launched the initiative retired during the implementation of the graduate programs, providing an opportunity for the incoming president to address the structural challenges that cut to the quick of the college's identity. While the transition presented a risk to the initiative's success, the new president supported it, understanding that the graduate programs would contribute to the college's long-term financial sustainability and extend its academic reputation. This advocacy has manifested itself through a strategic allocation of resources (both financial and human) and a concerted effort to ensure faculty and staff leaders understand the importance of the initiative for the college, as well as their role in its success.

Key leadership insight: initiatives that require deep changes to the identity of an institution call for the enthusiastic support of its president as well as its chief academic officer. When leadership transitions overlap with the implementation of a major initiative, consistent presidential championing is critical to its success. As you lead, consider taking the following actions: create regular opportunities to showcase presidential support in a variety of communication formats; foster cross-functional collaboration by emphasizing the initiative's contribution to the mission of the institution; and ensure there are multiple types of communication to reinforce the initiative's significance to the faculty and staff who implement it.

PROFESSIONAL SUCCESS: AMPLIFYING EXISTING STRUCTURES

Five years after the successful launch of SUMMIT, and two years after the successful launch of the graduate programs, Agnes Scott College continued to transform its curriculum and cocurriculum to prepare students for professional success, with an explicit focus on the early career advancement of our diverse population of undergraduate and graduate students. The college's goal is to cultivate students' professional success through a four-year experience that integrates the three elements of an Agnes Scott education: breadth (SUMMIT), depth (the major), and growth (professional success). Growth is achieved through a program that connects the student's academic experience to professional development through a scaffolded approach from the first semester, through their early postgraduate years, and beyond.

Ongoing financial pressures in higher education (especially for liberal arts colleges), public conversations about the value of a college degree, and families' expectations that their students' liberal arts education would lead to professional success all provide the impetus for this change initiative. Data from external consultants, institutional research, and trends in higher education informed the scope of the initiative, which has been supported by a private foundation.

From the earliest conversations and planning, the president focused the college on the importance of developing programs to enhance the professional success of students. Indeed, professional success quickly became a strategic presidential initiative with top-down administrative support, and the college created a committee structure and process to encourage faculty and staff buy-in. The chief academic officer appointed an ad hoc committee, the Committee on Professional Success (CPS), to focus solely on developing the proposal for this major initiative. Two people chaired the committee—a faculty member with some administrative responsibilities and an administrator with faculty status. Six additional faculty represented the academic divisions, and six staff members represented academic affairs, student affairs, and admissions. This configuration resulted in a creative, collaborative, and student-focused group.

The committee worked together for five months to develop a twenty-three-page proposal entitled "Breadth, Depth, Growth: Innovating the Liberal Arts for Professional Success at Agnes Scott College." Through a series of retreat-style forums, meetings, and presentations, the committee gathered information from sources across campus (including the offices of alumnae relations, admission, communications and marketing, and advancement); administered surveys to undergraduate and graduate students; met with department chairs; surveyed faculty; and consulted representatives from several learning centers, the library, and academic advising, among others. The committee presented preliminary ideas and data in a report to the faculty midway through the development process. It also worked diligently to communicate with members of the campus community, both to share and refine emerging ideas and to cultivate commitment to the initiative. The variety of opportunities for discussion and participation created bottom-up support and served to address concerns and misinformation that circulated about the plan.

The chief academic officer charged the committee with proposing necessary curricular and cocurricular changes that sometimes proved unpopular, posing some procedural obstacles for the committee. As an ad hoc committee charged with developing a transformative, college-wide initiative, its leaders had to consult with and connect to existing committees and processes. In doing so, they encountered instances of turf protection and ambiguities in responsibilities across units. For example, the initiative introduced new curricular and cocurricular elements to the general-education program, necessitating the elimination of existing requirements. While the committee's charge invited recommendations, it did not have the authority to suggest changes that were the purview of other committees, resulting in a structural impasse. This obstacle risked the committee's progress at several key junctures and required strategic thinking to ensure that innovative planning would not be lost.

The committee's charge to complete its work within four months created another structural antagonist. The time limitation meant that all stakeholder research and proposal development had to be completed in two months, with another two months to shepherd the proposal through the faculty governance process—including feedback sessions, revisions, and preparing the proposal for faculty votes. The ability to accomplish all of this depended on leadership of the committee by two cochairs who had an established working relationship, strong camaraderie, and trust. This foundation, combined with the cochairs' facility in navigating academic and administrative circles, made the ambitious time frame feasible.

Key leadership insight: transformative initiatives require collaboration among institutional stakeholders. The charge to the committee or body responsible for leading the initiative should clearly express who has the authority to make decisions when competing interests threaten to stall or derail progress. As you lead, consider taking the following actions: articulate and document the charge of each structure involved in catalyzing change, including its responsibilities, timeline, and decision powers; issue the charge from an appropriate source (campus-wide support ought to be charged by the president or provost, those limited to a specific division or to the faculty might be charged by the division vice-president, president of the faculty, or dean); appoint leaders who hold the authority necessary to achieve the initiative's goals (for example, an academic initiative ought to be led by someone with faculty rank); define expected outcomes before development begins (including assessment measures); and ensure that all aspects of the initiative are designed to achieve these outcomes.

CONCLUSION

As institutions launch transformative changes, it's important for leaders, both academic and administrative, to think of their institution's structures as catalysts in the change process. By purposely using organizational structures, leaders can develop, implement, and sustain transformative initiatives while remaining flexible and adaptive.

— *Takeaways* —

- Ensure that there are regular and repeated opportunities to showcase presidential support in a variety of communication formats.
- Appoint a leader who holds the authority to oversee all components of an initiative.
- Assume that the structures supporting the initiative's development and initial approval may differ from the structures that will support its implementation and ongoing sustainability.
- Clarify the charge of each leader and structure, including responsibilities, timeline, and decision powers.
- Define outcomes and goals clearly and early in the planning process. Remind stakeholders, especially those who plan and those who implement, of these outcomes and goals to ensure clarity and focus.

CHAPTER 19

Leading Collaborative Change for the Sustainable Future of Small Colleges and Universities

RON COLE AND JENNA TEMPLETON

Higher education in America is navigating an environment of increased competition for student recruitment and, according to projections, will continue to do so. For example, the Western Interstate Commission for Higher Education predicts a decline in high school graduates to start around 2026.[1] To compound the situation, the rising price of tuition and fees at public and private nonprofit institutions, despite greater discounting, has contributed to an erosion in the perceived value of a college education.[2]

Small liberal arts colleges and universities, especially those in the Northeast and Midwest, face the greatest strain. Pennsylvania, the state in which both authors work, is expected to have among the highest percentages of decreases in high school graduates over the next five to ten years, according to projections by the US Department of Education. Uncertainty caused by the COVID-19 pandemic and its economic implications—along with the persistence of systemic racism and divided political ideologies across the country—adds urgency to the work ahead in higher education.

In this environment, two institutions in western Pennsylvania, Chatham University (urban, with undergraduate and graduate programs) and Allegheny College (rural, undergraduate only), are building strategies of resilience with realistically targeted enrollment goals, investments in student success, and programs for new revenue. This chapter offers case studies from these two small, private institutions. We provide an overview of programmatic changes, but rather than focus on program details, we explore the processes employed to advance and manage change that can be of use to leaders at a range of other institutional types.

CHATHAM UNIVERSITY

Founded in 1869 in Pittsburgh, Pennsylvania, Chatham University was one of the country's oldest women's undergraduate colleges until 2014, when a transformation occurred. Now with a coed enrollment of over 2,200 students, Chatham grants bachelor's through doctoral degrees. Over its 150 years, the institution changed many times as it pursued its mission to help graduates enjoy productive, responsible, and fulfilling lives. The focus in the 1860s was access to education for women; in the mid-1950s a gateway program was added for older women, many of them single mothers. The 1990s and 2000s saw the addition of coeducational graduate professional programs that emphasize the health sciences and sustainability. In 2013 Chatham was facing significant declining undergraduate enrollment in the women's college, prompting the university to engage multiple stakeholder groups to explore options for a more sustainable future.

Innovation has always been an essential part of the university's culture. Change was needed once again to ensure continued resiliency in light of shifting demographics and enrollment trends. To begin the process, the institution decided to explore methods for bolstering undergraduate education, including the implications of opening the women's college to male students. Our goals were to grow the total number of undergraduate students and foster a sustainable and vibrant student body.

At the time of this process, graduate enrollments were three times those of the women's college undergraduates, which had declined to around 400. The last incoming undergraduate class as a women's college was only 90 students. Graduate enrollment was subsidizing the undergraduate programs at a rate projected to be untenable in less than five years. Internal studies found that fewer than 2 percent of high school girls indicated interest in women's colleges; therefore, it was and would continue to be arduous and unproductive to recruit from the reluctant 98 percent. Were the university to do nothing, undergraduate education would essentially disappear.

All levels of leadership and constituents were engaged in the process. The president convened a faculty study group to explore disruptive innovation by looking at multiple options for what could be a viable future, while the Board of Trustees simultaneously developed a task force. Both groups considered possibilities for becoming a graduate college, enrolling undergraduate men to the maximum required to remain a women's college, developing a separate, coeducational undergraduate college while maintaining a women's college, and moving to fully coeducational undergraduate programs. A series of town hall meetings locally and regionally were held for alumnae, and student meetings were held on campus, to discuss the options. Participants developed blogs and online feedback forums for continuing dialogue across all groups.

The study group representing the full faculty explicitly acknowledged that it was indeed time for change again at Chatham. The faculty supported the need and desire to meet the changing demographics and student interests in higher education and wanted to provide a range of choices in majors and courses, vibrant classrooms, and robust programs. The faculty noted that this coeducational option was not considered lightly nor was it a panacea.

The alumnae town hall meetings, while providing a venue for wide-reaching feedback, did not culminate in a singular voice. In fact, a group of younger alumnae created a Save Chatham advocacy group that held several small rallies in an attempt to stop the coeducation initiative. Surprising support for change came from older alumnae who wanted their alma mater to survive well into the future and continue to provide educational opportunities for a range of undergraduate populations. The undergraduate student government was split in its recommendation, though it recognized that the change would not have a significant impact on many of them.

The Board of Trustees reviewed additional data gathered by the president's council, including an analysis of enrollment at current and former women's colleges; a study of competitors where interested students enrolled if not at Chatham; consideration of Rutgers University's Douglass Residential College model; and examination of financial and enrollment projections for both single-gender and coeducational models. Based on all of the input, the Board of Trustees voted in May 2014 to move the undergraduate college to fully coeducational the following August. The trustees also directed the university to restructure its academic units, revise the undergraduate general education curriculum, and develop a women's institute.

Significant collaborative work across the university ensued. The restructuring of the academic schools resulted in revised dean positions. Previously organized by student type (e.g., undergraduate, graduate, sustainability), the schools were now realigned by discipline: health sciences; arts, science, and business; sustainability; and professional and continuing education. The president reassigned or appointed new deans to oversee each of the schools. The deans worked with the vice president of academic affairs to assign the departments to the schools and develop plans for the full restructure. A senior faculty member led the revision of the undergraduate general education curriculum. Nine men's sports teams were added, and the women's institute was established to continue the legacy of the women's college. Residence halls were reconfigured, longer beds ordered, student services and activities enhanced, dining hall meals and services revised, and new locker rooms added to the athletic and fitness center.

As a result of these thoughtful and engaging processes, the university increased the undergraduate enrollments to nearly match the graduate enrollments within three years, while creating a balanced institution that remains true to its mission. To sustain this new population, deans and other institutional leaders developed enrollment goals and allocated resources to achieve a stable and attainable undergraduate student body, which currently is approaching 1,200 students, nearly 30 percent male. For the first several years of this transition, sufficient capacity existed within the established course offerings to accommodate the growth. New majors, minors, and certificates have been developed over the past seven years. As capacity has been reached in many courses and programs, the institution has added new faculty lines to departments serving the largest number of undergraduate students.

Key factors in managing this change to strategically optimize enrollment included significant planning, personnel dedicated to the change management, multiple communication venues for constituents, and capturing the details of the process to compile afterward for continuous improvement and accreditation purposes. The most important factor was engagement of all levels of leadership—student leaders, senior faculty, president, president's council, and Board of Trustees.

ALLEGHENY COLLEGE

Allegheny College is an undergraduate liberal arts institution located in Meadville, Pennsylvania, about one hundred miles north of Pittsburgh. Founded in 1815 to provide access to education in what was then a frontier region of America, Allegheny continues its tradition of access, with recent entering classes exceeding 25 percent Pell eligibility and drawing from a diverse national student population. Allegheny delivers its mission to promote students' intellectual, moral, and social development through an interdisciplinary lens based on the tenets that students are prepared for the strongest outcomes when they know *how* to learn and that solutions for intractable problems are realized through *diverse* ways of knowing. These ideals have long shaped institutional culture, as demonstrated in this excerpt from the 1936 Allegheny College catalog, which contains ideals that could equally apply in our time: "The vocations of today are not necessarily the vocations of tomorrow. Every occupation is being influenced by the coming of the machine and the gradual re-organization of industrial and political life. For such an age, Allegheny believes that the finest vocational training any school can offer is a broad understanding of our social and economic order and a thorough knowledge of the laws and the science of learning."

Through the mid-1990s into the early 2000s, the full-time student body at Allegheny averaged about 1,850 students. After a period of growth in the 2000s, Allegheny, like other institutions, faced enrollment pressure around 2014 as the nation experienced a decrease in the number of high school graduates. While the college met its enrollment goals in 2016, the prospect of a decrease in high school graduates projected to start around 2026 prompted a robust evaluation and planning process. As a result, Allegheny chose strategically to return to a smaller student body while investing in new curricular and cocurricular programs. Within one year of this broad and inclusive process, the strategies were adopted and implemented.

The initiative began in the winter of 2017 with a retreat for the Board of Trustees, followed that summer by the president convening a multistakeholder strategic planning group of forty-five faculty, administrators, coaches, students, alumni, and trustees. This group was divided into three focus areas: access and enrollment, programs (curricular and cocurricular), and facilities. Each group in turn consulted with a range of other campus stakeholders as they developed strategies and recommendations for a sustainable future. By the end of the summer, the groups completed and distributed a comprehensive plan to the board and to the full campus community, with feedback and discussion facilitated through town hall meetings, online open-format surveys, and shared governance structures. The board unanimously adopted the proposal in October, and it was implemented during the remaining 2017–18 academic year. The plan included a realistic vision to systematically lower enrollment targets by a small percentage each year over five to seven years based on demographic projections—a vision that remained consistent with Allegheny's mission and commitments to diversity and access. In year one, there was an increase in academic quality and domestic and international diversity, and Pell eligibility was maintained above 25 percent for the incoming class. Alongside enrollment strategies, the institution established student retention as a top priority. Within two years, a collaborative process with nearly fifty participants from academics, student life, athletics, admissions, and student government achieved a 5 percent increase in first-to-second-year retention.

New investments included majors in art and science and in innovation, informatics, and business; an innovation center with connection to local business and manufacturing; two new sports teams and upgrades to athletics facilities; and campus-wide classroom enhancements. As part of this plan, the Board of Trustees unanimously approved a retirement incentive to balance staffing in concert with the new student body. While such a strategy would not work for all institutions, it was well received at Allegheny and was effective in spreading retirements evenly across the curriculum, allowing for only selective rehiring in areas of greatest staffing need based on enrollment trends. The subsequent academic plan, released in February 2018, maintained interdisciplinary breadth in the curriculum (aligned with institutional culture) and a consistent student-faculty ratio based on enrollment projections. A process for coherent and frequent communication was integral to successful implementation.

The communication and implementation processes began immediately after the summer 2017 working group completed its report. In August of that year the provost presented the criteria and goals for academic staffing to the Faculty Council, an elected body of faculty that serves as a liaison with the administration and advises the president and provost on staffing. In late August and early September, the provost met individually with each department or program chair to review the strategy and to provide information about projected staffing in their areas.

Throughout fall 2017 the Faculty Council was updated and consulted for feedback on faculty staffing. Deans in academics, student affairs, and enrollment provided feedback, and the chief financial officer worked with the provost to establish a multiyear staffing budget. Final components were shared and discussed with the Faculty Council in January 2018, and the plan was complete by the end of that month, after the close of the retirement incentive. A second round of meetings with the provost and department chairs followed to review changes that pertained to each department. The main points were also shared with the student government and alumni council. An overview of the staffing plan was presented in January at a meeting of all department and program chairs and then in February to the Board of Trustees and faculty. Throughout the entire process, the provost worked closely with the president to maintain alignment with institutional vision.

Chairs were naturally resistant to reduced staffing in their departments. This conflict was resolved once the administration acknowledged the impact, then showed the data and rationale for its decisions, and finally reimagined parts of the curriculum (i.e., shared courses between programs, which winnowed other courses). To facilitate this process, the provost hosted a half-day Curriculum Summit (with follow-up sessions) for chairs to bring concerns forward, anticipate problems, and collaborate on solutions. New academic programs were delivered through reallocation of faculty lines and by faculty from allied departments teaching courses in the new programs. Delivery of new programs did not depend on part-time or adjunct faculty. From the start, the prospect of change brought uncertainty among faculty and staff. However, key factors for managing this change have been open communication, building and following an inclusive process, and significant evidence-based planning.

Following the COVID-19 pandemic and under the leadership of a new president, Allegheny continues to evaluate its strategic position by reviewing enrollment targets and academic programs and following its roadmap for change processes. Additional change has included administrative reorganization into a new area for holistic student success with the appointment of a new dean for student success and of class deans. The student success area brings together what were separate learning support, advising, and student cohort programs. Budget reallocations and staffing reductions in other areas funded the new administrative positions. This change was evidence based and implemented to enhance student completion rates. Academic majors launched in 2018 continue to be growth areas, and the innovation center is expanding partnerships with regional manufacturers with co-op style courses and internships.

COMMON THEMES AND CONCLUSION

Common to each institution is a proactive Board of Trustees that has invested in innovation. The boards' inclusion of multiple levels of leadership was critical to success. Historical and national demographic data formed the foundation of evidence-based decisions that facilitated a process of collaborative change involving trustees, students, faculty, alumni, and administration.

The two institutions have also developed new partnerships in the form of postbaccalaureate articulation agreements that are mutually beneficial for student recruitment. Both institutions have adopted realistic enrollment strategies, pinned to sustainable goals that do not depend on growth in the number of traditional first-time, first-year students in the face of a projected decline in high school graduates. Lastly, each institution has enacted change in order to build on its strengths while remaining true to its identity and culture. Each institution also recognizes the importance of nurturing a culture of change for continuing improvement so as to navigate inevitable disruptions. In this regard, we believe that regular review of curricular and cocurricular programs will be more common across all areas of higher education.

The lessons learned at Chatham and Allegheny can serve as valuable case studies for other institutions that are considering their next steps. In particular, understanding change management has been fundamental to both institutions. The phases of change common to both cases are illustrated in figure 19.1.

FIGURE 19.1 Phases of transformational change

Denial
There's no need
for us to change.

→

Resistance
We won't change.

→

Acceptance
We're open to change
but not sure how.

→

Alignment
We're working in sync
toward a common goal.

Both institutions recognize points when the direction of change was temporarily reversed (i.e., moving from acceptance back to resistance for some stakeholders in response to particular issues), but the long-term progression has been toward alignment. Reaching alignment requires an inclusive process with frequent and consistent communication of plans and clear rationale for decisions in order to achieve a shared vision. Recognizing these phases has been key to developing resilience—the ability to effectively advance our missions in an ever-changing environment—at each institution.

— *Takeaways* —

- Know your institution before undertaking change—study, learn, and explore to develop a clear sense of the culture and authentic identity of the institution.
- Define the rationale for change clearly and use evidence-based reasoning to transition from resistance to acceptance.
- Engage not only deans and leaders but also faculty, staff, students, and alumni in the discussions and planning. The broader the transparency across stakeholders in the process, the greater the likelihood of achieving alignment.
- Be patient: genuine, important change takes time.

NOTES

1. "Knocking at the College Door: Projections of U.S. High School Graduates," 10th ed., WICHE (Western Interstate Commission for Higher Education), December 2020, https://knocking.wiche.edu/executive-summary/

2. See "Digest of Education Statistics: 2019," NCES, IES (National Center for Education Statistics, Institute of Education Sciences), accessed 27 November 2021, https://nces.ed.gov/programs/digest/d19/.

CHAPTER 20

The Institutional Shift toward Student-Centered Campuses

GINA HAUSKNECHT AND PAULA O'LOUGHLIN

Academic leaders now and in the years to come will need to map student trajectories through our institutions in a different way. In the faculty-centered model most of us were trained in, professional development was about research, classrooms were about teaching, and policy was about compliance. Students were expected to adapt to the norms and values of the larger institution. The essence of a student-centered institution is its orientation toward the multidimensionality of the students' experience rather than assimilation into the modes and mores of a majoritarian culture.

In this chapter we consider how Coe College in Cedar Rapids, Iowa, has shifted toward a more student-centered campus. The four areas we explore include understanding what today's college students want and need from us; examining how faculty development and evaluation can better scaffold student success; reconsidering how policies and processes such as transfer agreements and academic standing impact students; and collaborating between academics and student life for a more integrated campus experience.

UNDERSTANDING WHO OUR STUDENTS ARE AND WHAT THEY NEED FROM US

Our goal across institutions of all kinds is to prepare students for productive professional and public lives: we seek to send them into the world workplace-ready and upwardly mobile. In a word, the education we provide is "aspirational"—a term we used freely and proudly. But in words *not* typically used, we can also see this same education as integrationist and assimilationist. We have often implicitly or explicitly expected students to shape themselves to standards set by the most privileged and thoroughly prepared of their peers.

Our students come to us from all walks of life, with a wide range of experiences, needs, responsibilities, and challenges. Among the most prevalent of these challenges are financial precarity, first-generation status, academic underpreparation, family dysfunction, physical disability, or mental health diagnoses. In a deficit mindset, these characteristics might be seen as obstacles along the path toward a degree to be met with special programming or tracks or monitoring. Students with these challenges continue to enroll, and in growing numbers. But our students also come to us with valuable life experiences, "riches" that we should not just acknowledge but incorporate into how our campuses function. The opportunity now is not just to meet their needs—as necessary, daunting, and resource intensive as that can be—but to foster a strengths mindset across our institutions.

Students and their advocates expect to be seen on their own multifaceted terms, with distinctive assets. Increasingly, we understand our students not as clay to be molded into the finite number of shapes represented by our various programs of study but as self-determining individuals coming from and returning to a complex world. As institutional leaders, we need to help our schools and communities see the treasure in every student. Our work is not to turn our students into us but to prepare them to shape the world in their own image.

The expansion from a budget-conscious focus on retention to a fuller vision of student persistence is a critical example of how deans can and should productively center the student experience. Keeping students in school is becoming more visibly the work of all areas of the university, sometimes expressed in the phrase "Retention is everyone's problem." The other side of this coin—the student side—is persistence. A thoroughly student-centered approach operates in both modes: focusing on what the institution can do to retain students and how it can support them in persisting.

Recent outside forces have accelerated change, compelling innovation that has a distinctly student-centered character. Student vulnerability has never been so palpably on the faculty radar. The Black Lives Matter movement and the COVID-19 pandemic have vividly foregrounded student needs, engaging our campuses in new and creative ways of addressing them. At Coe College, and across academe, valuable conversations about anti-racism, mental health, and equity have generated reconsideration of course design and policies. Everything from deadline and attendance penalties to "trigger" and content warnings has been on the table.

While these can seem like small measures, and change often feels maddeningly incremental, the good news is that even a few well-chosen interventions across an institution can make a significant impact. It's critical that academic leaders maintain a holistic understanding of student success, integrate student-centered support into all areas of the institution, and communicate that student efficacy, well-being, and timely graduation are shared priorities.

RECALIBRATING FACULTY EXPERTISE
TOWARD STUDENT PERSISTENCE AND SUCCESS

To be an institutional goal, student-centeredness needs to be embedded in reward structures and governance. Consider how the existing evaluation processes and funding mechanisms on your campus do, or do not, scaffold a robustly student-focused faculty. The choices that underlie these structures determine what constitutes faculty work and what it means to be a college or university professor. The basic premises of student-centered pedagogy are not controversial on most campuses, whether two- or four-year institution, small college or state university.

Teaching at its best is intentionally designed to expand individual capacity and foster self-efficacy, not to transfer knowledge into compliant recipients being trained for a hierarchical, industrialized workplace. Yet at most four-year schools, the evaluation process demands that even those faculty who pride themselves on their teaching must prioritize research and scholarly or creative accomplishments. Even for non-tenure-track hires and adjuncts, the ubiquitous review of a CV routinely equates scholarly output with field knowledge.

For our institutions to enrich the lives of all of our students, we need to harness our faculty's intellectual capacity and passion for teaching and mentoring as much as for research. How much of a gulf exists on your campus between teaching and what faculty often refer to as "my own work"? Ideally, we can forge ways to bring these in alignment. The laboratory in the natural and social sciences is the obvious site where faculty share their research lives with their students. How else might you expand or create opportunities for faculty and students to collaborate? How can faculty think of—and be rewarded for thinking of—their work with students, including teaching itself, as more central to their disciplinary identities?

Moving beyond one's graduate research training to highly effective course design and classroom practices cannot simply be a matter of volunteerism and self-improvement. Academic leaders can engage their faculty in national conversations by funding participation in student- and teaching-focused professional development activities beyond the institution. At Coe we have tapped into the resources of regional and national consortia like Campus Compact, NetVUE (Network for Vocation in Undergraduate Education), the National Humanities Alliance, and Project NExT (New Experiences in Teaching). Start-up funds can be reconceptualized: some portion can be earmarked for teaching-related professional development. The legitimation of the scholarship of teaching and learning (SoTL) through its incorporation in evaluation processes now occurs even at major research institutions and needs to become the norm. Including mentoring activities and student engagement in adjunct faculty and staff productivity reports is another option.

Consider how faculty development activities, funding, and expectations are formulated at your institution. At Coe, faculty development has shifted over time from a primary emphasis on research to greater balance between research and pedagogy. Twenty years ago, virtually all internal faculty development grants were given for research projects; then a single grant was introduced to support course development. Now, 40 percent of grant moneys awarded encourage pedagogical projects. Ten years ago, pedagogical enhancement sessions were offered only on an ad hoc basis.

We have created a Faculty Development Committee that programs a range of gatherings that foster community around teaching. These include a well-attended annual retreat organized around a book from the scholarship of teaching and learning. Provided free of charge to participants, the retreat is supported with modest compensation, good food, and small gifts that keep the budget low while recognizing the value of faculty time. The evidence-based and resolutely practical books include Susan Ambrose and colleagues' *How Learning Works: Seven Research-Based Principles for Smart Teaching* (2010) and James Lang's *Small Teaching: Everyday Lessons from the Science of Learning* (2016). Among the most powerful texts has been Cia Verschelden's *Bandwidth Recovery: Helping Students Reclaim Cognitive Resources Lost to Poverty, Racism, and Social Marginalization* (2017). This book stimulated much conversation about the baked-in inequities between our students and the specific challenges that our classrooms pose to underserved students. Long since the retreat, faculty and staff have regularly referred to the book in various contexts.

REFRAMING CAMPUS POLICIES TO CENTER ON STUDENT EFFICACY AND RESILIENCE

As the previous example suggests, academic leaders can reap considerable benefits from helping faculty better understand the complexities of students' lives. Faculty across higher education have had powerful conversations in recent years as they have engaged more with the changing web of practices that constitute an institution's approach to diversity, equity, and inclusion. Creating more equitable campuses often means making systems visible that faculty may be unaware of but that have an outsized impact on student experience. Examples include the satisfactory-academic-progress system for federal financial aid and programs on your campus addressing food insecurity. Even the obstacles that the cost of course materials pose for some students may be hidden from faculty. Illuminating these dimensions of students' daily struggles can be critical in deepening faculty commitment to student success. Central to this effort is reaching beyond our familiar boundaries to listen to what our colleagues in other areas know about the complexity of students' lives today.

On our campus, we have shifted our focus toward students' lived experiences of our classes and evidence-based practices that promote resilience. The syllabus template provided by the provost's office, which we now update more frequently, has become an important tool for communicating not just the don'ts but also the dos. The emphasis has gravitated from the admonitory (e.g., FERPA and plagiarism) to the supportive (e.g., pointing students toward our food and necessity pantry, and a new, more accommodating approach to religious observance). We still require an academic integrity statement, but encourage faculty to explain its value to an academic community. Faculty are invited to consider whether the tone of their syllabi is hectoring and mistrustful, reflecting an assumption that students need to be kept in line, or communicating trust in the students' ability to make sound, informed decisions once they understand the educational purpose of course policies. The syllabus, as the encapsulation of both the content and the spirit of the course, is a primary site for establishing the degree to which the course centers and respects students and their learning at least as much as faculty performance of expertise. Each of these steps exemplifies how academic leaders can steer the campus toward student success.

Student life outside the classroom has also been reshaped in recent years by a focus on policies that build resilience, with a shift from enforcing compliance with academic standards to widening access and supporting degree completion. Accommodating the realities of students' lives means reexamining the time-honored premise that students would spend four years in a single higher-education institution immediately after high school, and that college would be the primary focus of those years. Increasingly, we understand that the students who start college with us may well graduate elsewhere. Academic leaders at two- and four-year institutions of all types need to understand our interconnectedness as we review our transfer policies for students coming to and leaving our institutions.

Along with making sure our own programs are transfer friendly, we can join other institutions in relationships focused on student degree outcomes, not on protecting our own turf. Students are often stymied by differences in institutional systems like financial aid and the academic calendar. Supporting the degree success of students who leave our institution ultimately will make us all stronger. We should reexamine policies concerning students who sit out (voluntarily or not) one or more semesters, to assure that our processes give them the best chance possible of degree completion upon returning. Some institutions have "fresh start" policies that allow students who have left with poor grades to rebuild their GPAs when they return. At Coe, we simplified students' experience with our academic standing process by aligning our internal standards with those dictated by federal financial aid. We also replaced a single, arbitrary deadline for academic probation with a rolling review of transcripts as students finish incompletes. We're considering how to bring our partnerships with student life into these conversations, mindful that student success is not just academic success and that a student's closest adult contact on campus often is not a faculty member.

The academic catalog can be a maze of policies that baffles students and sometimes even their advocates. Student-centeredness entails developing students' autonomy as they navigate our often-complex institutions. Professional and peer coaching, by providing guides and not just maps, empowers students to figure out their own way. At Coe, we partnered with College Possible's near-peer coaches and developed our own peer-tutoring model to include peer executive-function coaches. Consider, too, how you ask for and respond to input about the student's experience. Over the past several years, Coe has expanded the means for students to express their concerns, including an online drop-box, the creation of a student senate subcommittee on academic concerns that meets monthly with the associate dean for student academics, and syllabus language highlighting how to communicate with department chairs. We need to look at our institutions and processes through student eyes: students do not experience our institutions according to the firm boundaries of our organizational charts, often not even knowing who are faculty and who are staff.

REORGANIZING STUDENT SUCCESS STRUCTURES TO INTEGRATE ACADEMIC AND STUDENT LIFE

In many of the examples offered above, faculty can learn from our colleagues in student life, student financial services, the registrar's and advising offices, and student success initiatives. Collaboration between areas makes students' lives easier and more coherent; it can also help faculty and staff better understand our institutions and the students themselves. A holistic approach to student success requires reimagining institutional structures, removing barriers between our areas, and getting out of our silos.

One-stop student success centers are becoming increasingly common and are a prime example of an initiative for which collaboration is essential and requires thoughtful leadership. Because these centers are frequently, and necessarily, staffed across reporting lines, tussles can emerge over which area or unit will report on them. Further, to embed the academic experience more fully in students' lives often means locating these resources somewhere other than academic buildings—in some cases, as at Coe, in the library, but often in the student union.

As academic leaders, we need to create pathways for these critical partnerships. It is our responsibility to keep the focus on student success over and above any perceived threats to faculty or staff control. When Coe renovated the library to create space for our new Learning Commons, we engaged in a planning process with coleadership shared between the library director and the associate dean. Later, the Learning Commons joined forces with the alumni office to jointly develop parent programming to support student success, and with our career center to create an alumni mentoring program for first- and second-year students. These partnerships have resulted in other synergies and have modeled collaboration across areas of the college that previously were largely separate.

As with student success centers, academic leaders should work to build committee and other institutional structures that address the totality of the student experience. It's worth critically examining whether and how your institution's governance system itself supports a focus on student success. We refashioned our admission committee as an enrollment, persistence, and retention committee that looks at the entirety of the student path through Coe. Our "students of concern" committee is now an evidence-based group bridging academics, athletics, and student life. We created a retention data group with representation from academic affairs, student life, admissions, and the registrar's office and introduced an early-alert system run by a combination of faculty and staff. This system has proved fruitful not just in "catching" struggling students but also in involving faculty in conversations with student life and Learning Commons colleagues about how to support them. Members of these groups have developed a deeper perspective on the student experience and how their areas of expertise are actually complementary and not in tension with one another. Faculty, in particular, have come to appreciate to a greater degree the personal challenges faced by students from various backgrounds and how much these students enrich our campus.

CONCLUSION

Most of us were trained in academic hyperspecialization and a teaching model that defined student success solely in terms of career success, wealth achievement, and postgraduate degree attainment. Yet the long history of US higher education reflects commitment to the common good, not just individual advancement, and an increasing expansion of who is served by our colleges and universities and to what end. If institutions of higher education want graduates who reflect the broadest range of American society, we need to ask whether our policies and processes embrace that range or whether, in often subtle and hidden ways, they demand that students navigate and bend to structures not designed to help them meet their own goals. As academic leaders, we need to commit resources to a constant reinvigoration of our systems.

— Takeaways —

- The gifts and potential of a diverse student body enrich our work as educators. We need to appreciate that students coming to us with challenges offer us a wealth of opportunities to excel at our own central purpose of preparing the next generation of citizens.
- Faculty development needs to support learning as much as teaching, and this focus may involve a reconceptualization of the central work of the classroom. This entails an ongoing commitment to a broad base of faculty skill and knowledge beyond specialized graduate training.
- Institutional policies need to center on students' lived experiences, support access, and promote degree completion.
- Collaboration across the institution needs to be embedded as fully as possible in all student-facing structures and initiatives.

CHAPTER 21

Leadership at the Dean's Level in Community Colleges

VINCENT WIGGINS

Leadership in community colleges continues to be important because these institutions are a primary resource for a broad spectrum of individuals seeking out higher education to achieve their academic goals. Community colleges were initially developed to support students whose sole opportunity to earn a credential after high school was through such institutions and their resources. A complex political history related to community colleges often impacts the forward direction of support as leaders work with students to navigate the obstacles in this system.

The author of this chapter serves as a dean at Harry S Truman College in Chicago, Illinois. Under the leadership of Dr. Shawn Jackson, the institution's president, we have identified key focus areas that apply to all community colleges: enrollment, communication, and college culture. Success as a dean requires working with these three aspects:

- Enrollment: understanding the students' path prior to and during enrollment and at the completion of credentials, when the student could secure immediate employment in the workforce or transfer to a four-year college.
- Communication: understanding how to effectively receive from and share information with the internal and external stakeholders affiliated with the college.

• College culture: understanding the individual community college culture in order to create and maintain a welcoming, inclusive, and equitable space for the local community and institution, including students, faculty, and staff.

This chapter assists new deans and other administrators in understanding the expectations of the leadership role and offers advice on how to succeed. Topics include a brief history of community colleges and their current trends; insight into the role of the dean; students and their desired goals; important aspects of successfully working with faculty and staff; and major daily operations requiring significant time.

THE HISTORY AND MISSION OF COMMUNITY COLLEGES

Community colleges are a vital aspect of higher education. These institutions have existed in the United States for over a century, beginning in 1901 at Joliet Junior College in Illinois. In fall 2019, 41 percent of undergraduate students attended community college. Currently, there are more than a thousand campuses, the majority of them public, followed by independent and a small number of tribal institutions. They're supported by the American Association of Community Colleges (AACC).

The original purpose of community colleges was to provide educational opportunities for individuals after their K–12 experience. These students might not have the access to or resources for attending a four-year college. The mission of serving the community was a challenge for the colleges in their infancy, and continues to be, because they're often impacted by external forces, including budget restraints, that aren't always aligned with the needs of the community.

Over the years, the focus of community colleges has changed. They continue to serve the current needs of their communities, including offering certificate programs for students who need to develop skills for relevant academic career paths into certain industries or bachelor's degree–granting institutions in most states. Initially, community colleges didn't offer bachelor's degrees, but, according to the AACC, they now account for 1 percent of bachelor's degrees, 58 percent of associate's, and 41 percent of certificates nationwide. Although two-year institutions have much in common, cultural and industrial changes are occurring in some regions at a faster pace than in others, impacting community colleges in different ways. One of the major shifts affecting this entire segment of higher education is a significant decrease in federal funding.

US presidents have supported the idea of free community colleges since their founding. However, most regional political climates haven't been conducive to the plan, resulting in decreasing public funds in many states. As government support continues to decline, tuition increases to cover operational costs. As a result, leaders have explored other options for boosting funding to compensate for the decrease in government support. This shift requires deans to be proactive in their outreach by engaging in more events and initiatives to secure funds and to be flexible with their time commitments beyond work hours.

Another shift is related to student demographics. Initially, institutions were located in or directly connected to high schools to support graduates so that they would have immediate access to higher education. Over time, community colleges became independent of the oversight and leadership of high schools. In addition, recent data confirm that community colleges are more diverse in age, ethnicity, and other characteristics than their four-year counterparts.

The educational path of students interested in community college has also changed. Current trends favor more intentional alignment of student pathways in 2 + 2+2 agreements: junior and senior years in high school, two years in community college, and junior and senior years in a four-year institution.

OVERVIEW OF THE DEAN'S ROLE

The role of community college deans is both challenging and rewarding—as it is for deans throughout higher education. In general, deans are responsible for the operation of the college's academic affairs and accreditation requirements. This involves facilitating projects that include department chairs, program directors, students, faculty (tenured and adjunct), staff, and other college leadership (president, provost, vice-presidents, and deans in other areas of the college).

A dean supports the college's chief academic officers; serves as a leadership representative at internal and external events; and manages college resources, including the budget and other funding such as grants. The reporting structure is similar among all deans in that they work with associate deans and department chairs or program directors; oversee budgets related to academic departments; and lead special projects by working directly with the vice-president of academic affairs, provost, and college president.

Leadership is challenging because students follow paths through the institution that can lead to various outcomes after they receive a credential. A significant number of students are nontraditional and have limited financial resources and flexibility for achieving their academic dreams. Their circumstances and motivations vary: some aren't ready for a four-year college, seek a short-term credential to enter the workforce quickly, or are earning a degree in order to transfer to a four-year institution. This diversity is part of the ultimate reward for the dean in supporting students to obtain the resources necessary to accomplish their personal educational goals. The results of these efforts are often seen at graduation when students express gratitude for the college's help in overcoming the obstacles they faced in their journey to a credential.

Some of the most important mandates for a dean are to build relationships, understand the college's culture, and thoroughly understand the system and union contracts. Also, deans must create and maintain a structure and standard procedures that offer the flexibility needed to adapt to internal and external influences as these change in the political environment. To further develop as a leader, create a professional support system and enlist a mentor or mentors whom you can readily call upon as you navigate the different areas in your position.

As a dean, one must have a clear understanding of the college's mission and vision and also of oneself—including self-identification, personal philosophy, and the ability to manage stress. A valuable piece of advice shared by one of my mentors is that in order to be successful it's important to know your core values and pet peeves. This understanding will help you to create your professional character in your college and community while providing a sense of your expectations of others.

While managing a complex system and supporting a significant number of students who are at risk, the dean must manage personal stress in order to best serve the students and the college as a whole. Patrick Sanaghan identifies two important characteristics of an effective dean: staunch acceptance of reality and a clear sense of purpose and meaning.[1] Similarly, research by Linda Wild highlights the importance of identifying and managing the particular stressors that affect community college deans. Wild identifies two major factors that repeatedly appear in the data: "managing human interactions" and "intrinsic job demands." "These stress factors," she notes, "underline the importance for the community college deans to identify and hone their skills in human relations, communication, conflict-resolution, and management techniques."[2] Understanding these stress factors is important in succeeding in the aspects of deanship explored in the following sections.

COMMUNITY COLLEGE STUDENTS

The dean's principal role is to create and nurture a culture of success for students who come from diverse backgrounds. Every community college is unique: they're located throughout the United States in various communities and often work closely with high schools to provide higher education for students. Partnerships between high schools and higher education also provide opportunities for students to receive college credits prior to high school graduation by participating in dual-enrollment and dual-credit programs.

In most community colleges, open enrollment allows students with diverse backgrounds to seek a higher education. Serving a broad spectrum of students and managing operations are the dean's primary functions. Such management is often challenging because of the widely diverse array of students, including first generation, students of color, students in their mid-twenties and older, and other nontraditional characteristics not found as frequently in four-year institutions.

Students in community colleges also demand a more holistic approach because of the broad spectrum they present in college readiness and academic goals. This requires the dean to assess the support needed in the classroom, because the time in which to engage most community college students is limited. The majority of students commute and have other competing priorities that limit their flexibility in focusing on learning.

In developing one's holistic approach, it's important to understand the curriculum requirements that support student learning. These include the alignment of local, state, and federal guidelines and funding. In addition, the curriculum must correspond with industry and regional accreditation require-ments. This compliance calls for frequent reporting in order to document the relevance of the program and to meet learning outcomes required for students' success in the workforce and efficient transfer to four-year institu-tions. Accreditation aligns with the two major pathways for students seeking credentials: transfer to a four-year institution or to career and technical edu-cation (CTE). Community colleges are supported in performing their signifi-cant role in preparing students for the workforce supported by CTE programs that offer short-term and long-term credentials for employment in industries requiring specific licensures and certificates. These basic and advanced cer-tificates lead to an associate of applied science degree.

Community colleges confer the largest number of associate of arts de-grees that permit the student to transfer to four-year colleges or universities as juniors. For efficient transfer, deans have to work closely with partner in-stitutions to assure that course content is comparable to that of four-year institutions and that students take the courses necessary to a clear path.

FACULTY AND STAFF

The dean must focus mainly on collaboration with faculty and staff. Faculty are the subject-matter experts and the direct connection to the students. The staff are the frontline support to the students and have a close understanding of their needs. Working closely with all faculty and staff enables the dean to identify the direction in which to develop the curriculum and what holistic support should be provided to students. This ensures relevant education as part of the academic program.

A reflective partnership with faculty and staff is also important to provid-ing professional development opportunities. Ongoing support of colleagues can lead to their own success and to the success of the institution as a whole. As a leader, it's important to work closely with all colleagues to assist them with their involvement in committees and in leadership roles, such as depart-ment chair. Developing these reflective partnerships supports opportunities for faculty involvement and leadership.

OPERATIONS

Operations take at least 90 percent of a dean's time and energy and are critical to the institution's daily functioning and ensure that the needs of students, faculty, and staff are addressed in a timely manner. Operational functions, which build upon the three aspects noted at the beginning of this chapter, include enrollment, retention, completion, communication, college culture, and external influences.

Enrollment: understand prospective students, high school partnerships, nontraditional and reentry options, academic programs, and community perception to maintain a healthy enrollment, successful completion rate, relevant academic programs, and the community's positive perception of the college.

Retention: create and analyze qualitative and quantitative data to quickly make modifications to meet the needs of the students and industry demand. The key data components include, but aren't limited to, class scheduling, customer service and learning environment complements, student concerns, classroom observations, grade appeals, and syllabi review.

Completion: understand accreditation requirements, relevant curriculum, workforce partnership, transfer agreements, articulation agreements, advisory boards, and district guidelines.

Communication: develop, maintain, and revise communication with stakeholders to ensure everyone is aware of critical information and not overwhelmed with unnecessary flyers and email messages. Stakeholders include students, faculty, staff, academic departments, advisory boards, leadership, on-campus colleagues, and, if applicable, school district colleagues.

College culture: create and maintain a healthy culture that includes understanding the institution's structure, labor unions, and inclusiveness. In addition, professional development opportunities should be offered to faculty and staff to maintain a positive atmosphere.

External influences: identify external influences that impact the college's decisions, including community partnerships, advisory boards, and local, state, and federal governments.

CONCLUSION

My experience as a community college dean has been mostly rewarding but has also come with challenges. I find it satisfying to work with colleagues to create and maintain a culture of success for all students. To support them, I've found it important to build relationships, understand the college culture, and thoroughly understand the institution's system, including union contracts. To best serve students, the dean must manage personal stress that involves managing human interactions and intrinsic job demands. And to succeed, it's important to create a professional support system with colleagues and other leaders who can readily be accessed as you navigate the different responsibilities of your position. This support structure will also assist you in having a clear understanding of yourself, including self-identification, personal philosophy, and the ability to manage stress.

— *Takeaways* —

- The principal role of the community college dean is to create and maintain a culture of success for students who come from diverse backgrounds.
- A culture of inclusiveness should be engrained in the infrastructure of the college community and leads to institutional success in supporting all students and the community as a whole.
- The dean's role requires listening effectively and being an advocate who empowers students.
- The dean must understand that enrollment trends are changing and leadership must implement a plan to provide support and leadership to faculty and staff charged with operationalizing the college's annual goals.

NOTES

1. See Patrick Sanaghan, *Building Leadership Resilience in Higher Education* (Denver: CR Mrig, 2016), available at AI (Academic Impressions), https://www.academicimpressions.com/sites/default/files/0116-leadership-resilience-md.pdf.
2. Linda L. Wild, "Work-Related Stress Factors Affecting the Community College Dean" (PhD diss., Iowa State University, 2002), 98, https://lib.dr.iastate.edu/cgi/viewcontent.cgi?article=1409&context=rtd.

PART V

Leadership and the College

CHAPTER 22

The Dean as Supporter in Chief

Spreading Joy in Academic Communities

MARIA C. GARRIGA

"The main responsibility of a chief academic officer is to spread joy." I heard these words during a meeting for academic administrators. Those might not have been the exact words uttered, but they carry the spirit of what was said. At the time, my career as an academic leader was just beginning, and the words struck me as meaningful in many ways. "Surely, there has to be more to the job," was my first thought. Compliance issues came immediately to mind. Keeping accreditation agencies happy, making sure the academic side follows the many federal guidelines, and advancing intellectual initiatives are important responsibilities of a dean. But my musings quickly turned back to "Spreading joy? How hard can that be?"

In six years of holding different positions in academic leadership, my mind often comes back to those thoughts. Whether or not the *main* responsibility is to spread joy, academic officers are wise to foster an environment in which *well*ness is seen as the base of heal*th*. In this way, "wellth" provides the context for advancing student learning outcomes and moving the institution toward a practical application of its mission statement.[1]

Consider an analogy from my content area—teaching Spanish to speakers of other languages. Research in foreign- and second-language education tells us that culture must embody all learning activities; language can't be taught in a vacuum, and culture provides a unifying context in and out of the classroom. Culture influences vocabulary, grammar, and ideas; these, in turn, influence culture. Similarly, when a focus on wellth acts as the guiding value of personal and professional operations in the workplace, mundane academic tasks become grounded in human connectivity and take on special meaning. This goodwill, in turn, increases productivity and professional satisfaction.

Small, incremental changes in behavior and attitude are enough to create ripple effects and constructive interference in all areas of our lives and communities. This chapter presents seven simple yet important practices you can share through modeling to reduce stress, increase creativity and productivity, help your colleagues mindfully engage with their work and life, and spread joy among the academic community.

MIND THE GAP

Originally coined as a warning for travelers in the London Underground, the phrase "Mind the gap" has numerous cost-free applications for life. In order to effect change, one must be aware of the need for change: social gaps between colleagues should be considered before any further action is taken. What is the gap, or actual distance between the academic leader and the person they work with? Contemplate physical, affective, normative, and interactive distances between members of the team. Discussions about these perceived or real gaps are a good starting point for academic team tasks. It may not seem practical to walk to a faculty member's office for a quick conversation—e-mail and phone appear faster. However, the benefits of the short walk, a way to bridge one gap, are many. One gets an opportunity to stretch and to see the institution alive. Impromptu conversations with students or colleagues lift spirits and provide valuable information. I have the daily habit of walking with my administrative assistant to the mail room, and I walk with the provost on her way to meetings in other buildings. These short walks give us time to chat, and they showcase that we're a team that enjoys time together.

Social and personal distances can be narrowed by alternating the location of periodic meetings, rotating through seating arrangements and duties such as note-taking, and making sure all attendees know each other before commencing. Ice-breaker questions such as, "What is something positive that has happened in your life recently?" or the quirkier "If you were a kitchen appliance, what would you be?" also help narrow social distances. Thematically, efforts to bridge social distances can begin with a focus on universal principles. These are abstract, aspirational concepts about which the team can agree. Once the members have settled on a handful of universal principles, these become nonnegotiables and anchoring features of the discussion. Subsequent deliberations are then framed in relationship to the issues already resolved, serving as a reminder of team unity, past success, and empathy. The path to wellth is smoother when we act with the awareness that we are more alike than different.

Practice 1: Start each task or meeting with ways to notice and narrow any perceived gaps.

WORK-LIFE INTEGRATION

Quantitatively, professionals spend most of their waking hours at work. While traditionally there was talk of work-life balance, it is now recognized that balance is close to impossible. One is better off to refer to work-life integration. Community formation, personal well-being, and health are particularly suited to integration. Some may say, "I do not want my work to be integrated with my life." Nonetheless, the premise of this practice assumes that people work best in cycles: there will be times when work takes over your life, and times when life takes over your work. Our loved ones' needs and our own work emergencies will balance differently over time. There will be subtle pivots—as opposed to hard boundaries—between an individual's different personas. An academic leader should have the power to design their schedule to integrate all areas of life into a workday. For example, one of my fellow deans is at work by 6:30 a.m. and on the way home by 3:30 p.m., logging in from 8:00 to 8:30 p.m. for any follow-up needed. Scheduling life activities and work activities on the same calendar places them at equal levels of importance. Nonetheless, it's always good to take time exclusively for one or the other.

Many businesses, and some institutions of higher learning, have designed e-mail policies to protect employees as they compartmentalize their many responsibilities. In addition to limiting the use of the "reply all" and "forward" features, a policy may regulate use of e-mail after hours or during vacations, or even ration internal electronic communications to favor personal interactions. Several years ago, France modeled collective bargaining between employees and companies through a redesigned architecture for the timing of various matters of work and vacation, including e-mails. Might a similar national approach be welcomed in the United States? In addition to these discussions regarding electronic communication, an academic institution may experiment with "no meeting" days, or even a four-day class-scheduling week. These are creative, cost-neutral ways to increase employee satisfaction and wellth.

Experts in pedagogy note the directive to address different learning styles when designing a lesson plan. Teachers in training may be told something akin to "You do not need to address all learning styles in each lesson, but all learning styles must be addressed over a unit." Likewise, allow academic leaders (including yourself) the opportunity to weave many responsibilities into a workday, assessing balance only within a specific longer time block. Colleagues will quickly realize how the freedom to integrate the different realities of life contributes greatly to the wellth and good fortune of higher education as a vocation.

Practice 2: Spend time every two weeks assessing the integration of your work and personal life. Use both quantifiable and qualitative metrics. Consider looking into innovative industry practices for ways to increase employee satisfaction.

MINDFULNESS

Is your mind full, or are you being mindful? Mindfulness is arguably the single most important skill to cultivate in building the internal mental capacity needed to navigate hardships in academic affairs. Best known for a focus on the present moment, mindfulness also centers on an attitude of observation over one of judgment. It provides a context for other holistic practices that help make work meaningful. While formal mindfulness practices involve an intention of both set and setting during meditation, informal mindfulness practices can be attended to in everyday life. An astute academic leader will practice and promote both.

There are various types of meditation to suit distinctive types of personalities and occasions. A thorough discussion of meditation is beyond the scope of this chapter, but resources on metta, mindfulness, focused attention, open monitoring, contemplative prayer, and self-inquiry are easily accessible online.[2] Some universities dedicate spaces as meditation rooms, others hold daily Zoom meditation practices, and many provide a meditation app as part of their benefits packet. The academic leadership team will find that a regular meditation practice increases awareness of the self and sharpens perception. Sharing meditative experiences also shapes camaraderie in interesting ways.

Philosophers have argued that the ability to travel in mental time is the defining quality of human cognition. St. Augustine reflected on the passing of time, "The time present of things past is memory; the time present of things present is direct experience; the time present of things future is expectation."[3] He repeatedly used the phrase "time present," suggesting that mindfulness is the basis for all our thinking. From the vantage point of health as wealth, mindfulness practice is good for the heart (lowers blood pressure), mind (helps with memory and executive functioning), health (strengthens immune responses), and body (strengthens telomeres).

Practice 3: Commit to ten minutes per day of contemplative time and eventually let mindfulness imbue other activities.

TAKE IT OUTSIDE OR BE AN OUTSIDER

The literal meaning of "Take it outside" implies an escalation of violence that is continued outside. "Be an outsider" implies nonbelonging and a sense of loneliness. I encourage you to own the phrases by redefining their meanings. Time outside effortlessly lessens the power differential and inherent stress created by offices and assigned roles. We look more similar in nature.

Take pride in incorporating walking meetings and wall-less office hours as two tangible ways to bring the practice of *shinrin-yoku* (forest bathing) and its many benefits to your academic community. Space constraints during the pandemic forced institutions of higher education to reconsider or redefine teaching spaces. My institution created two outdoor classrooms and turned a traditional classroom into an open-concept learning space by keeping all access doors always open. Because students and faculty were pleased with the experiment, the practice will continue in the future, pending suitable weather.

The field of ecopsychology has long acknowledged that 120 minutes of weekly exposure to the outdoors optimizes health and psychological well-being. Incorporating nature and fresh air into academic life provides a robust investment in wellth, an inspirational model for students and staff who witness these interactions and supports sustainability in other areas.

Practice 4: Schedule two outside or walking meetings per week. Take this opportunity to get out of your comfort zone.

ESTABLISH A MOVEMENT PRACTICE

Most individuals associate the word "movement" with motion, action, development, change, flow, and flexibility. When asked to define the opposite of movement, one may think about idleness, repose, stagnation, rest, inactivity, or indifference. These insights are the results of group polling during a meeting of academic leaders at a national conference. Evidently, at the semantic level, the opposite of movement can seem as powerful as movement itself; in other words, it's good to move, but not moving can also make a strong statement. Leaders who strive to build consensus and advance the educational mission of their institutions figuratively move their institutions forward. For this specific practice, as in the discussion above, consider an expansive view of the word. First, one's mind turns to physical movement, but energy renewed through spiritual and social movement is also of considerable importance.

The natural sciences offer theories applicable to this wellness area. Inertia explains why objects stay at rest absent external pressure sources. Individuals are no different than objects in this regard. There needs to be considerable energy expended against us to get us to physically move. Similarly, a significant amount of psychic energy is required to move us spiritually. Considerable energy, education, humility, and self-realization must develop for someone to intentionally join social movements. The struggle to move is an exciting battle to fight, including, as the old adage notes, hills worth dying on. An academic leader who strives to act as supporter in chief must model a life that straddles different planes of movement.

For all movement practices, it's important to articulate an intention, a reason to get going. Consistency is key, so designate time to advance all three practices—physical, spiritual, and social. In a way, the physical movement practice is the easiest to promote as it can be broken into small increments of time and built into other activities. For example, use the restroom on a different floor. Balance on one foot while brushing your teeth. Stand up and pace the room each time you're on the phone. Limit scheduled meetings to either twenty-five or fifty minutes, and use transition time to physically move. Consider how your institution's strategic plan can contextualize spiritual and social movements and develop team metrics to advance those movement planes. Live a sense of agency when developing movement practices, and use the academic leadership team for community and support.

Practice 5: Intentionally set a movement practice that translates into increased efficiency at work and a happier lifestyle. Incorporate physical, spiritual, and social movement.

REEXAMINE SNACKS AND SLEEP

One point that the pandemic highlighted is that we don't need all those snacks. We can live without a candy jar and survive the meeting without donuts. Breaking bread together is a prime way to establish personal connections; but again, expand the conception of bread to include a piece of fruit, a hard-boiled egg, a couple of figs or dates, or a slice of cheese. Look to world cultural practices for ways to share nourishment and community. For example, the French paradox has been explained partially because they don't snack. Make water (from the tap, a water fountain, or sustainably packaged product) the drink of choice. A reconceptualization of snacks in the workplace will contribute to both wellth for workers and the institution's sustainability efforts. Intentional snacking contributes to financial savings and reduces use of disposable dinnerware.

Arianna Huffington makes people smile with the phrase, "Sleep your way to the top."[4] She means to encourage us to reexamine our relationship with sleep and to use quality and quantity of sleep as metrics in our assessment of personal success. Traditionally—nationally—slumber is prescribed for children and the aging, yet not often mentioned for working adults. My Spanish heritage contextualizes respect for sleep and acceptance of the nap. Once again, I urge you to expand your interpretation of snack and sleep practices through attention to global cultural customs.

Practice 6: Consider eliminating processed foods from the snack menu and instituting a ban on bottled or canned drinks. Prioritize sleep and consider a micronap.

CULTURALLY RESPONSIVE INTERACTIONS

Faculty members in educational fields are familiar with the concept of culturally responsive teaching (CRT). The basis of CRT is that the instructor should espouse positive perspectives, uphold high expectations, prioritize cultural context, engage in other-centeredness, and be a facilitator (versus leader) of all types of learning in the classroom. It's prudent for deans to expand these guidelines for classroom interactions to academic administration settings. Adoption of culturally responsive interactions allows the crafting of academic roles in cost-neutral ways to improve quality of life for all. It's also the right thing to do. An interesting project is for each team to engage in creating CRT-responsive metrics to be guiding principles in the evaluation of direct reports and supervisors.

A dean with the ability to see and promote the good in a project creates excitement and opportunities for the team, providing needed respite from the vicissitudes of life. Enacting the practices in this chapter fosters the development of powerful positive perspectives. Just as a teacher needs to expect high academic performance from students *and* provide the tools to deliver it, an academic administrator should include in periodic assessment a metric related to the availability of resources needed to complete a job. Industry speaks of "company culture," and higher education's culture should articulate and live acceptance and consideration of diverse viewpoints. Team conversations on institutional culture should precede assessment activities. The academic leadership pathway involves service to others; noting successful exercise of altruistic behaviors as part of personnel evaluations helps all to remember why they chose to be in higher-education administration. Summoning and discussing each team members' unique motivation for work builds team unity.

Practice 7: Contextualize culturally responsive interactions into your daily routines. Prioritize the tenets of CRT in operations within the leadership team and keep them in mind throughout the assessment cycle.

CONCLUSION

Lifelong vitality—the root of joy—is facilitated by securing an overarching purpose on the journey from health to wealth. A clearly defined sense of purpose and a commitment to celebrating joy in the small things in life can result in increased satisfaction both at home and at work. In embracing the practices explored above, it's important to remember that progress and attainment result from methodical practice. The journey from struggle to mastery of wellth isn't necessarily smooth. Use the rough times as chances to find inspiration and opportunities in challenges; build agency and mastery of good habits as tools to smooth the way.

Deans and other academic leaders may feel overwhelmed by pressures to embrace the practices outlined in this chapter in addition to solving the urgent issues that occupy their agendas. Physics tells us that energy is neither created nor lost but transformed. Yielding energy to these practices may feel daunting. Thankfully, these suggestions offer options and their implementation can be gradual. Consistency is everything. Small changes produce ripple effects and are additive in nature. A change in thought or behavior of 1 percent translates into a robust transformation. Two changes produce twice the modifications. Use the power of the 1 percent to enrich everyone's environment. Academic leaders should strive to spread joy as they advance the mission of their institution.

— *Takeaways* —

- When wellth is the guiding value of personal and professional operations in the workplace, mundane academic tasks are grounded in human connectivity and take on special meaning.
- The path to wellth is smoother when we act with the awareness that we are more alike than different.
- Live a sense of agency when developing movement practices, and use the academic leadership team for community and support.

• Efforts that amount even to 1 percent make a difference. They also grow and join with analogous endeavors to increase their power.

NOTES

1. The term "wellth"—found in the titles of self-help books, articles, apps, and websites—has been used in various forms for over a century, either as a combination of "wealth and health" or "wellness and health." For example, in the article "Money and Matrimony," (*Brooklyn Daily Eagle*, 11 November 1907), George Thomas Dowling wrote: "[Money] does not always make a man's condition well; many times ill. This is the meaning of the prayer for England's king, in the English Prayer Book, 'Grant him in health and wealth long to live.' The church is not on its knees uniting in its supplications that he may have more money, but greater well-being, greater well-th." The combination "wellness and health" was coined during the fitness craze of the 1980s.
2. For a definition of metta, see "Metta," *Yogapedia*, updated 26 November 2017, https://www.yogapedia.com/definition/7603/metta.
3. "The time present of things past is memory; the time present of things present is direct experience; the time present of things future is expectation." *Confessions by St. Augustine*, book 11, chapter 20, heading 26, https://faculty.uca.edu/rnovy/Augustine--On%20%20Time.htm.
4. See Ananta Ripa Ajmera, "Why Arianna Huffington Says 'Sleep Your Way to the Top' and 3 Proven Ways to Do So from Ayurveda," *Huffpost*, 22 April 2016, https://www.huffpost.com/entry/why-arianna-huffington-sa_b_9759076.

CHAPTER 23

Data-Informed Decision Making in Higher Education

PETE SKONER

The institutional decisions made by academic leaders affect student learning and success, faculty composition and effectiveness, and enrollment and financial stability. These decisions often include time constraints, involve competing requests for scarce resources, link multiple concepts with varying levels of complexity, require consideration of equity and inclusion, and are not always adequately justified.

The academic division is more successful with organizational and managerial decisions that result from a culture of planning, goal setting, assessment, analysis, and reflection. This chapter offers practical suggestions for academic leaders who seek to systematically and ethically measure, track, analyze, and use important data.

FOUNDATIONS OF DATA-INFORMED DECISION MAKING

Frederick Winslow Taylor was an early pioneer in using data for informed decisions. First among his elements of scientific management codified in 1915 is "Science, not rule of thumb."[1] Closer to the end of the twentieth century, W. Edwards Deming wrote in *Out of the Crisis* (1986), "Improve constantly and forever the system of production and service, to improve quality and productivity."[2] These applications of the scientific method and statistical processes were found mainly in industrial settings. Many of the same practices produce positive results when applied in service settings, including higher education.

In the popular book and movie *Hidden Figures*, scientist Katherine Johnson (1918–2020) displayed behaviors that effective academic leaders should emulate. Author Margot Lee Shetterly wrote of Johnson: "She listened closely to their [her supervisors'] instructions and, as was her habit, she asked questions. Not just questions designed to clarify the marching orders she had been given, but the kind of queries she had fired at her parents and teachers as a child, meant to broaden and deepen her understanding of how things work so she could create a more refined model of the world."[3]

Deans and other academic leaders are constantly facing decisions. Making them informed by accurate and timely data is ideal. When data are available, the main function of a leader is then to ask the right questions, as Katherine Johnson did. This interrogation leads to more effective operations and successful outcomes.

ADMISSIONS AND RECRUITMENT

Admissions and student recruitment require more time of academic leaders than in the past, at least for institutions in some sectors and geographical regions with increased competition for fewer traditional-aged college students. The dean's role in recruitment is to collaborate with the admissions office and the academic programs to establish enrollment projections for the annual recruitment cycle at the school, division, department, or program level. Projections should be developed using historical enrollment numbers from the most recent three to five years, along with moving averages, linear regression, or more complex modeling. Adjustment of model projections is based on societal trends, environmental scans of competitor programs, financial aid strategies, addition or closure of programs, and improvements to existing programs.

Several types of projections are possible depending on the purpose; these include expected, optimistic or best case, pessimistic or worst case, capacity, and break-even. After achieving consensus, enrollment goals need to be communicated clearly to everyone involved, along with defined expectations for each office and department. Many institutions use a customer relationship management (CRM) system for enrollment management functions. Deans and other academic leaders should receive summary reports from the system at regular intervals, perhaps weekly or monthly. These reports should show current-year progress in inquired, applied, accepted, and deposited students, compared to goals and to previous years. Robust systems would also provide dashboards to each manager, tickler messages when there are new students in any stage of an academic program, automated messages from deans or department chairs at ideal times to each potential student, on-demand reports, and summary yield and melt reports.

ACADEMIC PROGRAM REVIEW

Academic program review is important during normal times for continuous improvement and during turbulent times when resources are scarce. A comprehensive approach to measuring the effectiveness of each program should occur on a cyclical basis—possibly every three to five years. The process involves the department faculty completing a self-study that is reviewed by a cross-disciplinary committee, and results in a plan for the program moving forward. Options for the final recommendation include maintaining, enhancing, restructuring, or closing a program. Each factor affecting the decision about a program is assigned a percentage weight relative to its importance at each institution, rubrics are used for scoring, and numeric ratings are tabulated. For example, six factors include:

- Mission fit: the curricular or cocurricular features of the program that are consistent with the mission, vision, and strategic plan of the institution.
- External demand: new student enrollment, placement of graduates, career outlook from government or professional sources, and comparison to similar programs at peer institutions.
- Internal demand: number of major students, credits generated from all courses, and service courses provided for general education or other programs.
- Program quality, as indicated by student data (entering academic profiles, number of student publications or presentations, pass rates on

professional examinations, admittance rates to graduate or professional schools, employment and salary of program upon graduation); student learning data (scores on standardized disciplinary examinations, assessment processes and reports, and curricular improvements); curriculum data (program or specialized accreditation results, comparison to professional standards and peer institutions); faculty data (number, distribution within ranks, tenure status and percentages, turnover, terminal degrees, teaching effectiveness, grants, awards, scholarship, publications, and leadership in professional organizations); and facilities and equipment data (age, condition, currency, and appeal).

- Financial viability: student-to-faculty ratio, discount rate by program, tuition revenue generated, financial contribution amount and percentage, cost per student credit hour, and comparisons to other programs at the same institution and similar programs at other institutions.
- Opportunities for the future of the program, including planning process, curricular options, and capacity to improve or expand.

STUDENT RETENTION AND SATISFACTION

Student retention is improved through intentionality, analytics, and data-informed intervention. Predictive analytics based on the entering profiles of new students identify those at risk. Learning management systems (LMSs) are used to monitor, analyze, and report student behaviors. Tolerances are set to recognize outliers in student data, such as limited engagement in the course, excessive absenteeism, missing assignment submissions, and poor performance on graded assignments. System notifications are set to alert support staff, course faculty, academic advisors, or individual students. Faculty also submit early alerts when they notice changes in student behavior. Intervention comes from the course faculty or the student support staff.

Department chairs, other academic administrators, and support staff can have access to enter and view courses in the LMS to monitor specific students and entire courses. Dashboards conveniently display summary data for courses or instructors, and lists of specific students who may need attention. Georgia

State University is an example of a large, public institution that implemented processes to improve retention and graduation rates, especially for minority and underprepared students. Jean Dimeo notes:

> The institution's systems update student grades and records every night, and they review 800 risk factors for each of the 50,000 students on a continuous basis. . . . Based on system alerts, dozens of Georgia State advisers have held 200,000 meetings with at-risk students during the past five years. . . . The grand-scale efforts are achieving big dividends for the downtown Atlanta university whose student body is 60 percent low income and 60 percent minority, and whose learners are predominantly the first in their families to attend. . . . The overall efforts also have produced an additional $10 million per academic year in tuition and fees, because fewer students are dropping courses or leaving.[4]

With regard to student satisfaction, there are many sources and uses of data to consider, depending on the questions that arise. Many good questions surfaced during the COVID-19 pandemic. For example, most institutions asked students if online learning was effective or preferred. Google Forms, Microsoft Forms, and other similar applications enable one to quickly and efficiently survey large groups of individuals while maintaining anonymity. Some institutions conduct annual student satisfaction surveys. A worthwhile question to ask on almost any survey involves the Net Promoter Score (NPS); for example, "On a scale of 0–10 with 10 being most likely, how likely are you to recommend this institution to a friend, relative, or colleague?" The NPS score for the institution, or for a product or service, is calculated by subtracting the percentage of detractors (ratings of 0 to 6) from the percentage of promoters (ratings of 9 or 10), which can range from a low of −100 (if every customer is a detractor) to a high of 100 (if every customer is a promoter). NPS scores are described in materials available through the Qualtrics database.[5] Tracking metrics like the NPS and developing strategies for periodic evaluation over time will lead to continuous improvement.

CONSIDERATIONS OF EQUITY AND INCLUSION

Questions involving specific populations of students often emerge while reviewing data in educational systems, looking for gaps and outliers in outcomes, and planning for improvement. For example, in reviewing the retention of the entire student body, questions might arise about the retention of male students, first-generation students, or students of a specific race or ethnicity. Institutions respond by designing new systems or making improvements to support these special populations. Better support systems should lead to better outcomes for special populations and often benefit all students and the entire institution. Data collection and review are imperative for comparing outcomes before, during, and after system changes.

FACULTY PERFORMANCE

Faculty performance can be measured and improved through data. Each institution must agree on appropriate metrics, standardize data collection, report results so that faculty can compare themselves individually to institutional and professional norms, and then set goals for improvement. Student ratings of instruction are common, using a commercially available product or an instrument developed within the institution. These ratings provide quantitative data to compare averages from a specific faculty member or individual course to institutional averages. Commercial surveys provide additional references to averages from many institutions and by specific discipline. Equally important, the qualitative data from student comments are effective for review and reflection. Tracking the trends in student ratings over time ideally shows continual improvement.

Faculty performance is also measured through classroom observations and evaluation processes using rubrics for some level of standardization. Course-specific standardized student exams, such as those from the American Chemical Society, allow for comparison of student learning across specific faculty.[6] Some commercial products integrate with the LMS to track and compare frequency of course logins, timeliness of grading, and other measures of instructor interactions with students, especially relevant in online courses. Student grade distributions should be reported by faculty member, course, and department. Distributions can then be compared to institutional averages to identify outliers or student bottlenecks by quantifying the percentages of W, D, and F grades. Colleen Flaherty describes a model for assessing faculty performance in research through the use of bibliometrics, including paper counts, citation counts, and h-indexes.[7]

BUDGETS AND SPENDING

Spending compared to annual budgets can also be tracked effectively on dashboards. Tracking percentage of budget spent as the year progresses is helpful to prevent spending overages. In establishing budgets for future years, considering two or three years of actual spending and the previous year's budget informs reliable projections. George H. Brown and Del Doughty explore aspects of salaries and budgets in the following two chapters of this book.

CAPACITY FOR DATA-INFORMED DECISION MAKING

Academic leaders are typically experts in a field before advancing into leadership positions. Rising from certain disciplines, some leaders might already be prepared to manipulate data and make decisions informed by reliable information. Others should learn to value the potential of data systems and find institutional support for their development and use.

Many institutions employ trained data administrators to support all aspects of the university, including the academic enterprise. Titles for these positions include institutional researcher, data scientist or engineer, and business or systems analyst. These professionals typically have degrees in computer science, mathematics, science, one or more of the social sciences, or a related field. The software packages they use include Excel, SAS, Power BI, and Tableau. When there is a need for programming, the languages commonly used are Python or R.

These administrators can build data-gathering and -reporting systems, working collaboratively with the academic leaders who understand curriculum, students, faculty, and learning. The investment of time to reengineer processes for ideal data reporting can yield reports produced periodically or on demand in order to make the right decision at the right time. An individual faculty member, department chair, or dean can have convenient dashboards that display colorful, sophisticated, and powerful charts and tables to allow continuous monitoring of those key performance indicators (KPIs) that each institution or manager considers most important. Continuous review of numerical data, along with critical analysis, leads to identifying problems, trends, and opportunities.

When academic leaders don't have the personal expertise or the institutional support for analyzing data, they might assign faculty with release time to lead data collection and interpretation efforts. Or leaders can gain experience through professional organizations like ACAD (American Conference of Academic Deans) to provide discussions with peers. A third option is to contract with external consultants to build data systems to user specifications.

Whatever the case, deans without the competence or capacity for accessing data systems in order to make decisions are at a disadvantage compared to those who do. It is imperative in the current climate of higher education that resources are allocated in the ways most efficient for generating successful and sustainable results for both individual students and institutions.

BALANCING DATA AND EXPERIENCE

This chapter explores the reasons, methods, and outcomes necessary to inform decision making. Even the best data do not replace the experiences that people gain from years in academia. Typical academic leaders begin as faculty members teaching courses, engaging in scholarship, and serving their institution. They learn from colleagues and from practice, accept leadership roles within the faculty, and eventually accept part-time or full-time administrative appointments. They see decisions through the years that lead to positive results and others, in hindsight, that could have been more effective. Through all this, seasoned leaders develop an extensive knowledge base and intuition. The best expert systems should not replace the experienced decision maker but supplement and complement human abilities so that leaders make even better and more consistent decisions. Almost a decade ago, *MIT Sloan Management Review* asked: "Is there a perfect balance between experience versus data, [and] data versus experience?" The answer the authors provided is that "while an analytics equilibrium is determined, in part, by the individual manager's comfort level and experience with data, the organizational environment plays a significant role as well."[8]

Effective academic leaders are those who embrace a data culture while using personal and collective intuition—sometimes referred to in sports as the "eye test"—to affirm decisions, challenge findings by asking deeper questions, and continue discussions. Reviewing data often serves as the beginning point for more exploration and discussion. Involving colleagues in discussions on important data-informed decisions will capture the collective thinking of the group, lead to consensus, and result in optimal outcomes.

— *Takeaways* —

- Acquire the technical capacity to support the development, maintenance, and administration of robust data collection and reporting systems.
- Identify cycles for gathering, recording, and reporting the information needed for timely decisions. When data are unavailable for making an informed decision, gather the best data you can the first time, use that baseline data for future comparisons, and then improve on the process in successive cycles.
- Ensure that all academic decision makers have access to the necessary information in convenient formats. The goal is to provide the right information to the right people at the right time, while protecting individual privacy.
- Develop a culture of continuous review, reflection, inquiry, and improvement informed with data. When making decisions, always consider all students, including different races and ethnicities, socioeconomic levels, ages, and other student classifications.
- Make decisions and improvements based on data and institutional goals. Continue to monitor systems to close the loop.
- Celebrate successes as they occur.

NOTES

1. Frederick Winslow Taylor, *The Principles of Scientific Management* (New York: Harper and Brothers Publishers, 1915), 140.

2. W. Edwards Deming, *Out of the Crisis* (Cambridge: Massachusetts Institute of Technology, Center for Advanced Engineering Study, 1986), 23.

3. Margot Lee Shetterly, *Hidden Figures: The American Dream and the Untold Story of the Black Women Mathematicians Who Helped Win the Space Race* (New York: William Morrow, 2016), 178.

4. Jean Dimeo, "Data Dive," *Inside Higher Ed*, 19 July 2017, https://www.insidehighered.com /digital-learning/article/2017/07/19/georgia-state-improves-student-outcomes-data.

5. Qualtrics, "What Is NPS? Your Ultimate Guide to Net Promoter Score," *Qualtrics XM*, accessed 13 July 2021, https://www.qualtrics.com/experience-management/customer /net-promoter-score/.

6. "ACS Exams," American Chemical Society, Division of Chemical Education Examinations Institute, and University of Wisconsin Milwaukee, 2016, https://uwm.edu/acs -exams/.

7. Colleen Flaherty, "Academic 'Moneyball,'" *Inside Higher Ed*, 20 December 2016, https://www.insidehighered.com/news/2016/12/20/mit-professors-push-data-based -model-they-say-more-predictive-academics-future.

8. "Analytics and Intuition: Finding Equilibrium," *MIT Sloan Management Review*, 5 March 2013, https://sloanreview.mit.edu/article/analytics-and-intuition-finding -equilibrium/.

CHAPTER 24

Creating a Culture of Possibilities

Managing and Balancing Salaries across the College

GEORGE H. BROWN

Faculty and staff are the core of the academic enterprise. Instruction, research, advising, directing laboratories and studios, maintaining equipment, course scheduling, recruiting, enrollment management, assessment, and countless other activities central to serving students require dedicated faculty and staff. The most important job facing an academic dean is hiring and retaining an excellent college team to serve students and provide an educational experience that will transform their lives.

This chapter provides an overview of issues related to a dean's ability to manage and balance salaries across a college, including an examination of budgets and sources of funding, institutional policies and procedures, prevalent inequities, important data sources, and best practices for developing a prioritization plan.

BUDGETS AND SOURCES OF FUNDING

The most significant portion of college budgets covers faculty and staff salaries and benefits (the latter usually set as an additional percentage of salary). Most who assume a leadership role in higher education quickly learn that funding to facilitate the activities of a unit is limited. As Bright and Richards note, "In the realm of college finances and resources, several truisms prevail:

there are never enough resources to cover all or even most needs, there is much less flexibility in college budgets than any outsider could imagine, [and] the primary component of the recurring budget is salaries."[1]

While revenues, personnel lines, and time are finite, creativity is infinite, and an administrator's ability to work through limitations is a key attribute of success. Budgeting is a planning process in which creative problem solving is leveraged to achieve a balance between the needs of the unit and the availability of resources. To manage and balance salaries across a college, it's imperative that a dean invest time in fully understanding budgets, budgeting processes, the institution's culture of money management and expenditure, and the policies and procedures that govern spending, salary allocation, and personnel.

Public and private institutions differ significantly in the ways they function financially. Use of state funding is often restricted: some allocations are recurring, and others are tied to a fiscal year. Philanthropic support may be unrestricted or attached to an endowment where its use is determined by a donor agreement—possibly to fund a salary, in whole or in part, for a distinguished professor line or a director or chairperson position. Grant and foundation funding, which can be used for personnel if part of the proposal, may be used to buy out faculty time during an academic year or serve as extra compensation during summer months. If used for staff, grant funds may limit the duration of employment. Keep in mind that funding must be recurring if it is to support permanent personnel.

Institutions often have a cap on the maximum compensation a faculty or staff member can earn in a fiscal year, regardless of the funding source. There are always federal and state tax implications tied to salaries. The type of account to which funds are allocated may also add restrictions that limit fungibility. Depending on your institution, funding for exempt employees (such as faculty or administration) might not be usable for hiring hourly nonexempt staff who are eligible for overtime pay and hourly wages under the Fair Labor Standards Act.[2] It's best practice to fully understand all policies related to the use of budgets as well as those that guide personnel decisions. When setting salary levels, it's imperative to work closely with the human relations office, the provost, and the academic affairs budget officer.

GENDER AND RACIAL INEQUITIES IN COMPENSATION

In addition to understanding funding sources and policies that guide fiscal decision making, it's important to keep in mind that a budget, as Jim Wallis has noted, "is a moral statement of priorities. . . . It tells us, mathematically, what areas, issues, things, or *people* are most important to the creators of that budget, and which are least important."[3] Imperfect humans developed policies that reflected the perspectives, values, and prejudices of their society. Over time, racist, homophobic, and misogynistic thought was ingrained in many policies and practices, creating inequities in hiring procedures and salaries across higher education that, with effort, are currently being addressed. As Kendi observes: "Racially discriminatory policies have usually sprung from economic, political, and cultural self-interests, self-interests that are constantly changing. . . . Cultural professionals, including theologians, artists, scholars, and journalists, were seeking to advance their careers or cultures and have primarily created and defended discriminatory policies out of professional self-interest—not racist ideas."[4]

There are several potential inequities in managing and balancing salaries. For example, gender inequity is prevalent in higher education. In December 2020, the American Association of University Professors (AAUP) released a report analyzing data from the Integrated Postsecondary Education Data System (IPEDS) which found that even though women represent 50 percent of all faculty "[their] salaries . . . are approximately 81.2 percent of men's, with women earning $79,368 and men earning $97,738, on average"[5] The study also found that "full-time women faculty members remain concentrated in lower-ranked or no-rank positions"—adding more complexity to the gender pay gap.[6]

The IPEDS data also show that underrepresented minority individuals, those self-identified as Hispanic or Latinx, and Black or African American, "make up only 12.9 percent of full-time faculty members across the country, despite making up 32.6 percent of the U.S. population aged twenty-four to sixty-four."[7] These findings are echoed by Li and Koedel, who find that "Black, Hispanic, and female faculty are underrepresented relative to their U.S. population shares."[8] Their study also found that "Black and Hispanic faculty have significantly lower wages than White faculty, on the order of roughly \$10,000 to \$15,000 annually, or 8% to 12% of the average wage."[9]

SALARY COMPRESSION

In addition to gender and racial inequities in compensation, deans are also faced with salary compression that impacts senior faculty. Amy Stewart explains that salary compression occurs "when employees who have been in a job for a long time make less than new hires in the same position. . . . You see pay compression happen when starting salaries for new employees in a particular job title are set too close to the wages of your existing workers."[10]

To combat compression, institutions have traditionally allocated pay increases to coincide with promotions in rank. While the amount of the increase varies by institution, the assumption has been that between incremental increases, possible merit raises, and "bumps" with rank, salary compression should not be a significant issue. Unfortunately, annual and merit increases have been limited since 2008. The AAUP reported in its 2020 "Annual Report on the Economic Status of the Profession" that "among the 842 institutions that have participated in the survey from 2008–09 to 2019–20, average salaries for full-time faculty members have increased 1.0 percent since 2008–09 and less than 0.1 percent since 2015–16 after adjusting for inflation."[11] To put this in context, the US dollar has had an average inflation rate of 1.81 percent per year since 2008, producing a cumulative price increase of 26.19 percent.[12]

A CULTURE OF POSSIBILITIES

Personnel decisions, including salaries, impact human lives. Gender and racial salary gaps, salary compression, and limited annual and merit increases impact our ability to hire and retain excellent faculty and staff. By facing these challenges with careful fiscal management and thoughtful allocation, deans can directly address inequities present in salary distribution. But, as with many issues in higher education, solutions to complex issues require creativity, planning, and time.

Often in higher education, due to policy and limited resources, a culture of "no" prevails. "No, we can't fund this initiative. No, policy doesn't allow you to do that. No, we don't have funds to give you a raise." A culture of "no" leads to poor morale, disenfranchisement, low productivity, and poor retention of dynamic faculty whom the institution has invested time and resources into supporting.

I have found that a "culture of possibilities" helps to create transformational opportunities. A positive approach to resource allocation promotes a willingness to move the needle forward. At its foundation this commitment is predicated on the fact that we might not be able to do this today, but we can take steps toward realizing an objective and advancing a solution. This is not a false commitment. The world moves at the speed of trust. Making false promises for salary increases or other support, or kicking the can so far down the road it can't be seen or realized, will destroy your ability to lead. A culture of possibility is based on honest and transparent communication. Sometimes an initiative is simply impossible to realize: it doesn't fit with the mission or vision of the college, or it creates other inequities that impact the work of the faculty and staff. In these cases, honest conversation and creative thinking may lead to alternative choices that resolve inherent concerns while achieving an outcome similar to that originally proposed.

DATA-INFORMED DECISION MAKING

Having the data necessary to make informed decisions is critical to managing and balancing salaries. Beyond the factors related to budgets discussed above, productivity in terms of generated faculty teaching equivalent (FTE), student credit hour (SCH) generation, and assigned load (including service) are important data points to leverage in your decision-making process, especially when awarding merit increases. The office of institutional research should be able to help you gather this information.

You'll also need to access competitive salary data in developing a baseline for faculty salaries. The College and University Professional Association for Human Resources (CUPA-HR) publishes annual reports that contain current, reliable, and comprehensive salary, benefits, and workforce information.[13]

These data are aggregated by discipline through Classification of Instructional Program (CIP) codes, as well as by rank and tenure status. Important resources in determining appropriate salary ranges, these reports allow you to compare your current faculty salaries in relation to national ranges to see where differences exist. Again, it's important to understand how your institution uses CUPA data so you can interpret your findings in accordance with institutional processes and policies. For example, one institution may base salaries on median figures, whereas another strives to keep salaries around the seventy-fifth percentile.

PLANNING AND PRIORITIZATION

You have reviewed policies and procedures, explored salaries for disparities and compared them to national standards, and studied your budgets, including which sources of funding are available. The next step is to prioritize goals and implement your plan, depending on the source of funding, allocation, or reallocation. As Greg McKeown points out, "The word *priority* came into the English language in the 1400s. It was singular. It meant the very first or prior thing. It stayed singular for the next five hundred years. Only in the 1900s did we pluralize the term and start talking about priorities. Illogically, we reasoned that by changing the word we could bend reality."[14] Accepting that a priority is singular, we can ask ourselves a strategic question: "What *one thing*, when achieved, would fundamentally improve the balance of salaries across the college and move us forward?"[15] By focusing on the one action that will have the most significant impact on the college—revising curricula, building diversity and inclusion, nurturing innovation, or (as this chapter would suggest) balancing salaries—we can assure that the return on investment will be transformative. If you wish to encourage innovation, fund and reward innovation; if you wish to build diversity and inclusion, fund and reward faculty and staff who are engaged in diversity, equity, and inclusion (DEI) initiatives; if you wish to resolve pay inequities, focus your budget-planning process on equity and fairness and align resources to achieve that end. Without focus on a singular goal, progress will be limited because resources will be disbursed too broadly to have an impact.

A CASE STUDY: HYPOTHETICAL COLLEGE

To explore approaches to balancing budgets, the following case study is framed around a hypothetical college in a mid-sized state university. The dean of Hypothetical College completed a thorough analysis of the various data and, working with unit heads, developed a structured list of possible salary actions that allowed for phased implementation by taking advantage of incremental and merit increases, as well as retirements, reassignments, and rate reserve.

Table 24.1 represents salary allocations for Hypothetical College, the subject of our case study. In total, the college has an allocation of $6,825,340.00. The institution has authorized a 2 percent incremental increase, giving the dean $136,507.00 to allocate without restrictions. Incremental salary increases are based on a percentage of the total faculty salaries assigned to the college.

Based on this table, Hypothetical College has

- Twenty-five assistant professors with an average annual base salary of $55,000.00
- Forty-four associate professors with an average annual base salary of $61,485.00

TABLE 24.1.

Salary Allocations for Hypothetical College at State University

FACULTY	NO.	AVERAGE BASE	TOTAL SALARY	2% INCREASE	PRO RATA INCREASE
Assistant professors	25	$55,000	$1,375,000	$27,500	$1,100
Associate professors	44	$61,485	$2,705,340	$54,107	$1,230
Professors	30	$75,000	$2,250,000	$45,000	$1,500
Distinguished professors	5	$99,000	$495,000	$9,900	$2,000
TOTAL FACULTY	**104**		**$6,825,340**	**$136,507**	

- Thirty professors with an average annual base salary of $75,000.00
- Five distinguished professors with an average annual base salary of $99,000, exclusive of any endowments that support the positions

The dean could decide on an across-the-board increase of 2 percent for all eligible faculty, raising salaries for assistant professors by $1,100 over the nine-month contract, associate professors by about $1,200, and professors by $1,500 over the same period. But such a strategy treats all faculty the same and does nothing to solve inequities. Across-the-board increases don't allow the dean to reward faculty who advance the goals of the college, offer a financial incentive for those less engaged, or allow for corrective action on any salary gaps. Again, a budget is a moral document: how it's allocated communicates the priorities of the college.

The dean in our case study has made eliminating gender and racial pay gaps the salary priority the college will pursue—the *one thing* that would fundamentally improve the college and move it forward. Using the 2020 AAUP review of *IPEDS Data on Full-Time Women Faculty and Faculty of Color*, cited above, Table 24.2 aligns salaries according to faculty race and gender and identifies pay gaps represented in the IPEDS data. The table indicates that twenty-six associate professors earn above the average salary of $61,485, while eighteen faculty (three white males, eleven white females, two Black or Hispanic males, and two Black or Hispanic females) are paid less than that figure.

Because the dean has been part of the hiring process for all the assistant professors, establishing an equitable starting salary, and has found no major inequities in the salary at the professor rank, they have decided that $112,718 of the unrestricted salary increase would be used to make equity salary adjustments to this group of eighteen faculty, matching the current average salary for associate professors. This would leave approximately $23,889 for other salary priorities.

Implementing this broad equity adjustment means that some faculty will not receive a pay increase in this initiative. An open and transparent budget process, with a well-developed communication plan, is necessary to keep faculty informed and minimize resentment. Transparency and honest communication are key indicators in the college's moral compass and need to be in place before faculty see their paycheck stub. Explaining the full situation of

TABLE 24.2.

Salary Distribution and Gender and Racial Pay Gaps among
Associate Professors

FACULTY	NO.	SALARY	CUMULATIVE SALARY	GAP IN SALARY	CUMULATIVE GAP IN SALARY
White Males: Salary A	5	$67,000	$335,000		
White Males: Salary B	11	$65,000	$715,000		
White Males: Salary C	3	$54,416	$163,248	$7,069*	$21,207
White Females: Salary A	8	$65,000	$520,000		
White Females: Salary B	11	$54,404	$598,444	$7,081	$77,891
Black/Hispanic Males: Salary A	1	$67,000	$67,000		
Black/Hispanic Males: Salary B	2	$58,960	$117,920	$2,525	$5,050
Black/Hispanic Females: Salary A	1	$67,000	$67,000		
Black/Hispanic Females: Salary B	2	$57,200	$114,400	$4,285	$8,570
TOTALS	**44**		**$2,698,012**		**$112,718**

*$61,485 (average annual base salary of 44 associate professors) − 54,416 = $7,069.

salary inequities, showing the budget allocations without violating confidentiality, and presenting the goal of balancing salaries to eliminate gender and racial pay gaps with this incremental increase will go far in garnering the faculty's understanding and support.

The dean could also use merit increases to address salary gaps. These funds tend to be allocated based on defined criteria to reward exceptional faculty and staff. If the allocation guidelines allow it, extend a merit increase at the higher end of the allowable range to qualified faculty and staff who are also impacted by salary inequities. While this action may not eliminate all gaps, it's a corrective step that demonstrates a commitment to fairness and equity.

Retirements, reallocation, and rate reserve are additional ways the dean can address balancing salaries. As with financial issues, there are distinct differences in the ways institutions deal with replacing faculty and staff when they retire or leave the institution. If personnel lines and rate reserve (the difference between a senior faculty's salary at retirement or departure and the salary of the hired replacement) remains in the college, these funds can be pooled to serve personnel needs.

Imagine that two professors from Hypothetical College are retiring, one with a salary of $95,000 and the other at $75,000. The provost is allowing the college to fill these two vacant lines and maintain rate reserve. The dean plans to hire tenure-track assistant professors at $55,000 each. The total salary pool available is $170,000, with the new lines using $110,000. Because these are existing lines, benefits are in place, so there are no additional salary expenditures. This leaves $60,000 available in the college's rate reserve to reallocate to address wage gaps or resolve other personnel issues with new hires.

Depending on the institution, rate reserve can be escrowed to build up a needed pool to resolve more costly personnel issues. While escrowed, these funds could be used to hire temporary personnel. If your provost or president reclaims rate reserve, advocate for the funds by presenting a two-part plan that first details how the resources would be used to balance salaries, eliminate wage gaps, and strengthen programs and, secondly, defines the time frame needed for implementation. This plan demonstrates your leadership in retaining excellent faculty and staff and resolving salary issues before they escalate to institutional levels.

CONCLUSION

Read almost any book on leadership and invariably you'll find a section that highlights the importance of people in an organization's success. This is especially true in higher education, where engaged faculty and staff are vital in effecting positive change. I begin this chapter by noting that the most important job facing an academic dean is hiring and retaining excellent faculty and staff. Unfortunately, there are few leadership resources that highlight how to do this, leaving many deans to figure it out on their own. That was my experience. Learning how to reward hardworking faculty and staff, eliminate salary inequities, and fund innovation and DEI initiatives with limited financial resources kept me awake many nights and continues to do so with every new challenge. It's taxing to remain engaged with long-term goals—like managing and balancing salaries across your college—while a significant portion of your time is spent on immediate problems. A broader vision requires focus and determination.

I like to remind myself that I'm participating in an infinite game, one in which my job is to keep the long-term goal in play. The challenge immediately in front of me is just a challenge for today. But I have my eye on transforming the field for the future, so that my colleagues and I keep moving forward even in grueling times. We live in a culture of possibility. Academic leadership isn't easy, but it's very rewarding when we can be creative in solving problems, balancing the field by eliminating salary inequities, and supporting transformative innovation in our college through determined leadership.

— *Takeaways* —

- The most important job of an academic dean is hiring and retaining excellent faculty and staff to serve students and provide an educational experience that will transform their lives.
- While revenues, personnel lines, and time are finite, creativity is infinite and an administrator's ability to work through limitations is a key attribute of success.
- A budget is a moral document. Be aware of salary inequities, including gender and racial pay gaps and salary compression.
- Invest time in fully understanding budgets, budgeting processes, the institution's culture of money management and expenditure, and the policies and procedures that govern spending, salary allocation, and personnel.
- Work closely with the human relations office, the provost, and the academic affairs budget officer when making salary decisions.
- An open and transparent budget process with a well-developed communication plan is necessary to keep faculty informed of salary actions. Transparency needs to begin before faculty see their paycheck stub.

NOTES

1. David F. Bright and Mary P. Richards, *Academic Deanship: Individual Careers and Institutional Roles* (San Francisco: Jossey-Bass, 2001), 130.

2. "Wages and the Fair Labor Standards Act," United States Department of Labor, Wage and Hour Division, accessed 30 November 2021, https://www.dol.gov/agencies /whd/flsa.

3. Jim Wallis, "Truth That Bears Repeating: A Budget Is a Moral Document," *Sojourners*, 31 March 2017, paragraph 3, https://sojo.net/articles/truth-bears-repeating-budget -moral-document.

4. Ibram X. Kendi, *Stamped from the Beginning: The Definitive History of Racist Ideas in America* (New York: Nation Books, 2016), 9–10.

5. American Association of University Professors (AAUP), "Data Snapshot: Full-Time Women Faculty and Faculty of Color," 9 December 2020, 2, https://www.aaup.org /sites/default/files/Dec-2020_Data_Snapshot_Women_and_Faculty_of_Color.pdf

6. AAUP, 6.

7. AAUP, 3.

8. Diyi Li and Cory Koedel, "Representation and Salary Gaps by Race-Ethnicity and Gender at Selective Public Universities," *Educational Researcher* 46, no. 7 (2017): 343, https://doi.org/10.3102/0013189x17726535.

9. Li and Koedel, 348.

10. Amy Stewart, "What Is Pay Compression and How Do You Address It?" *PayScale*, 27 March 2021, paragraph 1, https://www.payscale.com/compensation-today/2020 /05/what-is-pay-compression-and-how-do-you-address-it.

11. "The Annual Report on the Economic Status of the Profession, 2019–20," American Association of University Professors, 5 May 2020, https://www.aaup.org/sites/default /files/2019-20_ARES.pdf.

12. See Ian Webster, "Inflation Calculator," US Official Inflation Data, Alioth Finance, updated 10 November 2021, https://www.officialdata.org/.

13. See publications prepared by the College and University Professional Association for Human Resources at https://www.cupahr.org/surveys/research-briefs/.

14. Greg McKeown, *Essentialism: The Disciplined Pursuit of Less* (New York: Random House, 2014), 16.

15. D. Mark McCoy, conversation with the author on strategic planning, 3 June 2021.

CHAPTER 25

The Line outside Your Door

Principles for Managing the College Budget

DEL DOUGHTY

Look at that line outside your door. It consists of people who want resources, namely, money from your office. One faculty member wants to attend a workshop in experiential learning. Another needs to hire a student worker to help him record a series of lectures. A third is there to ask if a small class can run in the summer. The lab coordinator wants to tell you that two of the hoods are broken and need repair. Standing right behind her is the director of admissions, who has a great idea for a recruiting campaign. Finally, there's a graduate student who wants to attend a conference in San Antonio next spring.

Those people are standing there because they, like everyone else, believe that you have more money at your disposal than you probably do. "The dean's office . . . the dean's office," they whisper to themselves and each other, "that's where all the money is."

Before you go out there to tell anyone in that queue anything regarding their requests, you would be well served to size up the modest resources you actually do possess. That's not something you can do by yourself, of course, nor anything you can do in a moment's notice, but since you're the one responsible for the accounts in your name, you need to be the one to initiate the process, and you need to operate from a few sound principles:

1. Find and manage resources.
2. Learn the mission statement.
3. Develop resources for managing resources.
4. Organize, but prepare for the unexpected.

For now, know that the line isn't going anywhere. Those folks will wait, and in any event the line will renew itself even if you answer everyone definitively this afternoon. Because everyone believes that you have more money than you actually do.

At times, you'll be tempted to look upon these people as annoyances. And some are. In time, you'll learn the ones who are always holding out a hand. But here you must fight the temptation to feel annoyed. Most of those in line have a legitimate point to make. They need resources to do the things that they're at the university to do. It's your job to find, distribute, and manage those resources. That is the first principle that you need to understand.

Consequently, the first move you need to make in this situation is to step out into the hallway and tell the people in line that you want to take a moment to get a good view of things before entertaining their requests and, they may rest assured, hearing them out thoroughly.

The people waiting in line want stuff. Whether they get what they want or not, they'll take comfort in a principled, informed decision on your part.

Now that you've bought yourself a little time, check your mission statement. Do you know it? Can you recite it, word for word? Can you paraphrase it two or three different ways? The answer to those questions should be a definitive "yes." As a dean, you should be your college's leading expert on mission and vision. Without a command of the mission, you're destined to be pecked to death by those requests out in the hallway. Then you'll have no money. The chief financial officer will send you an email with a red exclamation point beside it, and then the president's office will call. You'll worry. You'll lose sleep. You'll resent everyone, including yourself. After that, things might start to get really bad.

Learn the mission statement. That's the second principle. Beyond reciting it in front of a mirror, there are more interesting ways to do this. The first is to talk about it with people. Regularly ask others how they understand the mission. You might think that the words are right there in black-and-white and speak for themselves, but they do not. They're surrounded by oceans of white space and rivers of connotation.

If the word "scholarship" is part of your statement, ask the chemistry professor what that means to her next time you see her, and then ask the nursing professor, and then compare their answers. Better yet, when you talk to the nursing professor, tell her how the chemistry professor answered you, and see what she thinks about that.

This sounds silly, like it has nothing to do with money or budgets, but what's happening is that you have everyone thinking about the mission. If you have an old-timer on the faculty who was there when the mission statement was drafted, ask him why the framers used the word "scholarship" rather than "research," and whether the word "scholarship" was meant to include creative work in the arts as well.

The second way to learn the mission statement is to live it: "Become the living embodiment of the mission of the institution you serve." I took this advice years ago from a story about the sociologist David Riesman, and it has never failed me.[1]

You should take the very same approach to the strategic plan. Learn how to talk about it in such a way that a first-grader could comprehend it. When people start thinking in phrases like "SMART goals" and "continuous improvement" and "KPIs," they sometimes have the illusion of thinking rather than actually experiencing the plan. One is reminded of the saying often attributed to William James that "many people think that they are thinking when they are merely rearranging their prejudices." Beware.

Our third principle might be stated as "Don't go it alone. Develop resources, in the form of colleagues or software or books, to manage your resources." There are several points to make in this regard. First, an understanding of basic accounting terms goes a long way. If numbers aren't your strength, if Excel spreadsheets give you the hives, you need to do one of two things: get good and comfortable with numbers and spreadsheets or return to the faculty. I confess that I don't much care for spreadsheets myself—on aesthetic grounds alone, they're ugly. But I've invested time in learning how to use them, and it does help with the itching and swelling.

Second, you'll also be well served to learn how to use your institution's accounting software. At my current institution, we use a product called Canopy. It's fairly awful looking on a computer screen, but knowing how to use it means that you can find out things for yourself without waiting on others to tell you how much of the current fiscal year's funds are encumbered, how much actually spent, and what your account balances are.

Third, having a savvy budget specialist on hand is of great value. Hire someone with a knack for numbers and who enjoys delving into details; then, invest in that person's training and development. If you don't have the opportunity to hire someone in that role, find out who on your staff or faculty can fill it. College budgets, as part of the overall institutional budget, can be complex, and it helps to have someone nearby to talk to when fresh data appear. "Are you seeing what I'm seeing? What does this mean? Can that figure be right, or do you think that's a mistake?" These may be innocent-looking questions, but you would be unwise to handle them alone. Likewise, you will want someone around to solve problems and to help you navigate the rules that attach themselves to restricted accounts and to your institution's broader financial policies. Most of those are written down somewhere, even if the place runs on lore most of the time.

Fourth, no matter your disciplinary background, you as an academic will undoubtedly have an appreciation for research. It should not surprise you that the college budget, like all things, has a body of literature. You should explore it. You can get started easily enough by subscribing to trade newspapers, like the *Chronicle of Higher Education* and *Inside Higher Ed*, and scanning them for articles related to budgeting. Beyond that, there are a number of helpful books. My go-to is Dean Smith's *How University Budgets Work*.[2] Smith reviews and evaluates a handful of popular models (zero-based, formula-based, revenue-based, responsibility-centered), discusses the relation of the budget to the strategic plan, and explains implementation concepts such as underallocation, variance reports, and recapture.

The fourth principle is "Get organized, but expect surprises." In the course of the fiscal year, two key moments should get your attention. The first is the planning process or the actual making of your unit's annual budget. Again, although you may be the one leading or initiating the process, you can't do it alone, and you'd do well to take as inclusive an approach as possible. Do your best to make sure that everyone in your unit—regardless of rank, status, or background—has an opportunity to participate, review data, ask questions, and make requests. I have always liked the approach described in George Keller's *Transforming a College: The Story of a Little-Known College's Rise to National Distinction*.[3]

One way to ensure such broad participation is to develop and share a timeline that indicates who will do what and when. The timeline is a key driver. Make sure it begins far in advance of the fiscal year to allow ample time for requests, review, and revision. Drawing the timeline can be tricky because you'll likely find yourself working within three overlapping calendars (academic year, fiscal year, and calendar year). Ideally, the fiscal year will begin just ahead of the academic year, but often these calendar issues are beyond your control.

The beginning of the process should include a moment to look back at the previous year's financial performance, review mission statements and planning documents, and touch base with trends in enrollment, giving campaigns, and so forth. Particularly at the outset of the process, you may find it useful to implement planning forms or templates that help units think clearly and thoroughly about operations. Keep in mind that much of the work done in the trenches at this point is accomplished by those same people standing in the queue outside your door.

The second key moment in the budgeting process is the day when things fall apart—that is, the day that a crisis comes out of nowhere and threatens to upend your best-laid plans. No one knows when this day will arrive, and in some years it may not really happen at all, but you'd be foolish to pretend that it won't come to pass. For example, there might be a pandemic. Or fall enrollment might take a hit. Or the state legislature might tighten its purse strings in response to a natural disaster. Or all three. Contingency funds may offset some of the negative impact, but here you'll need to be calm, nimble, and transparent.

Let us now return to those folks in the hallway and invite them into our office. The faculty member who wants to attend a workshop in experiential learning will need about $2,500 to travel to San Francisco in August for training. As she describes the workshop's agenda and names off its "rock star" organizers and leaders, you can see that she is excited. And for good reason: the workshop does indeed look cool and exciting. And since experiential learning is part of the current strategic plan (Principle 2), you would like to say yes on the spot, but the fact is, it's late in the fiscal year, and this faculty member has already spent her allotted professional development funds. She knows this;

however, she also knows or believes that some other faculty members have not used all of their funds and so there must be some left over that she might claim. (This belief is common.) But in fact, the budget line for professional development is already running at 98 percent of costs, and spending $2,500 right now would put you over the line. What do you do? How do you respond?

An old proverb says that you'll be respected for the way that you say "no" and hated for the way that you say "yes." Thus, you'll want to affirm that the faculty member's excitement is warranted and laudable, then share the budget update. Describe the current financial position. At that point, if you do in fact think the program is worthwhile and exciting, you can agree to partial funding. You might encourage the faculty member to look at other offices, such as first-year experience, graduate research, or center for teaching and learning. After the faculty member thanks you and leaves, you can look elsewhere for funds (for example, you can see if there is anything to borrow from another operating account to supplement your initial offer), but there's no reason to do that on the spot and commit yourself to something that you will later regret.

The next person in line wants to hire a student worker. He's an older, tenured professor who assumes a certain sense of, uh, let us say "entitlement," which is perhaps why he doesn't go into a lot of detail other than to tell you it's something that he wants to do for his introductory survey courses. It's not a bad idea, and the professor is a good teacher. In this case, you know that you can't help the professor with his request, and you might say as much, but you can do something to help him (Principle 1). Find out exactly what he's trying to do, and why. Is the professor aware that the distance education committee has recently established a simple one-button recording studio for lecture capture? With an hour's worth of training, he might well handle the recording task himself. Or perhaps he only needs something as basic and lo-fi as a Zoom recording of a lecture, which he can do from his laptop. Being resourceful in this manner and connecting people to resources isn't a budgeting skill, per se, though it does help you get the most from your resources (Principles 1 and 3).

The lab coordinator then enters, fraught with worry about the malfunctioning hoods. Her department needs to be operable by the beginning of the semester, just weeks away (Principle 2—apart from any particular wording, running classes is what you do!). The cost will run around $3,500. She knows that she has already spent her current-year funds and is appealing to you for help. You know that you have $3,500 remaining in a contingency fund, which is just enough to solve the problem, but you had also been thinking about using some of that money to help the faculty member who wishes to attend the experiential learning workshop. Following Principle 3, which counsels you to learn the basics of accounting, you discover that you have two options. You might tell the lab coordinator to proceed with the repairs and pay for it using the contingency funds. However, you might also ask if the coordinator knows how the service company bills. If it provides an invoice after completing the work and gives you thirty days to pay, you may be able to pay from the next year's operating budget (though you may not, depending on the accounting rules—we're getting into the weeds on this one, but with more knowledge of how things work comes more options).

The professor who's asking for the small class to run tells you that the students really need it. If they can't get the class now, it will throw them off their degree plans and screw up their financial aid. He's right. Financial aid is complicated, and there's a lot wrong with the system that needs fixing, and of course you hate the bind that it puts students in sometimes, but here's the thing: the class has seven students currently enrolled, and the summer policy says that you need ten to let it run. You could just say that policy is policy and leave it at that. However, this question is worth thinking about because policies grow outdated. (Why is the policy ten? What is it based on? It's likely that no one knows the answers to those questions other than to say, "It's always been ten.")

First, you need to know your break-even point (Principle 3). Ask around about how to calculate that and you'll get varying responses. But you can't go wrong with some back-of-the-envelope heuristics. You need to know the cost of a credit hour and, more to the point, the cost that one in-state student will pay for this class. Let's say that's $1,000. Multiply by seven and you can see that the class will generate $7,000 in tuition. If you're at a state institution, you might also factor in formula funding. Perhaps that's $50 per credit hour per student. That adds another $1,050 for a total of $8,050. Now ask yourself how much it costs to run the class. What is the professor's salary? Let's say it breaks down to $10,000. Remember: you aren't in higher education to make profits for shareholders; you're in higher education because you believe in its mission, particularly the mission of your institution (hearkening back to Principle 2). At the same time, you can't afford to do things that are unsustainable, and understanding your breakeven will help you avoid doing that. In this case, running the class loses money. If the instructor happened to be a capable adjunct professor who earned, say, $2,500, things would look differently. The other thing to consider is the class itself. Is it a 100-level class that runs every semester? If so, the students can likely wait until it comes around again. Is it an elective? If it is, the students' advisors might be able to find a substitute.

Then the admissions guy comes barreling in with a bright idea. He's vibrating with enthusiasm. He wants to invite you to partner with him in putting on a series of luncheons with high school guidance counselors in three different cities! It will be fun! Enrollment will explode! It has worked elsewhere!

You will remain calm and ask, "Yes, but what will this cost me?"

"Nothing," he will say; "we're covering for the lunches. Check your calendar!"

"What about the travel?" Sniffing out hidden costs might be listed as a fifth principle, but really, it takes time to learn how to do this. He's mentioned some expensive cities—transportation and lodging costs could run upward of $2,000 or more if he's counting on you to cover that. That's not necessarily a lot, but these spontaneous expenses will nickel-and-dime you over a year's time and many of them will look stupid in hindsight. In the meantime, you'll still need to invest in mission-based or strategic priorities. So say no, say you'd love to but couldn't possibly. If he still thinks it's a good idea tomorrow, he'll likely return with a counteroffer to pay half. If that's the case, you might negotiate a little harder. You might, for instance, ask him to work a deal where you can target some strategic enrollment priorities.

At last comes the graduate student, young and full of fire. She's been working on a project that has found an audience at a regional conference, and you know from seeing her on other occasions that she really seems to be discovering her voice as a scholar. This conference is a big deal for her. You remember what that's like and really want to help but know that you're broke and you can't. There's nothing left in your pockets or under the sofa cushions. So you tell her to check with you tomorrow.

After she leaves, you stand up, walk down the hall, and take your place in line outside the provost's office. After all, that's where all the money is.

— *Takeaways* —

- As a dean, you're called to find, distribute, and manage resources effectively for your college.
- Get fluent in the mission and the strategic plan—doing so will keep you on course for good decisions.
- Don't go it alone—develop resources to manage resources. Learn the accounting system, stay current on rules and policies, develop a team of people with whom you can discuss data and reports.
- Get organized, but expect surprises.

NOTES

1. Robert Hendrickson, Jason Lane, James Harris, Richard Dorman, and Stan Ikenberry, *Academic Leadership and Governance in Higher Education: A Guide for Trustees, Leaders, and Aspiring Leaders of Two- and Four-Year Institutions* (Sterling, VA: Stylus, 2013), 7.
2. Dean O. Smith, *How University Budgets Work* (Baltimore: Johns Hopkins University Press, 2019).
3. George Keller, *Transforming a College: The Story of a Little-Known College's Rise to National Distinction* (Baltimore: Johns Hopkins University Press, 2004).

CHAPTER 26

The Role of the Academic Dean in Institutional and Specialized Accreditation Processes

ANN M. VENDRELY

Building a completely new degree program is an unusual way to start an academic career, but it's exactly what I did as a novice faculty member in 1998. At that time, I had prior experience as an administrator, but not in higher education. I had no idea how important it was to understand our specialized accreditation criteria and manage the relationship with the accreditation agency. We had a great team that spent many long days writing and rewriting documents, but we didn't have enough experience. Initially we were denied candidacy for our new program and placed on probation. A small team of faculty attended the accreditor's board meeting with additional documents and proposed changes. Finally, we met the requirements, so that students graduated from an accredited program and were able to move into professional careers.

Although it was a steep learning curve, I began to see the value that accreditation can bring, particularly because it's founded on peer review. This experience required that I quickly learn more about these processes. As I gained knowledge, I was invited to lead preparations for institutional accreditation, which expanded my role on campus and my understanding of other units. Later, I completed training to become a peer reviewer for our institutional accreditor.

This chapter presents some of what I've learned as an administrator working with accreditation for the institution and its specialized programs. While this content reflects my own experience and doesn't represent the perspective of any individual accreditation agency, I'll offer practical points about the accreditation process, such as preparing initial accreditation for new programs or institutions, accreditation reporting, working with sanctions, and ongoing evaluations. I also offer advice on how to lead your unit or campus through the process, including on-campus and virtual visits. I focus on institutional accreditation, but specialized accreditation uses similar processes.

BACKGROUND

Although often perceived as just another hoop to jump through, rather than a process that adds value, accreditation acknowledges that a college or university meets standards and encourages institutional excellence. It's a process led by peers, meaning that faculty, staff, and administrators work across the institution to apply the standards of the accrediting agency through self-assessment and peer review. The Council for Higher Education Accreditation notes, "Accreditation is review of the quality of higher education institutions and programs. In the United States, accreditation is a major way that students, families, government officials, and the press know that an institution or program provides a quality education."[1]

Seven geographically based accrediting agencies are private, nongovernmental organizations with professional staff whose purpose is to ensure quality education. Good standing with one of these agencies is required to receive federal funding, state funding, and tuition assistance for employees. As members in the accrediting agency, colleges and universities offer their support through payment of dues, participation in workshops and conferences, and provision of peer reviewers. The US Department of Education oversees the accreditation agencies.

In addition to the regional divisions, other specialized accreditors provide faith-based, career-oriented, and programmatic accreditation. In many other countries these duties are fulfilled by governmental agencies. Recent federal changes mean that these seven regional accreditors can now pursue

relationships with institutions outside their geographical boundaries; therefore, the preferred terminology of "institutional accreditation" is replacing
what used to be termed "regional accreditation." Further changes may follow
as these organizations seek to distinguish themselves and grow their membership beyond their geographic footprint.

Any institution accepting federal financial aid (Title IV funds) must be
accredited by one of the seven institutional (formerly regional) accreditors.
The dean plays an important role in meeting both institutional and specialized accreditation expectations. Much of this work occurs in the course of
supporting excellent academic programs but may also be a product of supporting programs with discipline-based accreditation and contributing to institutional accreditation processes.

THE DEAN'S ROLE

The dean's leadership in accreditation efforts includes preparing for reporting
and site visits, maintaining relationships with the accreditation staff, promoting best practices for assessment and improvement, and developing faculty
and staff to support these efforts. These responsibilities will vary based on
the campus size and organizational structure.

Each campus designates a point of contact for the accrediting agency
staff. The dean may not have direct contact but should be well informed
through conversations with the institutional liaison. Your institution should
communicate regularly with your accreditor when academic programs are
added or discontinued. Make sure you know who the point of contact for accreditation is and who is managing the annual updates on your campus.

Researchers have reported that Minority-Serving Institutions (MSIs) are
more likely to be cited for noncompliance and must develop institutional resilience for success with accreditation processes.[2] Institutional accreditation
was established before the development of special designations for MSIs, including Historically Black Colleges and Universities (HBCUs) and Hispanic-
Serving Institutions (HSIs). Precise reasons for the higher rate of citations are
unclear, but differences in mission, student populations, and resources could
account for some of the difference. Fernandez and Burnett's research found
that HSIs must practice "institutional resilience" as an adaptive process to

respond to reaccreditation. This involves developing inclusive structures, accepting small losses, and avoiding maladaptive tendencies.[3]

If you're directly involved in preparing accreditation documents or hosting a visit, you'll want to do your homework well in advance. Start with the criteria themselves. Where are they posted, and what guidelines are given for understanding them? Look for workshops or conferences hosted by the accreditation agency and read their monthly newsletters. Consultants are available to review documents before you submit them or prepare your campus for the visit. Much of this work can be done at a distance and for a reasonable fee.

INITIAL ACCREDITATION AND REPORTING

Initial accreditation for a new institution requires extensive documentation and an on-site visit. Becoming a candidate for accreditation follows a process similar to the one described later in this chapter for ongoing accreditation and can result in positive or negative outcomes.

In contrast, accreditation for a new academic program at an established institution has reporting requirements that depend on the degree of change and institutional status. For example, if the institution has prior approval for offering graduate programs, the process to add another one may be shorter than it was initially. Having a good relationship with staff at the institutional accreditor will facilitate these processes. They can suggest which of the forms and fees are required for the substantive changes your institution wants to make.

Accreditation requires a regular cycle for on-site visits, which occur every four to ten years. Your university will form a campus-wide committee to manage these visits and the additional reporting required. If the dean isn't on the committee, she should be kept apprised of the committee's work. Accreditation agencies are interested in the measurement of student success, the quality of learning, and return on investment (including cost and affordability). Accreditors look for evidence-based decision making that considers equity and inclusion outcomes.

Preparing the report involves creating a narrative to explain how your institution meets the criteria and then providing existing documents that support that argument. At one time, the documents for accreditation were long-flowing arguments with pictures and elaborate formatting, but not anymore. Digital processes make the documents shorter and more focused on the criteria. Some accreditors may still accept paper copies, but most have moved to online systems requiring universities to upload their narrative and supporting documents into a centralized website, which may involve a learning curve for mastering the software.

Often, there are limits on the number of words or pages that can be included. It's incumbent on the institution to present the best examples and most compelling arguments in a succinct way. A review team will read all of it; they appreciate clear and concise prose with relevant examples. If the evidence isn't clear, they have two options: dismiss your argument as not meeting the criteria or request that you provide additional information. Your campus-wide committee should be ready to respond to these requests for further information or risk being declared out of compliance with the criteria.

ACCREDITATION VISITS

After the report is filed, you may need to host a site visit to verify the evidence in your accreditation documents. The visit team will include faculty and staff from similar institutions with appropriate experience for evaluating your institution. To avoid any conflict of interest, the host institution has an opportunity to review the team members' credentials. The team will study all the materials prior to their arrival and use the campus visit to verify the accuracy of the report. They will consult a wide variety of people on campus and may specify a preferred order for the schedule. As they learn more about your institution, they may ask for additional examples and documents.

Your campus will designate one person to handle communication with the team chair. As you plan the visit, consider where the team members will stay (if in-person) and how they will get on and off campus. More important, you need to designate where meetings will take place and how to notify your university community. Some meetings will be open to all campus members, requiring a large gathering space, microphones, and speakers. Others will involve only one or two people and can be conducted in an office or conference room.

Members of the team may split up to meet with different groups during the course of the visit, so careful planning is needed. Be sure that the accreditors have time to travel between locations and address any mobility issues that team members may have. They may also request a private conference room, away from other meeting spaces, so they can consult with one another and review on-campus documents. It's usually a very full day or two while they conduct their visit. The campus liaison must check in regularly with the team to ensure that their questions are answered and additional materials provided.

In recent years, more visits have been held virtually, presenting a different set of challenges. Much of the schedule will be the same, with the accreditation team meeting with both large and small groups. Use of a video conferencing platform presents a key difference from in-person visits, however, as the right people need to be included for each meeting. A campus-designated host should ensure prompt start and end times, monitor meetings for appropriate behavior, and include scheduled breaks to allow everyone to step away from the screen for a while. The host should also track attendance for the visiting team so they can accurately document the participants in their report. Recording these meetings isn't permitted.

After the visit, the team has a specific timeline for preparing its report and sharing it with the institution. A draft is provided to administrative leaders for correction of "errors of fact." In this phase, the institution can't refute the conclusions, but can only make corrections to obvious errors such as incorrect titles or committee names. A final report is submitted to the institution summarizing the visit and responding to the criteria. The institution is given an opportunity to respond within a specified time. In some geographic regions, these reports are made public; in others, they remain private. The decisions about the institutional status are always publicly available. Maintaining compliance with the criteria is noted as fully accredited or reaffirmation of accreditation. Negative findings are also possible, which could result in sanctions, probation, or removal of accreditation. All of these processes involve additional steps.

NEGATIVE FINDINGS

An institution that doesn't comply with all the criteria for accreditation risks sanctions from the accrediting agency at different levels of severity, depending on the nature of the concerns. The first step might be a warning or notice. In this category, the institution doesn't meet all the criteria but has the capacity to make changes in a reasonable time to fully meet them. The next stage would be probation or show cause. In this category, several criteria are not met and corrective action is required within a specified time frame. Finally, accreditation can be withdrawn from an institution that fails to meet the corrective action within the specified time frame, or denied for an institution applying for initial accreditation.[4]

If the accrediting agency issues a sanction, there will be a clear timeline for returning to compliance. The institution will have an opportunity to respond to areas that are cited as not meeting the criteria, a process that begins with a written report and may be followed by testimony given in a hearing to a governing board. These are stressful situations; a representative of the visiting team may present their findings, and the institution is in attendance to respond. Decisions about accreditation status are generally made by a board, as designated by the agency. Those decisions are published on the agency's website and must also be published by the university.

SPECIALIZED ACCREDITATION

Interaction with specialized accreditation agencies is similar to that described above for institutional accreditation, as the two use similar processes. Differences include more specificity in the criteria that are related to the professional field or discipline, standards that are likely to be regularly updated. These criteria inform curriculum design and program review.

Specialized accreditation may require dedicated staffing, additional funding, or professional development unique to that department. These standards may thus require the dean to advocate for further staffing or facilities. The dean may also assist as programs revise their mission, student learning outcomes, or course sequences to meet accreditation criteria. The dean should be well informed about these criteria to advocate for the department with campus constituents and to mentor program leaders.

PROFESSIONAL DEVELOPMENT

After gaining experience with these processes on your own campus, you may consider participation as a peer reviewer. This important professional development opportunity for academic deans or department heads begins with an application process to review your qualifications and experiences. If accepted, you'll receive intense training on the standards for accreditation and the processes used by the accrediting organization. This training provides significant insight that you can immediately apply at your own institution because you will have a much better understanding of the criteria and how your campus meets them. After completing training, you'll be assigned to a team for a visit. Teams are usually a mix of experienced and novice members, so you can ask questions and learn from those who have more experience.

Institutions of higher education in the United States are remarkably varied in their organization, practices, and success. Each visit provides insights into how other institutions address the accreditation standards. Sometimes their practices meet the standards in a new way, other times they look similar to those at other institutions, and occasionally they don't meet the standards. Using that information, you write about what you found and hone your ability to apply the evidence to the standards. The best part of the process is forming new relationships with peers on the review team as you learn about their institutions and also share experiences of your own. You build a network of colleagues from across the country that become resources for future questions. Serving as a peer reviewer is time-consuming and challenging work, but I have found great value in it.

CONCLUSION

Accreditation is an important way the higher-education community serves itself and promotes quality. The academic dean has a significant role in assuring quality education through her normal work on curriculum development and on best practices in assessment, budgeting, and professional development for faculty and staff. Knowledge about specialized and institutional accreditation helps inform work toward educational quality and equitable outcomes. The dean can provide leadership for accreditation processes for new programs, ongoing compliance, visits, and sanctions. In addition, participation in accreditation processes can provide meaningful professional development for the dean and leaders at all levels.

Prior to accepting a faculty position, I worked as a manager in health care, so it isn't surprising that I gravitated toward an administrative role early in my career. Preparing documents, hosting a visit, and surviving the appeal process have honed my understanding of accreditation procedures. These experiences served as leadership development that helped me understand how to manage large, important projects. Working with accreditation has led me to greater administrative responsibility throughout my career, and I have found it to be fulfilling.

— *Takeaways* —

- Accreditation acknowledges institutional excellence through peer review processes.
- Deans can contribute to accreditation by organizing for reporting, which may include preparing documents and hosting visits.
- Promoting best practices in curriculum design, assessment of student learning, and faculty professional development contributes to accreditation success.
- For programs with specialized accreditation, deans encourage units to meet those specific requirements.
- Working with accreditation can serve as leadership development through an understanding of how to manage large, important projects.

NOTES

1. Council for Higher Education Accreditation, "CHEA- and USDE-Recognized Accrediting Organizations (as of December 2021)," https://chea.org/chea-and-usde

-recognized-accrediting-organizations. See also Council for Higher Education Accreditation, "About Higher Education Accreditation," https://chea.org/about-accreditation. This and other articles on the CHEA site inform much of the discussion in this chapter.

2. See Frank Fernandez and Christopher A. Burnett, "Considering the Need for Organizational Resilience at Hispanic-Serving Institutions: A Study of How Administrators Navigate Institutional Accreditation in Southern States," *International Journal of Qualitative Studies in Education* 33 (2020): 855–71.

3. Fernandez and Burnett, "Considering the Need for Organizational Resilience at Hispanic-Serving Institutions," esp. 864–65.

4. Congressional Research Service, "An Overview of Accreditation in Higher Education in the United States," CRS Reports, updated 23 March 2017, available at ERIC: Institute of Education Science, https://files.eric.ed.gov/fulltext/ED597874.pdf.

CHAPTER 27

Developing a Communication and Connection Plan for Success

FENG-LING JOHNSON

Effective communication is critical to a dean's success. Timely, clear, and consistent communication builds trust and strengthens relationships. A dean who is trusted can solve problems better, respond to emergencies faster, move initiatives forward with more support, rally their team to defuse a crisis, and achieve long-term success. Unfortunately, in the midst of myriad administrative demands, it's easy for a new dean to neglect the steps necessary for creating a comprehensive plan for effective communication or for building relationships within and outside the college. Having a plan enables deans and other academic leaders to systematically target and execute their communication events, build meaningful connections, and potentially raise their profile and refine their image in the community over time.

This chapter assists deans by identifying key constituents for communication and relationship building and by providing a framework for planning. It offers examples that can be modified to fit individual contexts.

KEY CONSTITUENTS FOR CONNECTION AND COMMUNICATION

Generally speaking, the key constituents for connection and communication can be grouped into four categories, though organizational structure varies from one institution to another. The examples below assume an academic dean in a typical public, four-year regional comprehensive university:

- *Upward relationships.* These may include the president, the president's cabinet members, the provost, vice presidents, and associate or assistant provosts or vice presidents. System administration fits into this category, though communication with system administrators is typically outside the scope of the dean or this chapter; however, a dean who serves on a system office committee may want to be intentional about communication with system committee members and cultivate those relationships.
- *Peer relationships.* These may include fellow academic deans, the dean of the library, the dean of students, and directors in student services (e.g., records and registration, financial aid, Title IX office, or offices of academic support services).
- *Direct-report relationships.* These may include department chairs, program coordinators, faculty, and academic staff in the dean's college.
- *Other relationships.* These may include administration and representatives in the collective bargaining units, student government officers, parents, alumni, the advancement officer, the alumni association officer, the college advisory board, a student advisory group, leaders of community organizations (e.g., local service clubs such as Rotary or Lion's Club, Chamber of Commerce, or workforce development groups), news media, the general public, colleagues at other institutions, colleagues from professional associations, and connections on social media such as LinkedIn.

A FRAMEWORK FOR BUILDING A COMPREHENSIVE COMMUNICATION AND CONNECTION PLAN

For a dean who is new to the institution, it's imperative to devote a period of time (e.g., the first two months) for meet-and-greet sessions where they can connect with key constituents. The goal of these meetings is to get acquainted, build connections, understand your colleagues' responsibilities, and establish common interests in potential areas of collaboration. Time invested in these meetings will be well rewarded with open doors for later conversations about mutual support and partnership. This applies to deans promoted from within as well, though the meet-and-greet opportunities would proceed with less introduction and formality and with more readiness for conversations on collaboration and partnership.

It's important that the new dean's plan include constituents in all four categories. A common pitfall for new administrators is the tendency to focus on only *one* of the categories in the first year and neglect the others, sometimes resulting in great cost to their success. For example, negative outcomes may result from focusing mainly on managing up (without intentional relationship building with peers or direct reports) or, conversely, focusing primarily on managing the direct reports (without sustained effort in building upward or peer relationships across campus). The key to success in communication and relationship building is to establish an effective, prioritized balance and implement it methodically.

A TEMPLATE FOR A COMPREHENSIVE PLAN

The template below provides a framework for articulating key questions: What, How, When, How Often, Who, and Why. In your work, include all four categories of constituents and distinguish ongoing regular interactions and communications from special-scenario communication and relationship building. Table 27.1 shows an ongoing connection and communication plan inside the dean's office, and table 27.2 presents aspects of broader communication.

In table 27.1, note that "How" refers to the medium of the communication: the event can be in-person, virtual, a combination of in-person and virtual; can be conducted via e-mail, e-mail list, or social media; can be an on-campus gathering; can be a newsletter, e-newsletter, or website news section; or can take the form of a presentation or town hall meeting. As for "When," it's important to think about the sequence of communications: Who needs advance communication among the stakeholders and constituents? What would a coordinated release of communication look like?

A SAMPLE FOR SPECIAL-SCENARIO CONNECTION
AND COMMUNICATION

I use the term "special scenarios" to refer to contexts that apply to some but not all deans, depending on their institutional circumstances. For example,

TABLE 27.1.

Ongoing Connection and Communication Plan

WHAT (MESSAGE)	HOW, WHEN, HOW OFTEN	WHO (AUDIENCE/ COMMUNICATOR)	WHY (PURPOSE)
Convocation college meeting	Beginning of the school year; once a semester or once a year	Dean (host), faculty and staff in the college	Launch the new school year; communicate about goals, priority initiatives, key data, and/or expectations; motivate and inspire
College leadership team meetings	Weekly or biweekly	Dean (host), department chairs, and/or directors	Provide updates, discuss and problem-solve departmental, programmatic, and college matters
One-on-one meetings	Weekly or biweekly	Dean and direct reports	Provide updates, discuss, and problem-solve issues in each department or program
Open house–style meeting (e.g., "Coffee with the Dean")	Monthly, quarterly, or once a semester	Dean (host), any faculty or staff members	Listen to concerns, build relationships, and promote team morale
Attending a department or staff meeting	As desired or appropriate	Dean (guest), department chair/ director (host), faculty and staff of a department or unit	Be accessible where the team is, learn about issues important to the team, etc.
Student advisory group meeting, if any	1–2 times per semester or per year	Dean (host), members of the student advisory group	Key updates on initiatives and programs; solicitation of feedback
Regular messages to the college community	Throughout the year; e-mail, newsletter, flyers	Dean to all or any groups within the college	To welcome students, faculty, and staff; recognize achievements; thank individuals; announce events, opportunities, and resources

TABLE 27.2.

Aspects of Broader Communication

WHAT	WHEN, HOW, AND HOW OFTEN	WHO	WHY
One-on-one meeting with the provost/vice-president (VP)	Weekly or biweekly	Dean and the provost/chief academic officer (CAO)	Updates, discussions
Deans Council	Weekly or biweekly	All academic deans, executive directors in academic affairs, associate/assistant provost or VP	Updates, discussions
Student government	Once per semester; more or less frequently as needed	Dean and student government leaders	Key updates on initiatives and programs; solicitation of feedback
Dean's advisory group meeting	Once per semester; more or less frequently as needed	Dean (host), dean's advisory group members (often from academic or local communities outside the university)	Key updates on initiatives and programs; solicitation of feedback
Other meetings	As needed	Advancement officers and potential donors, advocacy partners, community partners, etc.	Fund-raising, advocacy, community engagement, etc.

at universities where employees are organized in collective bargaining units, the dean may need to engage with union representatives on issues related to contractual and personnel matters. In this context, cultivating a positive, collaborative relationship with the union representatives is beneficial beyond the essential requirement of gaining an accurate understanding of union contracts. Other special scenarios may involve a unique initiative, policy change, new academic program, faculty or student accomplishment, or staffing change that requires the dean to communicate to pertinent university groups, and sometimes to communities outside the university.

A commonly practiced process for these scenarios adopts a concentric model, with the communication starting from the innermost circle and moving outward to the next circle and so forth. For example, it's common for a provost to share a new idea or initiative with the provost's council (or deans' council) to get members' reactions and thoughts. Deans are often able to anticipate potential objections or concerns that chairs and faculty might have. By considering the dean's feedback, the provost would be better able to tweak and frame the communication. Deans may then be charged with communicating the initiative to the chairs and directors for their feedback. After gathering input, the provost and deans may develop a consistent message, talking points, or fact sheets about the initiative to share with faculty, students, and any other pertinent groups.

As a dean considers a special communication scenario, it can be beneficial to follow a similar approach by first discussing the message with their leadership team, then tweaking and framing it based on feedback. Next, extend the process by including a student advisory group, the college faculty, or the college advisory board, thereby establishing a consistent message and talking points before wider communication to the university campus and beyond (via, e.g., press releases or other public communication). Keep in mind the key *Wh-* questions: Who needs to know? Who should the communication come from—the dean's office, the provost's office, or another office? What do people need to know and for what purpose? When should the communication be issued? Which medium is appropriate—e-mail, university e-newsletter, social media?

A SAMPLE SPECIAL-SCENARIO COMMUNICATION EVENT

The dean of academic administration oversees the Office of Student Advising, among other academic and student services. She has worked for two semesters with the vice-president of enrollment management, with the provost, and with academic deans to expand professional advising from first-year students only to first- and second-year students. In the implementation process, a communication plan needs to be put in place to ensure that everyone knows about the change and how it will impact them. What would this plan include?

- *Communication with professional advisors.* If professional advisors are engaged in this process, they will have many logistical questions in terms of timeline, location assignment, office privacy, advising caseload, work directions, effective date, and the like. How might the director of student advising be supported in this communication process with professional advisors?

- *Communication with students.* Students impacted by this change need to know who their advisors will be in the following year and where they can locate information about their advisor on the student portal. Who carries out the communication and through which medium?
- *Communication with faculty advisors who would be impacted.*
- *Communication with deans about information sent to students and faculty advisors.* Hold communication events with deans to coordinate implementation logistics.
- *Communication with faculty senate or faculty association, student government, the faculty as a whole, and the student body.*
- *Communication about website and material updates.* Who should communicate to whom and about what?

FURTHER CONSIDERATIONS

When developing and implementing a communication plan, in addition to identifying the purpose (why), speaker and audience (who communicates to whom), the message (what), medium (how), timing and sequencing (when), and frequency (how often), a wise dean would give careful thought to the location of the communication (where). For example, when communicating about a sensitive topic or information that could be difficult for a direct report, meeting in the direct report's office may better facilitate the communication because they would be more comfortable with and less threatened by a difficult conversation in their own office. This location also allows the dean to exit from the conversation smoothly, avoiding a potentially awkward situation of dismissing the direct report from the dean's office. Some situations may merit choosing a neutral meeting location—for example, at a café on campus—rather than either party's office. When deciding on the location for a communication, consider the power relationship of the two parties and the nature of the communication.

Another consideration concerns potential obstacles and possible responses. When dealing with a high-stakes or controversial communication event, it's helpful to consider barriers, opposing opinions, or concerns that others may have—and to be prepared to address them. It's beneficial to enlist colleagues who could be allies to support the idea from their perspectives or to help spread the message.

Some universities have well-developed institution-wide strategic communication plans. For example, the communications plan for Tufts University articulates the institution's purpose and scope, situation analysis, communication goals, key internal and external audiences, key messages, implementation activities, success metrics, communication functions and channels, and university and division communications contact information.[1] The key internal audience includes faculty, staff, students, trustees, and boards of advisors; and the key external constituencies include alumni, parents, prospective students, prospective faculty, prospective staff, donors and prospective donors, public and private funding agencies, public officials, host community residents, higher-education thought leaders, Tufts' competitors in higher education, news media, and campus visitors.

The "Strategic Communications Plan" at North Carolina State University was developed by a working group and advisory committee within the provost's office, "with input from stakeholders across NC State campus and guidance from University Communications" as "a road map [to guide] communications with the university community."[2] A comprehensive analysis highlights three main audiences: the "Primary Audience" ("Tier 1: Must have their support and ear"), the "Secondary Audience" ("Tier 2: Important, but not primary"), and "Other Categories" ("Tier 3: Nice to have"). A matrix for each includes the following considerations: audience description, desired behaviors, actions or thoughts, current mindset and level of engagement, barriers to communication, where audience members access information, and messaging themes.[3] A quick online search will yield a number of additional, varied university communication plans.

Finally, an academic administrator's communication plan can also involve supporting their colleagues inside or outside their institution, resulting in strengthened relationships. Writing in *Higher Ed Jobs*, Justin Zackal, communication specialist at Slippery Rock University, recommends these five communication strategies:

- "Lift Up a Stranger on Monday." Commend someone on an achievement or express appreciation for something they did. The positive vibes will make you feel good, make the other person feel good, and lead to future collaborative opportunities.
- "Check Up on Campus Events on Tuesday." "Break the chain of emails with an email that invites someone to an in-person event or commits you to attending an event." This can "improve your mood, expand your social network, and spark creativity."
- "Bump Up a Dormant Relationship on Wednesday." Check in with people and share a link to an article of common interest.
- "Sum Up Your Week for Your Boss on Thursday." Sending your supervisor a weekly update reminds them and yourself of your record of progress and accomplishment.
- "Start Up the Next Week on Friday." Email yourself a note about items to work on Monday morning and a note of encouragement for your own well-being.[4]

CONCLUSION

Deans who identify their collegial networks inside and outside the college and institution, develop plans for communication and relationship building, and implement those plans are more likely to have well-functioning teams, strong collaborative peer colleagues, supportive supervisors, and a well-connected professional network. Should a new dean inherit a dysfunctional team, it's imperative to create and implement a comprehensive plan for communication and relationship and team building.

Some of the best advice I have received from strong and accomplished administrators could be summarized as "You've got to have the right structure, have the right people in the right positions, and take care of those people. Once you have a healthy, well-functioning team, your initiatives and projects will succeed. Without it, they will not." A new dean will want to get to know their team members and assess the team's effectiveness and culture. If the team is not functioning well, then take time to build trust, right the structure, and cultivate a respectful and collaborative culture. This is hard, sometimes painful work but is absolutely necessary. Honest conversations about successes, challenges, struggles, and needed resources can take place through a variety of meeting styles, such as one on one, small group, department level, all chairs, and open-house events (e.g., tea, coffee, or lunches with the dean). This investment will pay great dividends for future cooperation and success.

— *Takeaways* —

- The four key constituents of communication are upward relationships, peer relationships, direct-report relationships, and other relationships.
- Consider the What, How, When, How Often, Who, and Why of communications.
- Give careful thought to the location of the communication event, taking into consideration the power relationship of the parties involved and the nature of the event. When communicating about a sensitive or difficult topic or information, choose a location that can best support both parties.
- Distinguish ongoing regular interactions and communications from special-scenario communications and relationship building.
- Secure the right structure, the right people in the right positions, and take care of them. Once you have a healthy, well-functioning team, your initiatives and projects will succeed.

NOTES

1. "Tufts University Communications Planning Guide," Tufts University (Medford, MA), accessed 16 December 2021, https://universityrelations.tufts.edu/wp-content/uploads/University-Communications-Plan_04-02-14_FINAL1.pdf.
2. "Strategic Communications Plan: Office of the Executive Vice Chancellor and Provost," North Carolina State University, accessed 28 June 2021, https://university-communications.ncsu.edu/wp-content/uploads/2016/11/FULL_PLAN_FINAL_MAY.pdf.
3. "Strategic Communications Plan."
4. Justin Zackal, "Send These Five Weekly Emails to Advance Your Career," *LinkedIn*, accessed 16 July 2021, https://www.higheredjobs.com/Articles/articleDisplay.cfm?ID=2717#.YLFTz-YqE6s.linkedin.

CHAPTER 28

Thriving as an Associate Dean

A Life-Cycle View

JAMES M. SLOAT

Associate deans answer a noble calling, albeit one that is often unnoticed.[1] They lead from a distinctly in-between position: structurally between the faculty and the administration; functionally between academic affairs and other administrative offices; and temporally between a faculty career and a senior-level administrative career. This chapter offers observations and suggestions designed to clarify both the job itself and the transitions into and out of the role.[2] This counsel appears in life-cycle form: entering the role, thriving in the ongoing work, and planning for your future as you leave the position.

ENTERING THE ROLE

For many people, entering an associate deanship can be among their most challenging professional moves.[3] Many other academic transitions appear to be more natural: from student to faculty to chair. Each of these stages occurs in the context of one's discipline and department, with a common vocabulary and with a defined set of responsibilities—such as scholarship, teaching, and service—that draws on prior expertise. In contrast, the move to an associate deanship can be unsettling, particularly if colleagues, responsibilities, and vocabulary change and you have limited previous experience in administration.

New associate deans may experience a recurrence of the imposter syndrome, which they may have encountered as junior faculty. They are trusted with significant responsibilities, often without formal training or orientation. At the outset, it can be helpful to know that you were *selected* for the position. Deans make these appointments intentionally—knowing that their own success will depend in part on the effectiveness of their associate dean(s). While you may have a sense of the skills you bring to the position, it may be worthwhile to ask your dean what they hope you will bring to this office. Their response may illuminate your forthcoming work. For example, they might say that your experience with departmental assessment will be helpful in an upcoming reaccreditation. Or they might have picked you for your understanding of the interpersonal dynamics of the social sciences departments. In either case, be assured that your appointment was by design and that this design can give specific direction to your work.

The transition from faculty member to administrator can be daunting. Many faculty value their autonomy and freedom. Some attach moral significance to their faculty work. As a result, you might be tempted to retain your faculty identity as long as possible. Resist this urge. Make the full jump—with both feet. Acknowledge and embrace your new identity as an administrator. While you need not abandon your soul in the process, you'll have to accept that your position and work have changed in several ways. You now have a "boss," perhaps for the first time in your career. Since you're serving at the pleasure of the dean, one of your central responsibilities is to make your boss look good by doing excellent work. Some of the assignments that you receive may not be your preference. As your calendar fills with meetings and appointments scheduled by others, your workday will likely be less flexible than it was as a faculty member: 8:00 a.m. and 4:00 p.m. may be regular meeting times. Since evening work may prove necessary, your experience with late-night grading may serve you well. Institutional "breaks" will be times to work on projects with a reduced schedule of regular meetings. Accept these new realities with grace rather than resentment.

Associate deans must develop a broader, *institutional* perspective. You'll be engaging a wider array of departments, disciplines, and issues. Though trained as a philosopher, you may find yourself working with statisticians on an institutional agreement about networked data services. In short, you'll be managing beyond your expertise—something that may be quite different from your previous work. In such cases, you'll be developing a new, multifaceted expertise: hearing, understanding, exploring, balancing, and prioritizing competing needs in a context of limited resources. Learning how to ask valuable questions, hear multiple perspectives, understand colleagues' needs and constraints, and unveil hidden presumptions will serve you throughout your career. In this way, associate deans are in the position to translate the institution's needs and constraints to faculty colleagues who imagine that "surely the institution can afford this—after all, look at the size of the budget." An emerging institutional perspective, combined with careful attention to what others share, will position you to make informed and equitable recommendations.

Associate deans have less power than the typical faculty member might suspect. We're rarely the "deciders" of important questions and seldom have control over significant budgetary levers. Our power (or influence) is often indirect. Having heard and understood many competing claims, we can "frame up" the essential choices for the dean. We also have greater access to information and decision makers. Consequently, we can gracefully offer thoughts, ideas, and suggestions that might inform bigger decisions. As translators, we can help resolve conflict by "discovering" common ground that was previously invisible or by proposing options for compromise that were unexplored. This indirect power is real—and should be exercised with wisdom and judgment.

When moving into the new neighborhood of administrative work, you will encounter a whole new set of colleagues who may have been invisible in your faculty role. Administrative staff at all levels become essential to your new duties. While most of these colleagues may not share an academic background, they've been working diligently in support of the institution's mission. To be sure, some colleagues will prove more cooperative than others, perhaps in surprising ways. When moving into a new position, there's great wisdom in taking the time to meet your colleagues, hear their stories, understand their work, and resist the temptation to tell them how to improve their office. Respect these colleagues; they know a great deal and can be very effective allies, even friends, in your shared efforts.

THRIVING IN THE WORK

Often, the on-ramp to an associate deanship is perilously short. It can be like merging onto a superhighway of rapidly moving colleagues, even while learning the features and limitations of the new position. As a result, you may find yourself very quickly immersed in projects, policies, processes, meetings, and decisions. It can feel overwhelming. The good news, though, is that you can draw on wisdom gained from your experience as a faculty member.

Much of an associate dean's work involves academic project management. You might manage an array of different projects which may have no connection to one another. All of them will need careful management so that you can draw on available information and dedicated people to reach effective decisions that advance the institution's mission. In facing this broad array of projects, it can be helpful to ask some diagnostic questions:

What is the problem we're trying to solve or the good we're trying to cultivate?

What is the institutional history on this issue?

What is the life cycle of this project? (Are you joining at the beginning, midstream, or near the end?)

What is my role in this project—leader, representing partner, facilitator?

Who should be involved, informed, consulted, reported to?

How will I know that the project is done? How can the effects be known and assessed?

The answers to these questions can help shape the ways you engage the work.

Associate deans also serve as the administrative contact for a variety of different institutional policies and processes. These may be familiar or new; clearly articulated or vague; sensible or puzzling. The first step is to learn policies and processes by taking the time to read a variety of handbooks (faculty, chairs, staff, student). While the prose may not elevate your soul, reading policies in context can reveal the underlying logic. When people turn to you with policy questions, your knowledge will allow you both to answer the question directly and to identify the source of the policy (for example, page 37 of the faculty handbook). This approach reminds faculty that they already have direct access to the policy in question, without irritating them by refusing to provide an answer to a direct question.

From time to time, you may be called upon to help define new policies or revise outdated ones. Policies have several important functions: they protect the institution and the community; clarify the "good behavior" that enables people to thrive; allow the institution to intervene in those (we hope, rare) cases when people are behaving poorly; promote fairness and equity by ensuring that analogous cases are treated similarly; and enhance efficiency by creating smooth pathways for common activities or decisions. In addition, an effective policy is

Clear. Everyone (especially those for whom it's unfamiliar) should be able to understand what the policy means.

Modest. You need not address every possible outcome; a more modest framing recognizes that circumstances may change.

Consistent. Similar cases should be treated similarly; be particularly mindful of any systemic advantages or disadvantages that might emerge from the policy.

Flexible. The policy should be adaptable to unusual circumstances without requiring an exception; it should resolve the significant majority of cases while preserving the opportunity for situational discretion.

Timely and timeless. The policy should address the current issue but still be helpful in the future.

Over time, effective policies help to shape an institutional culture in which people can work together both gracefully and confidently.

You will need to carefully consider your approach to meetings. If you use them well, meetings can be effective and not unpleasant. A good meeting saves everyone time because it brings together the critical people and essential perspectives necessary to address an issue. As you craft the agenda, it may help to think in terms of questions, tasks, and choices rather than topics. While general discussion can be illuminating, it can mushroom into soapbox diatribes or interminable detours. Many people struggle to paint effectively on a blank canvas. Associate deans can provide questions and assignments that allow group work to be done productively during the meeting itself. For example:

We've been working to clarify the differences between different faculty categories. Today, we'll be focusing on three questions about visiting assistant professors: (1) Should they have service responsibilities beyond their department? (2) Should they have access to institutional resources (like course development grants) beyond their department? (3) Should they be included in departmental curriculum revision efforts?

While *decisions* can effectively be made in meetings, *language* is often best distilled and crafted afterward. Associate deans can offer this valuable service. During the meeting, it can be difficult for the group to track and draft the discussion into workable policy language. By offering to manage the language and documents, an associate dean liberates colleagues to fully engage the discussion. Also, this approach ensures that formal language has a consistent voice throughout.

As part of their in-between role, associate deans often field concerns, complaints, and petitions from faculty who are dissatisfied with a policy, decision, or process. While such moments can feel uncomfortable, they also represent opportunities to engage positively rather than defensively. As a member of the dean's team, remember to represent the office and the institution in these conversations (even if you're personally ambivalent about the dean's decision). Listen to your colleagues to hear both specific concerns and underlying motivations; you will want to relay them accurately to the dean. Assume the best in your colleagues, and look to articulate shared values as a basis for a hopeful resolution.

As part of your work, some foundational talking points may smooth the way:

- "Thank you." Appreciation matters.
- "I'm really sorry that you've experienced this frustration." Empathy is critical   especially when other resolutions may not be possible.
- "I hear what you're saying; can I think about it and get back to you?" Reflection can sometimes prevent mistakes.
- "What do you think would be helpful in this situation?" Our colleagues may identify workable solutions that we don't anticipate.

- "At this point," or "Currently," or "Moving forward. . . ." Timing makes a difference, and future possibilities may be more attractive. It's rarely helpful to relitigate past actions or decisions.
- "Other colleagues see this question or issue differently." or "As it turns out. . . ." Colleagues can be adamant about their own views without being aware of other perspectives or conflicting evidence.

The associate dean's in-between position on projects and policies requires strong translation skills. We serve as important bridges for mutual understanding between faculty and senior administrators. At times, we help faculty colleagues understand broader institutional needs; at other times, we alert senior administrators to important faculty concerns. Clear and open communication in this work can build trust on both sides of the bridge.

PLANNING FOR YOUR FUTURE

Few (if any) people aspire to full-time careers as associate deans. Most often, an associate deanship is an important but temporary stage in a career. During this stage, though, you may find yourself fully extended—and without any evident time to think about your future plans. As a result, you might reach the end of your term without a ready plan for the next step.

Associate deans typically follow two main paths after their service: returning to faculty positions or seeking other administrative positions within the institution or elsewhere. The associate dean experience can clarify these future aspirations. Some discover afresh their love for teaching, scholarship, and the flexibility and autonomy of faculty life. Others have their appetite whetted in the dean's office and are eager to do further administrative work.

Since you might not fully know your future plans when entering an associate deanship, you may wish to take steps to enhance your options, including the following:

- Preserve your connection to your department. While you'll not be able to function like a full member of the unit, you may be able to continue relationships over occasional coffee. At the very least, you should continue to pay attention to developments (e.g., personnel, curricular changes) in your home department.

- Preserve your connection to your discipline. While you'll be busy with administrative work, you may be able to engage your discipline by reading abstracts or reviews and attending occasional meetings in your expertise, perhaps in alternate years. With a little bit of luck, you may find that the additional distance from your field gives you a helpful perspective on the broader trends and possibilities for future scholarship.

- Build an *internal* administrative network. Cultivate relationships with senior administrators at your institution. By understanding the challenges facing other parts of the institution, you'll not only function more effectively in your current work but also develop the nuanced understanding that will be essential should you seek a higher position.

- Build an *external* administrative network. Associate deans can work in isolation. Our successes are hidden, and we may not have safe venues for venting the frustrations that occur. Associate deans at other institutions can often provide perspective, commiseration, and helpful suggestions. Seek out these relationships, whether in cross-institutional collaborations or through individual outreach. Organizations such as the American Conference of Academic Deans (ACAD) can help you meet other associate deans as well as deans or provosts. A broad network beyond your institution can be invaluable when considering your options, identifying new opportunities, and pursuing other positions.

- Broaden your knowledge and vocabulary. Each discipline has terms that distill important developments and concepts. Administrative work is no different. Daily review of publications like *Inside Higher Ed* or the *Chronicle of Higher Education* will keep you abreast of current developments. Annual meetings of ACAD, the Council of Colleges of Arts and Sciences (CCAS), or the Association of American Colleges and Universities (AAC&U) can be efficient ways to gain broad exposure to the ideas and strategies that others are deploying effectively. These ideas may not only prove helpful in your current work but might also sharpen your vision and make you a stronger candidate for other positions.

As you pursue these relationships and networks, you'll likely gain greater clarity about your future aspirations. Trusted peers, mentors, close friends, and family all play their part in helping you discover and refine your future paths. To be sure, a clear aspiration does not ensure success along that path; however, strong networks, clear vision, and relevant experience will aid you in your quest.

CONCLUSION

Serving as an associate dean is a distinct and noble calling. Associate deans contribute significantly to the educational mission of their institution, often by cultivating the conditions in which others (faculty, students, and staff) can do their best work. In a relatively short period of time as an associate dean, you can help transform your institution by turning vision and ideas into action—project by project, policy by policy. Welcome to this calling. May you find the work inspiring.

— *Takeaways* —

- Make the full jump into administration. Embrace the challenges and opportunities of this new job.
- Pursue sustainable, common-ground solutions in projects and policies. Listen well to understand others' goals and work collaboratively for successful outcomes.
- Be a positive translator. Help bridge the divide between faculty and administration by facilitating mutual understanding.
- Build robust networks and relationships both inside and beyond your institution. This is human work; good relationships can make it humane.

NOTES

1. For the reader's convenience, I use the title "associate dean" as a proxy for the full range of titles (e.g., assistant dean, associate dean, assistant provost, associate provost, associate vice-president for academic affairs) that report to the dean or provost.

2. As with any advice, the particular salience depends on (and should be adapted to) one's own situation, skills, and temperament.
3. This article focuses on the transition from faculty to associate dean. Some associate deans have previously served in administrative roles (such as directors or chairs). While some of the examples and illustrations may prove unique, many of the ideas and principles should still apply.

PART VI

Leadership
and the Units

CHAPTER 29

Department Chair Development and Mentoring

JAMIE L. MULLANEY AND ELAINE MEYER-LEE

The literature on leadership in higher education is clear on one important message: "Department chairs matter."[1] As most deans know, chairs hold the potential to serve as change agents by leading academic initiatives, motivating faculty and fostering an environment where they can showcase their strengths and talents, and inspiring teamwork and collaboration through democratic leadership.[2] As Karen Brinkley-Etzkorn and India Lane note, chairs play a critical role now more than ever, in "an age of increased criticism, constrained resources, and a changing educational landscape in terms of increased institutional competition, the student population, and faculty and tenure issues."[3]

Yet it is hard to ignore another glaring takeaway from the research into the experiences of department chairs: many enter the role largely untrained and, once there, are often unsupported. Unlike other positions within academia, the chair role is often dutifully accepted as an obligation rather than purposefully sought. This chapter reviews some of the challenges of this role and suggests strategies for deans to use in mentoring these leaders. Deans who implement structures that support unit leaders not only shift the narrative of what it means to serve as a department chair but also alleviate the chronic issue of "amateur administration."[4]

CHALLENGES OF SERVING AS CHAIR

To understand the challenges of successful chair development, consider various metaphors that focus on perceived negative aspects of the job. Metaphors pertaining to entry into the position stress the undesirability of the role, such as a game of musical chairs in which faculty scramble not to be the one left standing.[5] Indeed, some faculty become chairs as a result of a rotational schedule or a leadership vacancy.[6] In one of our own experiences, members of a program jokingly use the shorthand "Stick!" when referring to how the next chair is determined—conjuring images of tenured relay runners finishing their lap and eagerly passing the baton to the newly tenured faculty rounding the track. In an episode of the popular TV series *CSI* (crime scene investigation), a dean is murdered and the main suspects are rival faculty vying to be chair. Clearly, the scriptwriters hadn't done their research!

Another metaphor for serving as chair is "whitewater rafting without a life jacket or knowing how to swim."[7] This ominous image highlights the dearth of tools chairs possess upon entering the role. In fact, lack of training appears as one of the most prevalent themes in the literature on chairs. Without explicit preparation and development, unit leaders find themselves relying on trial and error, which can lead to missteps.[8]

Chairs who receive effective training in leadership skills make up a small minority; the percentage of those reporting thorough preparation falls into the single digits.[9] This low investment in training for department chairs may stem from the position's temporary nature. Few faculty members aspire to or subsequently take on higher forms of leadership within the academy.[10] The majority return to their faculty positions following the completion of their term. In this regard, chairs constitute a built-in, short-term workforce in higher education.[11]

Another popular image of serving department chairs is that they are Janus-faced: looking simultaneously in the "opposite" directions of faculty and administration. Department chairs do not merely look both ways toward faculty and administration; they occupy a space between positions, forcing them to "swivel" and "shuttle" between their units and upper administrators. Sometimes they get caught in the middle or "torn between meeting the expectations of those they represent (i.e., the faculty) and those to whom they report (i.e., the dean)."[12]

The Janus-faced metaphor illuminates the sense chairs feel of being torn and needing to "straddle the often precarious line."[13] The line in question is the one that delineates faculty and administrator, or colleague and supervisor. The duality for chairs runs deep: many question who they actually *are*. Loss of self-identity may accompany the transition to the position when chairs confront the question as to whether they are faculty or administrators.[14] Existing in a liminal space "betwixt and between" makes it imperative for chairs to "maintain a double or dual consciousness," a predicament that, Freeman, Kakouti, and Ward note, "can be compounded when faculty only see themselves as temporary chairs."[15] The fact that chairs don't have traditional hierarchical supervisory relationships with their faculty means they need to become skilled in what is sometimes called "leading from the side."

EMBRACING LIMINALITY

The experience of liminality and resultant uncertainty for chairs has increased over time. According to Jeffrey Buller, department heads initially exerted more authority over faculty and resources than they do today. Over time, the top-down approach began to wane with a shift to more democratic practices.[16] Department chairs aren't alone in their struggles with having to work both up and down the ladder. Deans, too—although they occupy a higher leadership rank—must perform what Darla Hanley terms the "administrative dance," learning when and how to lead, follow, improvise, and create. Two key features of this dance include how to manage up and manage down. Mentoring for managing up entails demonstrating strong leadership and integrity, problem-solving, engaging in difficult conversations, advocating for faculty, and both advising and supporting one's boss. Mentoring for managing down includes "working closely with department chairs to position them as decision makers and leaders" who know "the 'hearts and minds' of the persons on [their] team."[17] Deans, then, are well positioned to mentor department chairs on overcoming the challenges of serving as bridges by communicating up and down.

Existing in a liminal space isn't inherently undesirable. In the original anthropological sense of the concept, liminality referred to a transitional state between one social identity and another as part of a rite of passage.[18] The literature on department chairs tends to frame this liminal position as ambiguous, confusing, and incomplete because chairs are neither truly faculty nor completely administrators. However, this liminality need not be a detriment. The challenge for deans and other academic leaders is to create a clearly defined role, meaningful in its own right. Given their elevated institutional status, deans wield the power and ability to enact structures and practices that can leverage this liminality in a way that allows chairs to truly lead from the middle.

DEVELOPING CHAIRS FOR NOW AND BEYOND

Specific training needs will vary depending on the size of institution, number of faculty, and range of responsibilities that administrators assign to the chair role. Notwithstanding operational differences across institutions, the general mission of a unit leader is, as Richard Bowman expresses it, "framing challenges, identifying opportunities, and managing resources. . . . Solving problems and enabling others to solve problems is the real work of academic chairs as leaders."[19]

A planned holistic approach to chair development must go beyond one-off efforts and could include short segments in regular meetings, internal reading groups or workshop/retreats, external events, written orientation resources, and informal or formal mentoring processes, all guided by periodic evaluation. While the precise content of these development efforts will necessarily vary across institutions, we recommend emphasizing the following themes in programming and materials: institutional perspective, relationships, data-driven problem solving, and fairness.

First, deans should encourage chairs to approach their work from a wider institutional perspective and to cultivate a shared vision of a sustainable future. Many articles and books encourage leaders to check their egos and not make the role about themselves.[20] Similarly, while it's expected that a chair will advocate for their own department, there are times when the focus shouldn't be on an individual unit. Providing chairs with insight into the broad workings of the institution will help them discern how their department relates to and is impacted by other units and the institution as a whole. Understanding broader perspectives also enables chairs to be more effective mentors and supervisors to colleagues in their department. In some situations, they must build buy-in for larger institutional goals that faculty perceive as being at odds with their personal wishes.[21]

The ability to have difficult conversations relies on good relationships, which the authors see as the second fundamental principle of the chair position. Like deans, chairs must sometimes make difficult and unpopular decisions. Starting from a base of strong relationships allows for a more complete understanding of how people may respond to decisions and the meanings they may attach to them.[22] Meeting with faculty early and often helps to build relationships that serve as a foundation when conflict or grievances arise. Deans can and should offer chairs training in conflict management and delicate conversations—moments that fare better in the context of trust.

Training chairs to use data in solving problems is a third essential aspect of creating effective leaders. Some studies suggest that chairs feel overwhelmed by the amount of information they receive from multiple sources. Chair meetings can foster data skills; deans can invite other internal campus professionals to lead these sessions. Leaders who know which data to use and how to work with it are better prepared to craft narratives around their decision-making processes[23]—another form of building trust and fostering relationships with their faculty. Data empower chairs to make more informed decisions in key aspects of their roles, such as hiring, managing the budget, tracking progress on goals, scheduling courses, and changing the curriculum.

Finally, deans themselves should be consistent and fair and hold their chairs to those same standards. Unlike serving as "just faculty," stepping into the role of chair brings a host of new responsibilities. On a practical level, a handbook on the position and a calendar of university deadlines are two small tools that can ease the transition into the role and reinforce consistency and equity. Chairs who understand their own job and can communicate it to their faculty are also better able to manage and protect their time (having one's time hijacked is a common lament of all leaders). Such awareness empowers chairs to prioritize and avoid responding to every issue that arises since there are few true emergencies.[24] Trust flourishes when deans and chairs lead on a larger-scale, more ethical level and in a transparent manner. In the absence of these principles, the sense of working for the common good is diminished, leading individuals and departments to feel it's their job to advocate for themselves.

BEFORE AND AFTER A CHAIRSHIP

Much of the literature highlights ways to improve life-work balance and build skillsets while occupying the role but ignores the time preceding and following the position. Faculty can be introduced to the role of chair in their first weeks at the institution. Orientation and onboarding sessions prepare new hires for their first year by reviewing learning management systems, campus policies and procedures, important deadlines, and required trainings. Similarly, early development beyond orientation can equip new faculty with information and skills they will need later in their careers. On our campus, we run a yearlong institute for new faculty that meets monthly. Much of the focus of these sessions centers on classroom and curricular issues (innovative pedagogy, high-impact practices, inclusivity, etc.) and how to balance scholarship and teaching.

We also spend time introducing faculty to campus offices—community-based learning, global education, and career education—with which they will partner frequently as they begin to advise and mentor students. We provide overviews of the preliminary, tenure, and promotion review processes and discuss crafting effective teaching statements, understanding and writing about classroom evaluations, and other topics. Many of these sessions do not relate directly to their first year as a faculty member; rather, the trainings are intended to increase awareness about campus culture and building institutional capacity. In a similar way, such sessions could orient new faculty to the role of chair in the form of leadership workshops (on topics such as managing conflict, assessment, or using data and metrics effectively) or could explore the specific work associated with chairing a program (just as we educate about advising students).

Sociologists refer to the "process of learning about role requirements of a particular status prior to actually acquiring that status" as "anticipatory socialization"[25]—a phenomenon that allows individuals to understand the nuts and bolts of a position, as well as its rewards, challenges, and coping mechanisms. Anticipatory socialization of all faculty for the chair role can happen through teaching and learning centers and through formal and informal mentorship from former department chairs. When pairing new faculty with mentors, leadership aspirations should be among the considerations. Anticipatory socialization carries the potential to create a culture of chairing that, over time, is proactive rather than reactive—such as the faculty suddenly realizing "We need a chair!"

Former leaders can also assist with mentoring newly minted chairs. Chairs who return to their programs after their term serve as invaluable assets in the unit. Some scholars recommend securing coaches outside the university to support chairs in a role that is "confusing, overwhelming, and lonely,"[26] but former chairs on campus can advise in a more tailored way as to lessons learned and challenges faced. They have developed valuable knowledge of institutional structures and culture. Moreover, tapping into the experience of former chairs affords meaningful opportunities for a faculty member in mid- or late career. To borrow a phrase from assessment, enlisting these individuals "closes the loop" and rounds out the academic experience by "inspiring down," that is, generating excitement and support for future leadership.

CONCLUSION

Mentoring chairs to embrace their position as not-fully-faculty and not-quite-administrators, including equipping them with an array of leadership skills, enhances the work they do, and develops their potential for higher administrative roles. As colleges and universities respond to the pressures of and changes in higher education, leaders may face challenges that didn't previously exist and for which there is no precedent or training. Trained leaders who have broad institutional knowledge and the ability to think beyond what will benefit their home disciplines can guide such initiatives as merging multiple departments or envisioning new organizational forms (such as our own institution's academic "centers"). The mentoring and professional development that deans provide for these challenging roles greatly impact chairs themselves, their faculty, and the entire institution.

— *Takeaways* —

- Challenges in developing chairs include their reluctance to accept the role, the frequency of turnover, and the liminality of the role between faculty and administration.
- Important themes in developing and mentoring chairs include embracing a wider institutional perspective or vision, investing in relationships, using data to solve problems, and encouraging principled decision making.
- Prechair and postchair periods are valuable opportunities to prepare faculty to more easily assume these roles and, later, to provide mentorship for it.

NOTES

1. Susan K. Gardner and Kelly Ward, "Investing in Department Chairs to Create Institutional Change," *Change: The Magazine of Higher Learning* (March/April 2018): 58–62.
2. Faiza Gonaim, "A Department Chair: A Life Guard without a Life Jacket," *Higher Education Policy* 29, no. 2 (June 2016): 272–86.
3. Karen E. Brinkley-Etzkorn and India Lane, "From the Ground Up: Building a System-Wide Professional Development and Support Program for Academic Department Chairs," *Studies in Higher Education* 44, no. 3 (2019): 571–83.
4. Brenda Lloyd-Jones, "Department Chair Leadership Skills," review of *Department Chair Leadership Skills*, by Walter H. Gmelch and Val D. Miskin, *Journal of Educational Administration* 50, no. 2 (2012): 245–48.
5. Lloyd-Jones, 245.
6. Sydney Freeman Jr., Ibrahim M. Karkouti, and Kelly Ward, "Thriving in the Midst of Liminality: Perspectives from Department Chairs in the USA," *Higher Education* 80 (2020): 895–911.
7. Gonaim, "A Department Chair," 274.
8. Jeffrey L. Buller, *The Essential Department Chair*, 2nd ed. (San Francisco: John Wiley & Sons, 2012), 4.
9. Lloyd-Jones, "Department Chair Leadership Skills," 245.
10. Gonaim, "A Department Chair," 282.
11. Gardner and Ward, "Investing in Department Chairs," 59–60.
12. Freeman, Kakouti, and Ward, "Thriving in the Midst of Liminality," 897.
13. Gardner and Ward, "Investing in Department Chairs," 59.
14. Gonaim, "A Department Chair," 282.

15. Freeman, Kakouti, and Ward, "Thriving in the Midst of Liminality," 897.
16. Buller, *The Essential Department Chair*, 100.
17. Darla S. Hanley, "The Administrative Dance: Managing Up, Down, and Across," in *The Resource Handbook for Academic Deans*, 3rd ed., ed. Laura L. Behling (San Francisco: Jossey-Bass, 2014), 144–45.
18. See Arnold Van Gennep, *The Rites of Passage* (Chicago: University of Chicago Press, 1960).
19. Richard F. Bowman Jr., "The Real Work of Department Chair," *Clearing House* 75, no. 3 (2002): 159.
20. See Gary E. DeLander, "Lessons from a Recovering Department Chair," *American Journal of Pharmaceutical Education* 81, no. 3 (April 2017): 1. See also John Griffith, "Department Chair Leadership: From Theory to Best Practice," *Department Chair* 31, no. 3 (Winter 2021): 15.
21. Gonaim, "A Department Chair," 283.
22. Angela Lumpkin, "Enhancing the Effectiveness of Department Chairs," *Journal of Physical Education, Recreation, and Dance* 75, no. 9 (November/December 2004): 45.
23. Virginia Coombs, "Productive Relationships with Department Chairs and Program Directors," in *The Resource Handbook for Academic Deans*, 3rd ed., 243–44.
24. DeLander, "Lessons from a Recovering Department Chair," 1.
25. Lisa McIntyre, *The Practical Skeptic: Core Concepts in Sociology*, 4th ed. (New York: McGraw-Hill, 2008), 267.
26. Wendy W. Cook, "The Department Chair Coach," *Department Chair* 31, no. 3 (Winter 2021): 11.

CHAPTER 30

No Small FEAT

Fostering Effective Administrative Teams

DARLA S. HANLEY

Deans and other academic leaders foster administrative teams that advance their unit, shape the student experience, and support college-wide initiatives or goals. Depending on institutional structure, these teams include department chairs, directors, coordinators, administrative support staff, social media managers, marketing professionals, technology specialists, and recruiters, to name only a few. Groups are designed to engage combinations of people to work together (inwardly facing) on ongoing initiatives, projects, curricula, or programs. They're also formed to engage beyond campus borders (outwardly facing), including interactions with alumni, potential donors, accrediting agencies, professional organizations, friends of the institution, and the community. Administrative teams range from small and intimate groups to large and potentially unwieldy bodies—depending on the institution's organizational structure, the nature of the work, the vision for the project, and resources.

Within units, administrative teams are responsible for addressing big-picture institutional ideas, the smallest unit details, and everything in between. These groups call on their members to share content expertise, use people skills, demonstrate a command of technology to support the work, employ critical and creative thinking, and so much more. For deans, putting people together and forming groups is one thing, but fostering *effective* administrative teams is the critical part of this equation.

First, let's define effective. In this chapter, "effective" means teams of people working with a dean who perform their assigned tasks at a high level and produce intended results. Second, the word "team" describes people working within a unit to perform specific roles that contribute to the greater good. Administrative teams are made up of people working individually and collectively—independently and together. They're organized, play on the same side, and are focused, adaptable, committed, and resilient.

Effective administrative teams are curated and nurtured by deans and other academic leaders at many levels. These groups are positioned for success when team members are assigned to appropriate roles, are informed of expectations, and are empowered to take risks and perform tasks with confidence. Further, they are strengthened when diverse perspectives are represented and dissenting opinions expressed. All of this flows from the dean and from everyone knowing the what, why, and how of the work.

WHAT: BUILDING THE DEAN RELATIONSHIP

Communication is central to all relationships, including dean relationships, and takes many forms. Every day, deans set the stage, the tone, and the example for their administrative teams with their use of language, choice of communication modality, and actions. They build professional relationships with others as they share content and determine how information is distributed (e.g., individually, to a group, in person, verbally, in writing, formally, or informally) and how it is documented, if applicable.

The dean's communications-related decisions shape their engagement with administrative teams and contribute to form a "dean relationship" with individuals and groups of colleagues. This working relationship, when healthy, encourages colleagues to play to their strengths, learn from each other, work collaboratively for the betterment of academics and the overall student experience, and advance the institution. Its formation requires deans to have a vision and create opportunities for shared experience—to purposefully develop teams that are confident, trusting, and respectful. It also requires deans to build (or mend) bridges among team members along the way.

When considering the communication options used to forge professional relationships, deans must reflect on the topic at hand, the people involved, and the potential impact on the institution, its work, and reputation. They categorize each topic through such lenses as routine academic matter; exciting new initiative or opportunity; sensitive topic or difficult conversation; requirement of accreditation or other official mandate; budget, facilities, or resource need; upper administration priority; or crisis. Deans also give thought regarding whom to include based on their roles, responsibilities, expertise, and skill set in order to form productive and diverse groups. All of this results in strengthened connections and teams that come together to create, problem-solve, facilitate, innovate, and celebrate.

Deans further their professional relationships with colleagues as they engage with team members in one-on-one check-in meetings, regularly scheduled group sessions, and informal conversation as they "walk the campus" and stop by areas or offices. Each of these connections brings something distinctive to the dean relationship.

The one-on-one provides space for deep dialog between two people and the sharing of individual career goals, challenges, and other sensitive topics in a more private setting. It creates a place where the dean can offer advice and guidance to a team member in a confidential context and show support in ways that may be awkward in a public arena.

Regularly scheduled group sessions provide a forum for sharing information, soliciting input, and team building among colleagues (with a formal agenda distributed ahead of time and minutes taken to document the session). These meetings are most effective when the dean leads them to include a balance of telling and discussing, asking and listening, and identifying and resolving.

In addition, the informal nature of the walk-around engagement contributes to building rapport with individuals or small subsets of teams and often results in valuable exchanges that wouldn't occur around a conference table or in a formal group setting. These interactions are both strategic and spontaneous, allowing the dean to be seen as they show interest and presence in their unit.

In order to generate the best results, deans, like other academic leaders, need to strategically think ahead as they work to build professional relationships. By drawing on prior experience, they're able to use lessons learned to manage stakeholders and address issues. The professional exchanges between the dean and team members also require the dean to consider tone, emphasis, and the emotional charge of the communication so as to shape its impact.

Thus, knowing when to add enthusiasm, how to de-escalate conflicts, and avoid unintended consequences is an essential component of the dean's skill set.

Professional relationships within and among administrative teams are strengthened by shared experience and by developing a joint record of unit success and institutional accomplishment. Deans create the opportunity for shared experience in unit meetings, committees, task forces, councils, and work groups. They also support shared experience via annual events, informal gatherings like group luncheons, and unit retreats. Each of these collective experiences brings people together to address unified goals and provides opportunities for decision making, original contributions, and consensus building. The manner in which the dean creates and facilitates shared experience contributes to the interpersonal relationships fostered within teams and across the unit, and forms a group dynamic. Stated another way, the stronger the individual relationships are among team members, the stronger the team and the dean's unit becomes.

Just as great teachers know the students in their classroom, deans need to know their team members and meet them where they are as they guide them to where they want them to go. This awareness is central to the dean relationship and requires the dean to listen attentively, see each person and their individual strengths and areas to improve, and evaluate work based on actual observations. Team members benefit when deans offer true support, provide valuable resources, and facilitate professional development that positions them for success. Moreover, really knowing the members of the team takes thoughtful effort and a desire to make their unit a great place to work, study, and learn.

WHY: WORKING WITH PURPOSE

Fundamentally, a dean's work is about students and advancing academics and the educational process. This underlying purpose propels decisions and actions and helps shape the work of the unit. It also guides the way effective administrative teams function.

Fostering effective teams requires deans to know their institution and work with purpose to skillfully frame issues, opportunities, and challenges. Like all academic leaders, deans need to consider how their messages are expressed and to which administrative team(s) the information is directed. They need to think about how messages may be received within the contexts of institutional politics, systems, and community. Further, in each exchange, the dean's words and actions generate optics, establish possible precedents, and symbolize values. Deans need to respond, not react, whenever possible and always remember that messages from them come from their role as the leader of the unit. Simply put, framing influences the professional engagement of everyone in the dean's unit, the relationships formed, and the outcomes achieved.

Deans work with purpose by offering ongoing input and support to contribute to their team's engagement and growth. This constructive feedback changes the manner in which people think and work. In an academic institution it takes many forms, including verbal debriefing sessions following an event (e.g., the close of the academic semester; the launch of a new program or initiative; accreditation review site visit); appreciation e-mails or cards articulating the team member's strengths and contributions to a specific accomplishment; and formal written performance reviews for the employee's file. The dean's feedback creates a record of their support and documents the team member's professional contributions and development. Among the most important work completed by the dean, these words show appreciation, acknowledgement, expectations, and encouragement.

Each dean, unit, and institution is unique, with its own vision, mission, and set of values. These assets inform the work and support the reasons decisions are made and why actions are taken. Therefore, it's critical for deans to know themselves as leaders and managers, know the heart of their institution (e.g., a research focus, a teaching focus, niche programs, specific student populations served), and be able to articulate the purpose of their offerings and unit to develop their teams. As part of this work, deans draw on strengths up, down, and across an institution to make it a place where history and traditions are embraced and where innovation and forward thinking are rewarded. They balance working within the cross purposes of serving as a sage academic pedagogue steeped in educational best practices and an academic entrepreneur pushing boundaries and changing with the times.

Working with purpose requires clear directives, long- and short-term goals, assessment, and reflection. Deans empower effective administrative teams to work with purpose when they impart clear expectations; provide resources, tools, and professional support; work with transparency; and offer recognition when goals are met. Teams are guided by deans to contribute to routine or ongoing projects (e.g., curriculum, scheduling, recruitment, accreditation), to work that is singular in nature (e.g., search committees, new facilities design and opening), and to unexpected events (e.g., planning for instruction during a global pandemic, a crisis on campus). This means that deans need to coordinate and assist their teams to prioritize and work within the arc of the academic year—recognizing that the purpose and workload of a unit varies greatly across, for example, the recruitment cycle, registration period, summer session, and spring break. They also need to encourage teams to accept new tasks when sudden issues or new opportunities arise, always do what they can, and see the value of their contributions.

Specifically, deans guide their administrative teams to purposefully complete tasks linked to the first moment they connect with prospective students and families through the students' educational journeys and continuing with alumni relations. Students are the reason deans and other academic leaders work—and are the centerpiece (and purpose) of all efforts. Accordingly, it's essential for deans to view their role through a student-centered lens, noting that students today differ from those of the past. This requires an awareness of student needs and an ability to position faculty and administrative teams to address them. As part of this work, deans need to identify and articulate the value of the experiences offered within their unit as distinctive and rewarding, and develop a shared narrative with their administrative teams that illustrates why the work is done, why students enroll, and why education matters.

Over time, deans cultivate and encourage effective administrative teams to function with knowledge, skill, and choreographed actions, knowing the "why" behind the work. Understanding purpose is part of this success.

HOW: LEADING BY EXAMPLE

Deans lead by example as they strive to build professional relationships, work with purpose, and advance the student experience. How (the approach deans take to attain outcomes) occurs only once a dean and their administrative teams know the what and why of their work. Thus, the how embodies all steps, procedures, systems, practices, and other actions taken that allow the dean and their colleagues to realize goals. The how is also linked to the dean and their administrative team's professional style, preferences, and reputation.

Professional style and preferences within the dean's unit take many forms. They can appear in ways that are casual or formal, open- or closed-door, introverted or extroverted, subtle or flashy. The dean's style and choices significantly shape the approach and emerge in written, verbal, and nonverbal communications; within an office climate; or in unit-sponsored events. Accordingly, deans need to recognize these elements as drivers that influence the working lives of their administrative teams along with the outcomes achieved for their institution.

The reputation of a dean, unit, and institution takes time to develop and stands on established records of professional engagement in which original ideas and initiative are offered. In addition, strong reputations are developed when deans and their teams strive to offer high-quality performance in all contexts and work with consistency and follow-through. The thoughts and opinions held about a dean and their unit are created from large public-facing actions, high-level involvement on campus, and quiet behind-the-scenes gestures of support. Thus, reputations include objective data and subjective perceptions—blending measurable information with viewpoints and beliefs of how things seem. This means it's essential for deans to create an accurate portrait that highlights the strengths and accomplishments of their unit, and use it to tell the story to team members and other stakeholders.

Every day, week, semester, and academic year, deans show their teams *how* to effectively work within the culture and structures of their unit and institution. By example, they demonstrate a manner of engagement that invites administrative teams to be present and take pride in their work. They facilitate team members in understanding and agreeing on processes for completing tasks, and they foster a climate of mutual accountability where all team members contribute their "fair share." Deans also create a setting by establishing realistic deadlines for projects with measurable outcomes. Throughout all of these efforts, deans advocate for their teams and units and strive to provide the resources needed for them to perform their roles efficiently and move forward. This requires the dean to implement informed actions and decision making while supporting others with respect, compassion, integrity, and energy. When they set this type of example, their team benefits from working with a skilled, competent, and effective leader.

In many ways, the dean is a model for their administrative teams showing how to represent, engage, and celebrate their work to make things happen for and with students. Strong deans also show humility and take ownership of mistakes or missteps as they model professionalism and navigate original work, leadership, and management in their setting. In doing so, a dean leads by example and organically fosters effective administrative teams that rely on one another and on the dean. They work together in concert and navigate issues with a shared sense of the team (people), unit (place), and impact on students, teaching, and learning (purpose).

NO SMALL FEAT: *FOSTERING EFFECTIVE ADMINISTRATIVE TEAMS*

Everyone wants to be part of something that is effective and successful—including deans and their administrative teams. Within units, deans mentor, inspire, and position effective administrative teams to contribute to the task at hand. They encourage professional dean relationships with individuals and groups that set a tone as they strive to create work environments where the exchange of ideas is encouraged and all contributions are welcome. Further, deans strengthen effective teams by creating opportunities for shared experience and space for reflection, evaluation, and discussion. They strategically use communication as a tool as they thoughtfully select language, determine appropriate framing, and craft feedback to guide colleagues as they respond, resolve, advocate for, and advance the work.

As leaders, deans are responsible for ensuring that all members of their unit know their role and are empowered to perform it— to engage together to realize the what, why, and how of the work. They model essential qualities and abilities and see their reflection in the achievements and outcomes generated by their teams. Fundamentally deans, like all academic leaders, foster effective administrative teams through attentive listening, keen observation, and awareness. They assign tasks within the context of their institution, the arc of the academic year, team expertise, resources, and priorities. Moreover, by acknowledging professional style and preferences, building on reputation and prior success, and continuing to learn and evolve, the dean with their administrative colleagues stands ready to navigate whatever challenges present themselves.

Finally, effective teams are all about their members. Deans assign colleagues to roles and in combinations by putting people together to complete specific tasks. They see colleagues for what they bring to the table and position them to perform excellent work. Along the way, they observe team members (individually and in groups) and offer essential guidance and feedback as they generate intended results throughout an academic year. Together, they unite on behalf of students to advance academics and the educational process. Through all of this, deans assist team members in continuing to grow and contribute as professionals, being part of something that is meaningful to them and beyond.

The complex and rewarding work of a dean and their *effective* administrative teams drives institutions. When done well, team building illustrates extraordinary skill, achievement, and performance. Fostering effective administrative teams is no small feat.

— *Takeaways* —

- Effective teams are all about their members.
- As leaders, deans are responsible for ensuring that all members of their unit know their role and are empowered to perform it—that is, are able to engage together to realize the what, why, and how of the work.
- Effective administrative teams are cultivated and encouraged to function with skill and choreographed actions.
- Deans lead by example as they model essential qualities and abilities and see their reflection in the achievements and outcomes generated by their teams.

CHAPTER 31

Reimagining Difficult Conversations as a Form of Leadership

BRIDGET KEEGAN

There are as many books and articles about having difficult conversations as there are difficult conversations that you'll have as an academic leader. There is no one-size-fits-all solution or strategy, though there are numerous useful approaches, such as motivational interviewing or appreciative inquiry.[1] Difficult conversations are the part of academic leadership that no one likes—most of us dread them. Yet they can be a place where, surprisingly, you can make a profound difference as a leader. Instead of treating them as something to be endured, it can be helpful to approach these encounters as a way to have a positive impact on your colleagues and your institution. Reframing difficult conversations as a way of demonstrating your values, and your institution's mission and values, may not make you dread them less, but the process may allow you to see them as contributing to your effectiveness as a leader.

The root causes of difficult conversations vary. Perhaps a problem has gone unresolved or even unaddressed over time. Or tension may be caused by the sheer complexity or "baggage" around an issue. Most difficult conversations are difficult because they are, fundamentally, about loss, or fear of loss. That loss may be very real and tragic, such as the death or serious illness of a student or colleague. Or it might be the loss of a position, resources, status, or an opportunity such as promotion. Other categories of difficult conversations such as negotiations or advocacy for resources for an individual or unit—put one at a risk of loss if the discussion doesn't go well. Loss is at the least unpleasant, at worst painful and traumatic. What's more, people tend to see any kind of change as a loss. Acknowledging the emotional dimension is an essential first step because, in difficult conversations, emotion rather than reason can predominate. One might hope that academic professionals, who value reason and who teach and research using critical thinking, would approach challenging conversations with those skills. But when it comes to matters that involve or threaten loss, academics are also human.

Instead of offering prescriptive advice, in this chapter I provide an inventory of questions to ask yourself. While some may seem obvious, difficult conversations might evoke emotions for you as a leader as well as for your colleague. Having a checklist can help you be intentional rather than just emotional.[2] I have attempted to put the questions in a general order, but you may not have the luxury of time to ask and answer them all if called to a conversation quickly. However, some can be considered in the abstract so that you have a foundation to build upon, no matter the circumstances.

Finally, in what follows I focus on difficult conversations rather than difficult communications, though the two have much in common. Communications, such as announcements or directives, are often not immediately interactive, though they may lead to conversations later.

IS THIS MY CONVERSATION TO HAVE?

This most critical question is surprisingly easy to forget. As any academic leader who has served for more than a few weeks knows, many different problems present themselves to you on any given day. They may come from those you oversee (faculty, staff, students) or those who oversee you (your supervisor, the Board of Trustees). They may come from outside your unit (an office, such as student life) or outside the institution (parents, the public). Your approach will vary, depending on whom you are called to have the conversation with. Nonetheless, the critical question to ask yourself is whether *you* are the one who *should* be having the conversation. In other words, is this problem *yours to solve?*

Most academic leaders enter administration because they're proactive problem solvers. Your first instinct when an issue lands in your office is likely to roll up your sleeves and deal with it. But when I remember to ask myself this question, I often discover the conversation may not be one that *I* need to have. Or at least *not now*. I'm not suggesting you avoid difficult conversations; rather, asking whether or not it's *your* conversation may facilitate better outcomes for all involved. Having a discussion that is not yours may lead to worse outcomes or more complicated subsequent conversations. An obvious example is a legal matter, such as one involving Title IX. Although you want to be helpful and transparent, your role may impose constraints that, if ignored, could jeopardize you or the institution.

How do you know whether it's your responsibility to have that conversation? Being intimately aware of your institution's policies and procedures is a first step. Keep a set of desk references, and familiarize yourself early and often. The faculty or student handbook, collective bargaining agreement, and university bulletin (if it outlines academic policies) are excellent resources to keep handy. Know the individuals specifically tasked with communicating on behalf of the institution, such as the university's communications director or, if it's a potential legal matter, the general counsel, and have them on speed dial. If a crisis or scandal occurs, external inquiries from the press or the public should always be referred first to these individuals. I also recommend familiarizing yourself with your institution's crisis plan (if available to you).

If you aren't sure that it's your conversation, ask a colleague—your supervisor, the general counsel, or a fellow dean or chair. It may turn out, in fact, that the conversation is one that *no one* needs to have. Allow me to illustrate with a memorable example. Early in my tenure as dean I learned that students (or their parents) believe that they should go "straight to the top" if they have a complaint about a grade or other academic matter. I have saved myself countless hours by directing them to policies in the student handbook. A few of those grade appeals did eventually become my conversations (as per the process), but 99 percent were resolved by the instructor or department chair.

IS THIS MY CONVERSATION
TO HAVE *NOW*? IF NOT, WHEN?

I received one of the wisest pieces of advice in my career when I first became a department chair: whenever possible, wait twenty-four hours before responding to an inflammatory e-mail. I was surprised how often the situation resolved itself in that time frame. While in some cases responding immediately is required, there may be other circumstances when jumping on an e-mail thread only fans the flames. If you get an e-mail equivalent to a "Howler" (*a la* Harry Potter),[3] it's always best to avoid responding through e-mail; call or visit in person instead. As we all know, individuals sometimes adopt rhetorical postures in e-mail very unlike how they will interact with you *viva voce.*

Reminding yourself of the difference between the urgent and the important is also good practice. While you'll need to determine more gracious ways to say it, "Your poor planning or bad judgment doesn't constitute my emergency" is a helpful mantra. There are times when the urgent and the important overlap. You don't want to delay a difficult conversation, but it's likely that the more important a conversation is, the more you'll need to get additional information. Thus, it's beneficial not to react immediately. Sometimes all that's needed in the moment is a quick acknowledgment with a promise to follow up later.

Another question about timing relates to logistics: depending on the conversation, scheduling it at the end of the day—or at the end of the week— may be helpful. That said, most people have justifiable preconceptions about what happens at a meeting set for 4:30 p.m. on a Friday, which could be counterproductive.

WHAT ARE MY VALUES AND HOW DO THEY INFORM MY COMMUNICATION STYLE?

I work at a Jesuit institution, an order founded by St. Ignatius of Loyola. A core component of Ignatian spirituality, practiced by Jesuit priests and shared with all who work and learn at Jesuit schools, is the concept of indifference. A few sentences won't do justice to the philosophy, but in general it means not getting attached to any person, thing, or outcome—including one's own "ego ideal" or self-image. Similar concepts are found in the philosophy of Stoicism and in Zen Buddhism. However, in the Ignatian tradition, the aim of indifference is to allow oneself a radical openness to the workings of the "greater good" (in a Christian context, a larger divine plan). At the end of the day, indifference may be a fancy way of saying "Don't take it personally." You're having the difficult conversation because of the role you're in. If there's negativity, then it's likely directed at your position (chair, dean, or provost), not you as a person. Put more positively, if I see myself as an agent for the mission of Jesuit higher education, which aspires to create a more just and equitable world, then I can frame *everything* I do in my role—both the fun and the daunting—within a higher purpose.

Another element of Ignatian spirituality I rely upon is the concept of *cura personalis*, or care for the whole person. Again, this concept is multifaceted, but in this context it helps me to be empathetic and curious about the person with whom I'm having a difficult conversation. Unfortunately, in these situations it's all too easy to see someone as the sum of whatever bad decisions or situations brought them to you. *Cura personalis* reminds me to put myself in the other person's shoes. It may not make the problem that led to the conversation go away, but it makes me mindful of my emotions and my potentially unproductive preconceptions.

The practice of assuming the other's positive intent is also central to Ignatian spirituality. Admittedly, there are situations where this approach may be excruciatingly hard to take. But the premise forces me to step outside of my prejudices and see outcomes of the difficult conversation that I might not have imagined. As a quick example, faculty members in my college prize teaching reductions above any other form of compensation, and we have clear policies about what level of enrollments allow program directors to qualify. A faculty member who was asked to direct a very low-enrolled graduate program came to me to request additional course releases before he would accept the assignment. My first instinct was to feel as though I was being held hostage. However, I stepped back and asked him why he felt he needed them. I learned that the previous program director had presented the work in a way that made it sound far more time-consuming than it had to be. When he and I discussed how the work could be done more efficiently, we came to an agreement that we both felt happy about, even if it didn't include as many course releases.

Reflecting on which of your personal values—or dimensions of your institution's mission—you wish to remember in difficult conversations can help you see the *greater good* these interactions might have.

WHAT DOES A SUCCESSFUL OUTCOME LOOK LIKE?

For you as a leader, a successful outcome might simply be getting through this conversation. However, based on your answers to the questions explored above, are there other ways to identify values or "hidden goods"? Can you have the conversation in a way that makes the colleague or student feel heard, respected, and valued, even if they don't like the message you're sharing? Are you able to discover something you weren't aware of? It may be helpful to convey the goals of your conversation at the start, along with your openness to learning. Consider this statement, for example: "I have some difficult news to share, but I wanted to discuss it with you so that you could ask questions and share your perspective."

At the same time, as suggested above, it's important to ask yourself if what you have is really a communication rather than a conversation—at least not a conversation yet. Academics love to debate ideas, but do you want to invite the give-and-take of an argument, or do you just need to convey instructions (e.g., "Please cancel these low-enrolled courses.")? A difficult conversation might need to follow (e.g., "Why are there so many low-enrolled courses in your program?"), but you could get better outcomes if you separate the two.

WHAT DO I NEED TO KNOW AND HOW DO I NEED TO PREPARE FOR THIS CONVERSATION?

The more difficult the conversation, the more essential it is to prepare for it. What conversations do you need to have before or after (with the general counsel, the Title IX coordinator, Human Resources, the provost, or the president)? Some of this preparation will take the form of consultations to provide you with useful data or background. In general, if there's trouble brewing, it's wise to inform those higher in the chain of command (a step that can, occasionally, help refine your answer as to whether this is *your* conversation). There are many cases in which protocols and policies exist: knowing and observing them are critical and can remove stress and ambiguity.

Ask yourself whether you need to know anything about the person(s) with whom you'll be conversing. Are other factors impacting them personally or professionally, such as a failed grant application, health issue, or divorce?

A wise mentor once told me that being an effective academic leader draws on many of the same strategies as effective teaching. Just as you wouldn't go into a class without a plan, it's useful in advance to map out your points, rehearse what you're going to say, and consider how you hope the conversation will flow. Think about responses the other person might have and how you'll respond. If they start to cry, scream, lash out, or go silent, what will you do? Are you prepared to call the meeting to a rapid conclusion? Envisioning scenarios is critical, but don't get too attached to any one of them. If you can, especially if the stakes are high, talk them over with a trusted colleague or your supervisor. That said, be aware of the need for confidentiality around many areas that usually constitute difficult conversations.

Beyond whatever scripting or rehearsing you do, include time for the other person to talk or ask questions, as well as time for you to listen—authentically. You may need to create the space for some repetition on your part. If it's a conversation about a piece of bad news, the other person may need to hear it more than once to fully process it. Likewise, if they want to bargain or negotiate, you'll want to make sure that you can feel comfortable holding your ground.

Finally, think about how you envision the conversation ending. You may need to prepare yourself to state this explicitly. We all have colleagues who need to get in the last word. Are you comfortable with either letting them have it or thinking they have it? Whenever possible, avoid ending the meeting with an apology, too often the default for women leaders. Instead of saying, "I'm sorry about . . . ," say, "Thank you for making the time to talk with me about. . . ." If you understand that difficult conversations are a part of your role, you're less likely to feel the need to apologize for having them. Depending on the circumstances, be careful about suggesting that you're personally responsible for the particular difficulty under discussion.

WHAT LOGISTICS DO I NEED TO CONSIDER?

Being called to an administrator's office might conjure feelings of anxiety akin to being called into a middle school principal's office. It may be easier for someone to hear bad news in their own environment. But don't get a reputation for delivering bad news only in a person's own space. Also, factor in the need for confidentiality. If the conversation is one that you are scheduling, be mindful how you do so. If your assistant is making the appointment, give as much information as you can about the purpose and don't put your assistant in an uncomfortable position of having to be mysterious. You can be general, such as mentioning that the meeting is about a "concern" or "to discuss a personnel matter." If the person presses for more information, it's best to say, "I'd prefer to discuss the details in person."

Having difficult conversations face-to-face is always preferable, even if it feels more uncomfortable. You may sometimes have to speak on the phone or meet by videoconference. Avoid an e-mail "conversation" and don't send texts. Exceptions may occur when it's a wider communication or if it's important that wording be precise, accurate, and documented. Even then, writing is generally better as a follow-up.

Who needs to be there? Based on your research and your university's policies or protocols, you may need to have the union representative or ombudsperson present. What if the other person wants someone with them? What if you want a witness? Perhaps you need to have public safety alerted and nearby. Can the conversation be recorded, and should you be explicit about whether that is permitted? Last but not least to consider, do you need to have a box of tissues within reach?

Choreographing the nonverbal component of the meeting makes a difference. Consider in advance where you want people to sit and do your best to direct them there. Is there a way that you can make everyone more at ease? In general, I go out of my way to be unfailingly courteous and professional, even if the other person may not be. Politeness may be disarming in a positive way, especially in contexts where someone is expecting a fight.

How will you respond if the temperature of the meeting heats up? Do you know what your triggers are, and can you monitor your own stress response? Another piece of treasured advice came from a wise woman who worked for the CIA. If you feel yourself wanting to cry, move your tongue in your mouth the way you do when you are flossing. Apparently, there is a physiological effect that counters the "sob reflex." Regardless of the reason, I've found it to work on more occasions than I can count.

NOW THAT THE CONVERSATION IS OVER, WHAT ELSE NEEDS TO HAPPEN?

As you conclude the discussion, be sure to anticipate whether it's appropriate to invite follow-up or further questions. Will you need to document the conversation? Are additional actions required? In general, making notes immediately after the conversation is helpful—not only if you have to produce official documentation but also for your own records.

Finally, check in with yourself—how are you feeling? If possible, schedule something stress relieving after a difficult conversation, such as a good workout or coffee with a friend. Reflect upon what you've learned and what you could do better next time. That said, don't castigate yourself if the conversation wasn't perfect. I guarantee you'll have plenty of future opportunities to improve.

CONCLUSION

As academic leaders, we're all invested in the transformative power of education to change individual lives and our communities for the better. We celebrate learning as growth, even when it happens slowly or unevenly or when learning may be forced upon us. When you approach difficult conversations in a reflective and intentional way, you learn things about yourself as a leader, about the people you work with, and about the institution you serve. Difficult conversations are unavoidable but can be an invaluable way of demonstrating your commitments as a leader.

— *Takeaways* —

- Most difficult conversations are about loss or fear of loss. Emotion rather than reason can predominate.
- Reframe difficult conversations positively as an opportunity to enact your values as a leader.
- Whenever possible, take time to prepare for a difficult conversation in advance and to reflect on it afterward.
- Approach a potentially difficult conversation with a checklist of key questions to help prepare yourself and ensure productive outcomes.

• Remember, in most difficult conversations, you're representing your institution or your unit. The majority of the time, it's not about you personally.

NOTES

1. Originally designed for counseling, motivational interviewing (MI) was created in the 1980s by two clinical psychologists, William Miller and Stephen Rollnick, and used to help those struggling with addiction to negotiate behavioral change. It has been adapted for nonclinical situations such as coaching and even parenting. Appreciative inquiry (AI), like MI, takes a positive approach to the capacity of individuals and groups to grow and change. While the theories and techniques associated with both approaches are rich and extensive, both encourage taking an "interrogatory" position in conversations and asking questions rather than making statements or judgments. In the academy, AI has been applied to student advising with positive results, as is documented in the work of Jennifer Bloom and colleagues.

2. Atul Gawande, the surgeon and writer, makes a compelling case for the use of checklists in *The Checklist Manifesto* (London: Picador Press, 2009). According to Gawande, even highly trained professionals, such as doctors or pilots, benefit from having checklists that can help them avoid mistakes when faced with complex circumstances.

3. See a clip from the film on YouTube, https://www.youtube.com/watch?v=fBziSx7RtqY.

CHAPTER 32

Mentoring to Build a Pipeline of Academic Leaders

PAULA O'LOUGHLIN, ANGELA ZISKOWSKI, AND ANGELA BOS

Mentoring matters, yet as academic leaders we often think only of its critical role in supporting faculty success. But mentoring is equally important in developing the next generation of academic leaders. Very few current leaders, the authors included, started out planning for administrative roles. Mentors can recognize a faculty member's potential as a leader and carefully develop both skills and interest. It's imperative that senior leaders in academia prioritize the mentorship and development of junior and mid-career faculty as a key component of their positions. Committing to mentorship adds to the academic leader's portfolio and provides a wealth of benefits. Mentoring within your own institution is fulfilling because you support the growth of colleagues whose work and leadership in turn support your students. Mentors also have the opportunity to pass on the values that we believe are critical for higher education. On a pragmatic level, you may get help with a task on your to-do list by delegating and supporting a mentee who is taking on a project. Mentoring academic leaders reduces the global stress at our institutions by effectively distributing our work among a cohort of rising leaders. In addition, promising leaders help relieve stress when there are sudden departures of key figures.

We address this topic from two different perspectives: a provost who is highly engaged in mentoring academic leaders, and two rising faculty leaders whom she has mentored. The provost's perspective serves as a how-to for mentorship of faculty leaders. The faculty viewpoint highlights ways in which rising academic leaders can proactively work toward achieving their leadership and career goals.

AN EXPERIENCED MENTOR'S APPROACH
TO GUIDING ACADEMIC LEADERS

A primary mandate for current academic leaders is to develop the next generation of leaders. Central to this mentoring is the mind-set of helping others to discern their own aspirations with regard to their next professional steps.

Mentoring future leaders begins with the first conversation with your faculty. Rather than approaching the conversation as a supervisor focused on the faculty member's responsibilities, reframe the purpose of the initial talk to focus on listening and getting to know the person and their goals. For example, after they speak about what they do, ask, "What is your favorite part of your responsibilities and why?" or "Where do you want to be in five years?" Don't hesitate to directly ask if they've ever thought of taking on a leadership or administrative role. Some people may read these open-ended questions as a form of threat. Be prepared to explain that the purpose is for you to get a sense of how you can help them grow.

The right moment for this conversation varies widely. If you're new to an institution, it may naturally evolve with faculty who were on the search committee who hired you or who lead governance bodies. In other cases, your awareness that you're working with a future leader may occur more gradually as you get to know people. It may become clear as people work through the tenure process or through annual reviews that certain individuals have the ability to think strategically, take an institution-wide perspective to thorny issues, or bring people together to solve challenges. Others are incredibly detail oriented and suited for managing specific projects or elements of portfolios.

Things are a little more challenging if you've become an academic leader within your home institution and you want to mentor others on campus. Your new position will offer a more institution-wide perspective of people's abilities and showcase the strengths of rising leaders you didn't notice before.

While your role within the institution has changed, others may not immediately see this. In such circumstances, these intake conversations could happen more gradually.

Whether you're rising from within or were an external hire, it's important for you to let the faculty member know during this initial conversation that you're going to support their goals, whatever they may be. Their ultimate goal may not be your preferred outcome (for example, leaving the institution or replacing you), but that's irrelevant. Nothing kills a rising academic leader's interest faster than the idea that you're undertaking this mentoring to feather your own cap or to manipulate the faculty member. In many cases, the rising leader will politely decline your offer of mentorship because they have other priorities (e.g., wanting to achieve tenure or full professor). That's OK and to be expected.

Your responsibility is to open the door to a conversation that both of you can return to over time. Taking on a leadership role has to be their choice and not a decision you make for them. No one wakes up one day and says, "I want to be a leader." Rather, they come to understand over time that academic leadership as something they enjoy or excel at. They may have considered the possibility but didn't know how to ask the question or may have been afraid of the repercussions. They may be getting negative feedback from their faculty peers about their interest in leadership, navigating their colleagues' negative impressions of administrators, or receiving little positive feedback for their leadership efforts (except for being asked to do more). It's critical for you to affirm their interest and skills.

Once someone has expressed a willingness to explore academic leadership, there are several other steps you can offer as a mentor. Based on their goals, it's important to talk about how to build their skill set—and CV—appropriately. If someone has never had the chance to run a department or program, this could be a first step. Conversely, someone who has run a department or subfield within it could be encouraged to consider broader, institution-wide opportunities. Perhaps your institution is about to begin an assessment cycle, strategic planning campaign, or presidential search. If so, consider nominating your mentee for duties in these efforts. Every opportunity helps them learn about the work of an academic leader. Serving as a faculty member on an executive-level search for the institution has helped solidify interest in administration for many academic leaders. If at some point your mentee formally seeks an administrative position, you can mentor them through the roller coaster ride that applying for academic administrative jobs is. Take time to explain how search firms work, what the line authority is, and so forth.

Set up regular one-on-one meetings in which you check in with your mentee about what they're learning. These can be casual coffees so that they know you're paying attention. If they're leading a program that's a direct report to you, these conversations can become part of those meetings. The topics of your discussions can vary considerably based on their interests. Some mentees have found it useful to hear about how the mentor makes tough decisions. Others want to know how to determine when they're ready to go to the administrative "dark side." In other cases, you might reflect on something new that has come across your desk and ask them for feedback.

There's no script for these conversations. In some cases, you might explain the difference between managing and leading—and that neither is really possible without the other. Be sure to affirm that these are exploratory conversations and you just want them to identify their path and plan. Saying "yes" doesn't mean they're forever doomed to administration, and saying "no" doesn't mean you as the mentor will ever think less of them or stop suggesting opportunities. You may need to address the trope that "going to the dark side" means selling out. Or you could talk about your own or a colleague's journey to leadership.

Beyond one-on-one check-ins, consider bringing together your mentees as a complete cohort or in small groups for development activities alongside other administrators. Prior to the pandemic, I would bring together my associate deans and faculty program directors about twice a year for food and conversation. Each time, I give them a challenge or activity. One of the most popular was a version of an "inbox exercise" based on a day in my life. This exercise sets up a scenario in which I have fifteen minutes or less between meetings, people waiting outside my office, phone calls to return, a series of critical e-mails, and a president who needs something. My questions to the aspiring leaders included the following: How do I triage the various emergencies? Who do I deal with and why? What do I delegate? What tasks are my responsibility alone and what is a real emergency?

Another helpful activity for rising leaders has been sharing challenges drawn from my own experience at other institutions (with names omitted and some details changed) and then letting them figure out how they would address them in my role.

You may also connect your rising leaders with others in higher education to give them alternative perspectives and additional mentors. Too often, faculty members gain experience in one kind of institution or system and assume there is a single decision-making matrix or organizational chart that everyone in a dean's role will use. You can further develop your rising academic leaders by connecting them to a peer cohort of faculty who are interested in leadership so that they can support one another's leadership aspirations. The Council of Independent Colleges (CIC), Higher Education Resource Services (HERS), and the American Council of Education (ACE), as well as consortia such as the Associated Colleges of the Midwest, Great Lakes Colleges Association, and Big Ten, all run professional development programs. Or you can create your own group, possibly by teaming up with a neighboring institution. Such a program doesn't have to be highly organized but can still give your rising faculty leaders collegial support.

Administrators should also consider mentoring rising leaders beyond their own institution. ACAD, for example, offers the chance to serve as a peer mentor. While institutional governance structures vary, all academic leaders fundamentally engage in the same work. The benefits of mentoring outside your organization are the same as those within your institution. There's no set path to how these relationships start, just as there wasn't a guide for the mentors who looked out for you in your discipline or field. You may know someone from professional work, perhaps a former colleague or student.

Provosts and deans should be intentional about facilitating the development of faculty who demonstrate leadership potential. By investing in our faculty as mentors, we can help our institutions build leadership capacity.

BEING MENTORED IN ACADEMIC LEADERSHIP

In this section, the faculty viewpoint is offered by two rising faculty leaders who have benefited greatly from the thoughtful, personalized mentorship described in the prior section and who hope that more administrators will engage in similar efforts. There's a real need for administrators to initiate conversations in order to cultivate the pipeline of leaders for their institutions. Most faculty have never talked with a senior administrator about the ways they want to contribute to the institution—or how they wish to be supported in their development. Deans and administrators play a major role in encouraging faculty members to develop as leaders. Faculty members from marginalized groups in the academy, such as women, BIPOC, LGBTQIA, first-generation, and international faculty may underestimate their leadership potential—and can be particularly responsive to the encouragement of trusted administrators.

Some administrators, however, may be less inclined to actively mentor faculty toward academic leadership. In this case, faculty members shouldn't wait for a dean or senior administrator to identify them for a role or seek them out as potential leaders. Many models of successful mentoring emphasize proactively seeking out a wide variety of mentors to support your development. Numerous opportunities and significant growth come from seeking advisors and mentors and sharing your interest in academic leadership with them. The earlier you express interest in such roles, the more opportunities your mentors have to facilitate your preparation to succeed in them. For example, if we as deans aren't aware of a faculty member's desire to move into leadership, we may not consider them to serve when a valuable opportunity arises. Serving on a committee for institutional reaccreditation is a critical, high-level responsibility available only once in many years. It's ideal for a dean to have a pool of individuals who would benefit most by such an experience. Your mentor may connect you with other opportunities, such as serving on searches for presidents, provosts, and other senior-level positions. Reviewing CVs and participating in interview processes from the other side of the table are excellent ways to prepare for a position you may envision having in the future.

With the guidance of mentors, faculty can position themselves to develop in ways that will help them achieve their leadership and career goals. If you're strategic about using institutional service to gain experience in tasks that are universal in academia, performing these roles will provide opportunities to develop skill sets and experiences that are easily transferable and appealing to other institutions. A faculty member could opt to serve on the college finance committee, allowing them to gain experience with the senior-level, macro view of the institution's financial workings and build a knowledge base that's relevant at any institution.

Committees centered on retention or admissions could also offer similar broad and transferable experiences. The added benefit of this service is that it often includes working closely with individuals from other areas of the institution: staff in various offices, administrators, or even members of the Board of Trustees. In some cases, when a faculty member observes a need and wishes to address it, a dean can support the effort by providing funds. This is a win-win for all involved: the dean gets results on an identifiable problem that the faculty member is invested in solving, and the faculty member develops their leadership capacities.

Finally, faculty who take external leadership opportunities can thereby broaden their experiences and skill sets. They may later stand out in an applicant pool for a senior-level academic leadership position. All faculty members' disciplines have national organizations (for example, the American Historical Association) that have their own committees, initiatives, and leadership positions. Likewise, serving on a local school board or government council provides myriad experiences in working with a diverse set of people who have competing interests, budget challenges, and multiyear goals. Working as a volunteer for nonprofit organizations or leading local fund-raising efforts provides excellent experience that can be leveraged in an application for an administrative position. Such work should be encouraged, valued, and highlighted. Wider engagement of every type brings a faculty member's skills and experience to the institution at which they're seeking a leadership position. Faculty members often serve in these capacities off campus and would do more if it furthered their growth or promotion at the institution.

CONCLUSION

Approaching legacy and succession in a selfless way is among the most important gifts we can give to our colleagues, students, and institutions. One of the fundamental responsibilities of academic leadership is to build a pipeline for the next generation of leaders, for our own and other institutions. The energy we put into this work ensures not only a reliable workforce for ourselves but also stability for our institutions. Serving as a mentor affords us the unique opportunity to transmit our learned experiences and guiding principles from one generation of higher-education leaders to the next.

— *Takeaways* —

- To build a pipeline of future academic leaders, deans need to prioritize mentoring by encouraging faculty leaders to identify their goals and to facilitate their development toward achieving them.
- Essential steps to this mentorship vary, but might include having a first conversation with rising leaders about their goals; presenting them with relevant opportunities within the institution to build their skill set; meeting to see what they're learning; connecting them with mentors and opportunities beyond the home institution; and mentoring them through the job search process.
- Mentoring is a relationship; thus, it works best if the rising leader is actively involved in curating what they want to learn.
- A few strategies for success for rising leaders include being savvy in building a variety of mentors; choosing committee and service work that helps build skills that are transferable across institutions; and leveraging volunteer and community work that requires important real-world skills needed for administration.

PART VII

Leadership in the Future and in the Past

CHAPTER 33

Embracing New Joy

Returning to the Faculty after the Deanship

LISA JASINSKI

Among the hundreds of college presidents, provosts, and deans who depart their administrative positions every year, a substantial number elect to return to the faculty rather than retire outright. Concerning the prospect of resuming a faculty role, Ronald Ehrenberg, former academic vice-president at Cornell University, advised his peers, "When you go back [to the faculty,] remember that your administrative experience has fundamentally changed you; you are a different person and you have to do different things."[1]

Further underscoring the theme of difference, Larry Nielsen, former provost of North Carolina State University, characterized returning to the faculty as involving many overlapping significant changes, such as adjusting to a new (and often slower) pace, doing a different type of work, and cultivating new relationships with professional colleagues.[2] To better understand these differences and how former senior academic leaders navigated these transitions, I interviewed more than fifty former presidents, provosts, and deans at four-year institutions who returned to the faculty.[3] Their stories demonstrate how returning to the faculty can be an opportunity to advance personal goals while continuing to serve others.

The majority of former senior leaders I consulted characterized the transition in their roles as positive, affirming, liberating, and rewarding; few lamented the loss of power, status, or salary. Returning to the faculty can be an opportunity for self-directed reinvention. Many leaders stated that they felt more "present" and "balanced" upon resuming their faculty role. Exiting the administrative ranks need not be something dreaded or delayed, they argued. The change is something to enjoy. There are many ways to find meaning, purpose, and delight in this transition, especially when you align your faculty work with the things that matter to you most.

KNOWING WHEN IT'S TIME TO STEP AWAY

When asked how they knew it was time to take a new direction, former senior leaders often pointed toward several contributing factors. For a few out-liers, the decision was quick and decisive: departing for personal reasons (e.g., a serious illness) made for a straightforward choice. Deciding to step away is rarely this one-dimensional. Afforded the luxury of determining the terms and timing of their exit, most leaders chose to depart when factors in their own lives neatly aligned with those of their university. In deciding when to step away, academic leaders might ask themselves:

- Are we approaching a major milestone, such as completion of a strategic plan or fund-raising campaign, that will allow me to leave on a high note?
- Is my staff in a good place? Am I leaving my successor with a capable and functioning team?
- What else is happening with the senior leaders at my institution? Would a new president, VP, or dean be better served by selecting their own cabinet? Can my staying on—for another year or more—provide stability during other transitions?
- Is this job still interesting? Do I feel challenged and rewarded? Am I still having fun?
- If I keep going at this rate, will my mental and physical health suffer?
- Am I the right person to be in this office at this point in my institution's history? Are my skills the right ones to help move us ahead?
- Can I put off writing that book another year?
- Do I feel called back to the classroom?
- What opportunities am I passing up by continuing to be an administrator?

- What will continuing to work (or stepping away) mean for my spouse or partner? Does continuing to serve in this role come at the cost of not spending quality time with my children or grandchildren? Do I need more flexibility in my schedule to care for my aging parents?
- Am I staying in this role because deciding what to do next is scary? Am I staying because it feels easier to stay than to go?
- If not now, when?

Returning to your faculty life affords the chance to rethink how you do things. In the spirit of Ehrenberg's advice, it may be helpful to recognize the ways that you can operationalize professorial responsibilities differently than you did earlier in your career. A critical aspect of any life transition is making choices: choices enable us to get "unstuck," negotiate obstacles, and move forward. Given that universities provide few explicit expectations for what a former senior leader *ought* to do upon returning to the faculty, abundant opportunities for choice await. For instance, while your faculty contract might enumerate your teaching responsibilities, other details—like research or service expectations—will likely remain vague. Returning to the faculty will almost certainly give you considerable latitude to decide how to use your time and energy.

FORGING YOUR PATH

Former academic leaders can shape their transitions by taking stock of institutional contexts, personal goals, and individual skills. Some ex-deans I interviewed took pleasure in revisiting former research agendas or embarking on new ones. Although preparing to teach for the first time after an extended absence can pose a learning curve, one former dean at a research-intensive public university described returning to the classroom to be both "fun" and "invigorating." Freed from the responsibility of speaking on behalf of their institutions, some leaders exercised their faculty voices in print by writing op-eds or for a popular press. Others tested the waters of the job market, applying for open administrative positions or engaging in consulting work before fully committing to their faculty contract. Each of these choices holds the potential for intellectual and professional satisfaction.

Another way to approach the transition from administrator to faculty is to identify things that you find rewarding and that add value to your institution, colleagues, local community, or academic discipline. Four tried-and-true win-win strategies are explored below. In deciding which to adopt, former leaders should exercise the skills they honed as senior administrators: reading subtle situational cues, listening to others, being strategic with their time and energy, seeking out feedback from trusted colleagues, and keeping their egos in check.

PROVIDE LEADERSHIP ON CAMPUS

Exiting the deanship need not mean abandoning your commitment to serve. Agreeing to lead a project or initiative is one way that former administrators who return to the faculty continue to give back to their campuses. For example, one former chief academic officer at a small private institution described why he agreed to play a key role in his university's reaccreditation: "The dean asked me to take on, with the help of another person, the collection of data and composition of our [accreditation report]. I think that's just kind of the right thing for me to do. I know the institution inside and out, and now, in a faculty role, I can bring a certain kind of perspective to the writing of that report that probably nobody else in the college could do."[4] He framed this as an "appropriate form" of university service because it leveraged his institutional knowledge, relationships, and organizational skills while never undermining his successor's authority. Writing an accreditation report had the added benefits of taking a time-intensive task off the new CAO's plate and allowing a new generation of faculty leaders to play prominent roles in standing committees.

Other administrators who returned to the faculty remade themselves into *different kinds* of campus leaders. Some became department chairs. Others directed programs (such as an in-house leadership development workshop or a speaker series) or continued to use their technical knowledge by participating in groups like the institutional review board. Some volunteered to participate in social events hosted by the alumni association. That your time in the dean's suite has come to an end doesn't mean that your time to be a campus leader is over.

BECOME A QUIET MENTOR

One of the least-visible but most common ways that former leaders continue to serve their campuses is through quiet mentorship. The modifier "quiet" describes a particular form of mentorship practiced by many former leaders: guiding and advising using a particularly light touch. Rather than telling others exactly what to do, providing all the answers, or doling out unsolicited advice, quiet mentors gently aid others in drawing their own conclusions. While chairing a committee or writing an accreditation report is a visible (and vocal) form of leadership, every day is filled with informal opportunities to lead quietly: being a sounding board for a faculty colleague, asking clarifying questions to allow others to reframe their thinking, or offering positive encouragement in the face of a setback.

One former leader described using her administrative experience to help her department chair craft a more persuasive budget request. Another former dean helped arrange an introduction between a junior colleague and a senior scholar in the field. A former provost at a public university explained how he exercised quiet mentorship in the context of his department meetings: "I can put a perspective on questions that the department has that they would have difficultly coming to themselves, simply because they haven't served in that role and seen the situation from the point of view of an administrator. I try real hard to let the department find its own way, but if they come to me and say, 'What do you think?' then I'm more than happy to share what my experience would help with."[5] It can be tactful to adopt a posture like this one, a willingness to help when asked, to ensure that your colleagues feel comfortable tapping into your expertise (should they choose). At the same time, it merits repeating that you should exercise a light touch to avoid appearing overbearing or too eager to advise.

SERVE YOUR COMMUNITY OR PROFESSION

Former senior administrators sometimes look beyond their institution to serve or lead. Stepping up to serve local community organizations or professional societies can, in turn, raise the profile of your university while giving you a realm in which to flex your administrative muscles. While it can be challenging to quantify reputational benefits, former leaders explained how their efforts—both as scholars and citizens—enhance institutional prestige. One former president of a midsize private university recounted how he divided his time upon returning to the faculty: "On the one hand, I am writing a new book, which was the opposite of the scatteredness that being a president involves. I love the focus and the control and the concentration. On the other hand, apparently, I still feel the organizational impulse. It's the collective impulse, and I'm chairing the board [of a local nonprofit]. This is the same kind of mind-set and the skill set, I think, that the presidency offers. I think if I had only been writing a book, I would have been unhappy."[6] This former president found fulfillment by engaging in two energy-intensive pursuits: writing a new book and volunteering on a community board. By reengaging his research program and lending his practical expertise to a local charity, this former president found what was for him the perfect balance: a worthy scholarly endeavor paired with service that elevated his university's standing in the community.

Other former leaders looked beyond their campuses and took on leadership roles in their disciplinary societies, joined nonprofit boards, or made themselves available to mentor aspiring leaders. In many ways, off-campus leadership can give you the best of both worlds—the rewards of being part of something larger than yourself without fear of stepping on your successor's toes. This approach can be especially appealing for leaders who felt pressured to resign and are eager to create space between themselves, their institutions, and their former administrative peers.

WHEN IN DOUBT, DEFER

A successful leadership transition is often shaped by what a former dean does *not* do or say. Deference, silence, humility, and strategic absence are often winning strategies when navigating the liminal spaces between administrative and faculty roles. When pressed, many former leaders reflected that doing *nothing* proved integral to their eventual return to the faculty. Hanging back enabled ex-deans to give space to their successor and to their colleagues. Being physically away from the campus during a sabbatical not only allowed others to adjust to a new leader but also freed the former administrator to rest and resume personally and intellectually rewarding pursuits. Mastering the self-discipline required to maintain a low profile goes a long way in helping faculty colleagues see you as a peer. One former provost advised: "It's best not to bring that [administrative] persona into the departmental dynamic. . . . It's just not going to help you integrate into the group if you're always acting like you used to be the provost. It's not helpful."[7] There are many ways to be deferential; examples include agreeing to teach a large introductory course that others may be less excited to teach; abstaining from controversial departmental votes; moving into an unoccupied office rather than demanding renovations to an existing one; and refraining from voicing any opinions about your successor—in public or in private.

(RE)DEFINING THE ROLE OF A FORMER LEADER

These examples illustrate how senior academic leaders who return to the faculty used their talents and exercised restraint to advance their own goals and the missions of their institutions. Former leaders were at liberty to define their faculty roles according to different, even contradictory impulses. Some performed their roles as primarily inward focusing, mentoring departmental colleagues and serving on university committees, while others found satisfaction by engaging externally with local nonprofits and national networks. Some continued to exercise their leadership skills in organizations, while others filled their time with the more individualistic pursuits of teaching, research, and doting on their grandchildren.

In approaching your return to the faculty, be generous with yourself. Many former senior academic leaders told me that it took two years, if not longer, to find their footing on faculty soil. Along the way, they recalibrated their expectations, tried new things, took risks, and eventually grew more confident with their status as a former administrator in faculty clothing. In time, they got better at structuring their days and deepened their appreciation for the autonomy afforded to them.

As you complete your administrative responsibilities, don't be afraid to embrace the many and varied opportunities that lie ahead. In taking stock of your options, it can be prudent, when possible, to seek out win-win strategies for advancing your own goals while benefiting others. Returning to the faculty will never be a one-size-fits-all prospect; indeed, much of the joy is found by embracing your own path and honoring all the ways that your administrative service has changed you. Most importantly, have fun. You've earned it.

— *Takeaways* —

- As you transition from leadership to the faculty, leverage the skills that made you effective in your previous role—flexing institutional knowledge, building relationships across campus, exercising interpersonal acumen, providing organization and structure, celebrating the wins, and using humor to break the tension.
- Adopt a light touch when inhabiting a new position in the social architecture of a department or college.
- Stepping *away* from senior academic leadership is a chance to step *up* in other places and ways. Direct your efforts beyond the campus walls to support causes and groups that matter to you. Recognize the power of external networks to provide a safe harbor if your exit was fraught with political and interpersonal tension. Use the flexibility of your faculty schedule to take on added responsibilities at home.
- Temper the impulse to be *too* helpful or a know-it-all. Remember: inaction can sometimes be the best course of action, both for you and others.
- Give yourself time and permission to make the transition back to the faculty gradually. It may take a few years and a few backsteps to find your stride. It's not a race.

NOTES

1. Ronald G. Ehrenberg, "Being a Quadruple Threat Keeps It Interesting," in *Faculty Career Paths: Multiple Routes to Academic Success and Satisfaction*, ed. Betsy E. Brown and Gretchen Bataille (Westport, CT: Praeger, 2006), 120.
2. Larry A. Nielsen, *Provost: Experiences, Reflections, and Advice from a Former "Number Two" on Campus* (Sterling, VA: Stylus, 2013).
3. Lisa Jasinski, "Stepping Down? Theorizing the Process of Returning to the Faculty after Senior Academic Leadership," *Journal of Research on the College President* 4 (2020): 45–61.

4. Lisa Jasinski, "'From the Center to the Margin': Theorizing the Process of Returning to the Faculty after Senior Academic Leadership" (PhD diss., University of Texas at Austin, 2018), 237.

5. Jasinksi, "'From the Center to the Margin,'" 243.

6. Jasinksi, 242.

7. Jasinksi, 189.

CHAPTER 34

The Role of the Dean
of the College (1964)

WILLIAM C. DeVANE

Editor's note: The speech below was delivered at the ACAD conference held at the Mayflower Hotel in Washington, D.C., on January 13, 1964, and was printed that year in the *Proceedings of the American Conference of Academic Deans*. It was later included in *The Academic Deanship in American Colleges and Universities* (Arthur J. Dibden, ed.; Southern Illinois University Press, 1968). Finally, as ACAD looked to its seventy-fifth anniversary, the speech was published again, in *The ACAD Leader* in October 2018.

William Clyde DeVane (1898–1965) served as dean of Yale College from 1938 to 1963. Upon his retirement in 1964, he was the longest-serving dean in the institution's history to that time. Press reports of his retirement noted the numerous projects he looked forward to finishing, among them his *Higher Education in Twentieth-Century America* (Harvard University Press, 1965). Sadly, however, DeVane's essay for ACAD was among his last published works. Shortly after his retirement he passed away on August 16, 1965, at the age of sixty-seven.

One of DeVane's opening remarks is notable: "I think we do not often remember that deans, in the American use of the title, that is, as connected with a college, are recent creations . . ." Ephraim Gurney (1829–86) was appointed dean of the College Faculty at Harvard in 1870, an event often cited as the foundation of the modern concept of academic deanship. Thus, the office itself was just short of a century old at the time of this speech in 1964.

In his remarks, DeVane speaks familiarly, pulling the reader into the historical sweep of leadership through the use of "we," "us," and "our." Leadership has a noble history, a lineage that we are a part of and that we guide into a new century. Each of us in our own way brings guiding light into what DeVane calls "this wild and dark world."

The swift movement of time has done some strange things to the title of dean. Once, the dean was a clergyman, head of a cathedral, or chapter, by title set over ten monks. As we think of our faculties at home, most of us would have a hard time reckoning ten monks in those secular bodies, or ten who even had the appearance of monks, to say nothing of the monkish habit of obedience. But if it comes to that, not too many of us are clergymen, and our offices have little of the cathedral air about them, nor are we as a profession usually credited with clerical virtues. More often than not, the feature ascribed to us by the faculty is illegitimacy.

On our part, I think we do not often remember that deans, in the American use of the title, that is, as connected with a college, are recent creations—perhaps creatures of a day. Our office in this sense is hardly a hundred years old. We are the product of the nineteenth century in America, called into being by the university movement in higher education which burgeoned in the late 1860s. Before the War between the States the college usually got along with a president, a treasurer, and a librarian who was also a teacher. It was the growing size of the colleges late in the nineteenth century, together with the growing complexity of the institutions as they took on university stature and pretensions, that called us into actuality. Before that, we were merely senior tutors, or a hope in the overtaxed presidential heart. But once we were visible, we made ourselves indispensable, and by the end of the nineteenth century every college, no matter how small, had one of us.

With our accession to office—an all-purpose office—we almost at once began to take on many of the duties, attributes, and colorations of the president. The old president of the college, who was usually really a clergyman, was often the father of his flock, both of his faculty and of his students. He suffered the pangs of dispensing student discipline and cried aloud about it. Governing the student body, said Ezra Stiles, one of the old breed of presidents, was like trying to control a wildfire, and "the only diadem a president was likely to gain was a crown of thorns."[1] In his better mood, Stiles taught his senior class a course in moral philosophy, but managed to work in some sessions on the Hebrew language, because, he said, he would not like to have his boys go to heaven and not know the language of the place. To control and discipline the faculty was also his task—often a very painful task as the consequences of the president's decisions were serious and lasting. Above all, however, the president in the old regime was a mythical figure who attracted legends and stories to himself, and if he was not sufficiently eccentric, his students affectionately created the legends about him. I suppose the modern psychiatrist would say that the old president was an almost perfect father image; and what else they might say about the poor old gentleman will not be suggested here.

But here is the point. The early dean inherited most of the characteristics and attributes of the old president, as well as many of the duties. A recent book has a significant title, and I hope you will ponder every word of it. It is this: *God Bless Our Queer Old Dean* by William Storrs Lee.[2] There is affection in that title, along with condescension toward a Walter Mitty grown old. That perceptive man, James Thurber, made the dean a hero in his play *The Male Animal.* But well beyond sterling qualities, heroic virtues, and innocent moral triumphs, the dean was a mythical character to the students of a later time as the old president had been before him—something to be treasured nostalgically by alumni as a part of one's college days. I need hardly tell you that the myth had frequently little to do with the reality. The faculty who knew the dean knew this, and often had other terms than those used by the students to describe the dean's character. In any case, no harmless eccentric could possibly have done what the dean of the college was expected to do in an academic year. Just the same, the dean was, and is, the figure in the complex, modern institution who preserves best the human values of the old college and its president. We modern deans came into a goodly heritage, and we must remember gratefully such men as the magnanimous Dean Briggs of Harvard, the hospitable, wise and kindly Deans Keppel and Hawkes of Columbia, Jones of Yale to whom God deigned to speak, Gauss who left his imprint upon Princeton, Norton of Pomona, and many, many more throughout the land.[3] About these men the stories of innumerable quiet charities, and even more precious understandings, clustered. The office, I think, has a way of inducing benevolence, and sometimes wisdom.

As for the dean's duties, they were never precisely defined, and often one could only say that a dean is one who performs decanal duties. Generally, the man defined the job by his interests. In most cases he holds his office for a term of years on appointment by the president, and in that sense is the president's man. At the same time, he is usually drawn from the faculty, and most often remains the faculty representative in the hierarchy of the administration. And it is this ambiguous position that is sometimes the source of his acute distress, as he tries to maintain concord between an impetuous president and a recalcitrant faculty.

In the changing academic scene, the office of the dean has evolved in the same way that the presidential office has done. As the institution grew larger and more complex the president receded intellectually and personally from the faculty and the students. Most of the president's energies went into dealing with the alumni, making speeches, serving on national committees, soliciting money, and performing other such painful and public tasks. The conduct of the college at home has in this way descended upon the dean—and then in the course of events the dean himself has receded from the students in part, and becomes an academic dean, with associates and assistants dealing with the many other phases of the college. This is often only a partial recession; for the dean stays on the campus and is seen daily, and is appealed to by students and faculty as a court of higher authority than the assistant or associate dean. As chief officer of the college, or academic dean, the dean is responsible for the total oversight of the undergraduate phase of the institution's educational operation—the health, morals, quality, and personality of the college and its personnel, its policy, its finances, and its standards, though some of these functions may be delegated. But delegation merely eases the daily burden, and does not relieve the dean's obligation of responsibility for the welfare and health of the total college.

By all odds, the most important aspect of the academic dean is his relation to the faculty. This is an aspect of the task that he cannot delegate, though if he is wise he will get all the help he can. In dealing with the faculty the dean is least like the myth the students may have created about him. Here the deepest personal characteristics of the dean must come into play. His wide knowledge of the academic world is here invaluable. In recruiting a faculty, which with the help of the departments is his major task, he must know where good physicists are educated, and where good historians, where men are trained who have no time for anything but research, where teachers are bred who will never learn more than they now know and will become less and less effective as teachers. And it is well if the dean knows where to look for that priceless man or woman who is both scholar and teacher, and has the extra virtues of personality and the capability of becoming a loyal member of the college community—loyal not to himself, but to the enterprise. In short, the dean must have antennae and know where to look. Not less, he must know how to look. It is well if the dean shall have had, somewhere in his career, the experience of observing or working in a first-rate institution that knows quality and is not willing or compelled to accept the mediocre. He must smell out the future to know what the candidate for appointment will be in fifteen or twenty years, and what the discipline the young man professes will be in the same twenty years. It is perilous to make an important appointment, for example, in a science like physics where the fierce pace of change may make the person under consideration obsolete sooner than his expensive instruments become outmoded. The qualities most valuable to the dean in the appointive process are knowledge, intuition, and sometimes persuasion. This is to ask a very great deal of mortal man, and if the dean can find somewhere a crystal ball which will let him peer into the future a quarter of a century ahead he can sleep better; the mistakes he makes in appointments, or allows to be made under his supervision, will often haunt him that long. Unlike the physician, the dean cannot bury his mistakes.

Now the care and feeding of the faculty in his charge is a different matter and calls for some different qualities. It is still extremely valuable for the dean to know the academic world widely and well. But with the faculty on the campus the prime quality necessary is understanding. The dean must understand his faculty in the mass and deal openly and frankly with them. His integrity must be beyond question. He must understand with sympathy, and yet with firmness, the individual in the faculty, as well—the conditions of the teacher's life, his imagined necessities and his real ones, his anxieties and his ambitions. In the light of his appraisal of the worth of the man and his value to the college, the dean must do everything he can to see that in justice and under the rules of fair play the best members of the faculty get what they legitimately want in terms of salary, promotions, leaves of absence, teaching schedules, and other such matters. And in doing this, the dean must always keep in the forefront of his mind the good of the institution rather than his own affections. But, as all deans know, the academic world is not an Eden inhabited only by the wise and good. We do not have to look far to see selfishness, malice, and greed in a faculty, and less often more vicious evils, such as cheating and treachery. More often a member of the faculty is guilty of sharp dealing, prejudice, petty hates, or of seeing his own desires and virtues out of all perspective; and occasionally they become manipulators to get offers from other colleges, and threaten to resign. It is sometimes wise to make use of a quotation from a folk jingle that each of us learned in our youth: "If he hollers, let him go." Kiss him goodbye, if you will, but never take him back! In dealing with the faculty it is frequently better to be admired than loved.

Perhaps I have almost persuaded you that the academic dean is a composite of all virtues, a really magnanimous person. But I hardly need remind you that the world is of another opinion. I have never fully understood the instinctive animus that many faculty members feel at the mention of the dean, but there must be something to it—it is so universal. The dean, of course, can be drunk with power. He can be high-handed and arbitrary. He can play favorites. He can even be stupid. All these things he does, no doubt, consciously or unconsciously, arrogantly or reluctantly, for he is human and fallible, for he often must be the executioner, the hangman, and seem to the faculty member to be "the smyler with the knife," as Chaucer phrases it. The dean may be compassionate, but he cannot be queasy, and if he is to last long in his job he must be able to put the painful matter out of his mind at night. But departments and professors can be arbitrary, too, willful and self-seeking.

Perhaps the greatest difficulty I have had as dean is in trying to get departments to consider the good of the college as a more important matter than the advancement of the discipline which they represent. Especially in the universities has the loyalty of the department and the professor in the department shifted today from the college to the subject of their teaching and research and its national or international associations. This is most noticeable in the sciences, but has spread to all disciplines. The dean, who is committed to his institution, has to continually seek ways to circumvent this centrifugal loss of loyalty, and this calls for perseverance, patience, and skill. In such a Balkanized faculty it is difficult to preserve the freedom and morale of the college as a whole, and at the same time attain purpose, order, and proportion.

The second great area of direct interest of the academic dean is the area of policy. Here the dean must be an academic statesman of the most skillful kind—a prime minister who holds his leadership by persuasion and votes. Traditionally and properly the control of the curriculum is normally assigned to the faculty, but in actual practice the course of study is guided and managed by a committee responsible to the faculty. The dean is invariably a member of this committee, and frequently its chairman. In any case, he has the immense advantage of continuity. The composition of the committee changes year by year—sometimes the dean sees that it does—but the dean is always there. He thinks about the curriculum steadily, as the members of the committee rarely do. The faculty and even members of the committee on the course of study will normally think of the problem piecemeal, course by course, or the departmental offering. The dean must think of the curriculum in its totality and proportion as well as piecemeal, and must scrutinize the quality and appropriateness of each course, and if possible curb the endless proliferation of courses. If a bold new arrangement in distribution or concentration is proposed, it is usually the dean who has thought of it. If a change is proposed in the honors program or the calendar, or in the terms of financial aid, or admissions, or athletic policy, it is likely that the initiating idea has come from the dean. It is sometimes fortunate if the faculty realizes where the ideas come from only after the vote is taken.

To be effective in this area of college policy the dean must know many things, and exercise some unusual qualities. He must know the general history of higher education in America, where its component parts came from and why, how the college and the university developed, when and why at that particular time. And in that perspective he must know where the college is now in the total educational establishment, what are its prospects, and what its dangers. This is especially important now as the college once again is facing the question of its survival in its traditional form, and under pressure from advanced credit below and early specialization from above, is in danger of becoming a junior college or of being swallowed by the graduate school. The college must now say what it should be and why. I think that wise management of the curriculum may be the key to the situation. Even more intimately the dean must know the peculiar history of his own college; for colleges, like people, have personalities and special characters, and are made by the conditions of their history.

In the making and control of the curriculum the special qualities the dean must exercise seem to me to be three: imagination, restraint, and persuasion. I have probably said enough about the first, and shall only add that the imagination must be curbed by judgment concerning what is possible, both humanly and politically. When one thinks of restraint in a faculty, one remembers Mark Twain's comment on honesty: "Honesty," he said, "is the rarest of virtues. Use it sparingly." But in the desire of the faculty to expand the course offering of the department, for one reason or another, there is never any restraint. Our bulletins and catalogs aspire to rival the publications of Sears Roebuck. Left to the faculty, or even the committee on the course of study, there is seldom any sense of form in the student's education, seldom any sense of discrimination between the important and the trivial. I have seen the case where a faculty was offered a general raise in salary if the course offerings were reduced to make a raise financially possible. The faculty would not do it. If there is to be any restraint in the endless proliferation of new courses, it usually must come from the dean.

The third valuable quality that comes into play is persuasion. When an imaginative program of studies has been constructed, having the virtues of form, order, proportion, and discrimination, it is necessary to persuade a faculty, preoccupied by its own studies and vested interests, to accept the plan—possibly with some small sacrifice of sovereignty on the part of the department or the individual for the general good. But mere acceptance is not enough. The faculty has to operate the program, and if there is no enthusiasm for the plan it cannot be a success. To win such enthusiasm will call upon all the statesmanship the dean has, and some other qualities that might be thought more political than statesmanlike. I have sometimes said that the most useful of a dean's characteristics are patience and low cunning.

In a complex organization like a modern university, the dean needs persistence, ingenuity in stating his case, freedom to maneuver, and good luck when he sits down at the budget table with his rival deans of the graduate and professional schools, the provost, the treasurer, and the comptroller to plan the expenditures for the next year. He must know why it is more important to strengthen the Department of English than to provide a new professor for the Law School, why better pension arrangements are more important than an athletic field house, and why the enrollment of the college must not be increased without an equivalent increase in the size of the faculty. These are behind-the-scene matters, seldom immediately visible to the community, but of much consequence. The hardest matter for the dean to learn here is that there are cases and times when he should not win if a wholesome corporate spirit is to be preserved. The good of the university is more important than a victory for the dean or the college.

The third great area of operations for which the academic dean is responsible is the world of the student. This area is usually delegated to an associate or assistant dean, called variously the dean of students, the dean of men or women, and so forth. But the responsibility for the satisfactory conduct of the office, remains with the head dean. And here the dean must exercise tact and judgment in dealing with his associates and also with the faculty, as discipline and standards are applied and rewards and penalties made. The faculty will almost invariably be dissatisfied with the operations of the office. The dean's office is always too soft with the students, and at the same time unreasonably severe. Here is a useful rule of thumb: when a member of the faculty gets too obstreperously critical, put him on the committee which dispenses discipline. After a little experience, he frequently becomes an ardent special pleader. As for the faculty members who cannot get to their classes on time and are invariably late with grades and reports, there is little that can be done except to catch them when they are young and make them think that you are keeping a record of their delinquencies. Here a loud strong voice, a scowling countenance, and a fist that can bang the table are of inestimable value.

By divorcing himself from the intimate association with the students, or being divorced by the sheer business of his office, the academic dean suffers a loss which he does not always appreciate. It is well that the dean should make every effort to keep in touch with the students by teaching a class, having some of them in his home, or meeting frequently with them in their organizations. I confess that some of the happiest recollections I have had in my career as dean have been friendships made with students, or occasions where the innate gaiety and honesty of the student have been suddenly apparent. For example, I remember with delight a conversation I had years ago with a student, the son of a classmate, who came to see me about his academic condition, at his father's request. During a little preliminary persiflage it became clear to me that he was in danger of being drafted by the army. I had not then seen his record, so I asked him if he were in the top half of his class. "Oh, no sir," he said, "I am one who makes the top half possible." A better story even longer gone by is the one told about a predecessor of mine, Dean Wright, who was called on at his home by a returning alumnus, whose greeting was, "You don't remember me." Leaning forward to see him better in the dark, the Dean responded, "The name escapes me but the breath is familiar."

But those lighthearted days have gone for the academic dean, and indeed, even for the dean of students, and for the undergraduates, too. We have moved into a grimmer world. But neither years ago nor now was the discourse between the dean and the student always a gay one. There was always the necessity for the dean to find out and listen carefully to the poor earnest student who could not make the grade, the student who was financially destitute and too proud to ask for help, the student who had to be rescued from his opinionated and strong-handed father, and the student who was in desperate need of friendship, and possibly psychiatric care. These things, now cared for by expert counselors, physicians and psychiatrists, wardens and masters, are the very stuff of life. They were painful enough to see and hear at the time, but in escaping from them one loses one's touch with humanity at its most appealing stage. I wonder, sometimes, if the brisk, competent, modern student who possesses the world, now, has escaped those agonies of adolescence, or if behind his glossy assurance he, too, ever is lonely, or knows himself to be small and helpless in this wild and dark world.

A few observations upon the dean's various relationships, and I have done. Between the president and the faculty the dean is between the upper and nether millstones. He has the duty to inform the president of the true state of things in the faculty—things which the president sometimes would rather not hear. He must convey to the faculty, often, things the faculty would prefer not to hear. Above all, he must maintain his own independence and integrity if he is to be of any use. It is often a delicate position he occupies, and he must be prepared to be blamed by both sides. Toward the faculty he must be eminently just and deal evenly, but yet make distinctions. He had better know the pecking order in the faculty and yet never use it. There is a very imperfectly followed chain of command in most institutions. A few years ago the new captain of the Naval ROTC came into my office and announced, a little belligerently, that he was bewildered by procedures in the university. "What," he asked me, "is the chain of command here?" Just then one of our most distinguished professors came by the door, and I said to the captain, "See, there is a professor! He is responsible only to God." It is well if the dean shall be a scholar in order that he may speak on even terms with the faculty, whose highest respect goes to scholarship. But once he has become dean he will seldom have the chance to be a scholar again. The duties that the dean performs daily are antithetical to the scholarly life. His life is harder, more continually demanding, and full of constant crises. His pay is less, in spite of the legend to the contrary, than that of many professors—in some places less than the football coach. He is as likely to be blamed as praised. One may fairly ask why anyone should accept such a job. For myself, I have a point or two in answer. First, there is in some of us qualities of personality that demand to be exercised if we are to be whole men. Next, there is a kind of loyalty which is old-fashioned today and may, I admit, be foolish. But a man needs something beyond himself and his family to give his life to, and a college seems to be of manageable size; and he may better the place by his efforts.

NOTES

1. Ezra Stiles (1727–95) served as the seventh president of Yale College from 1778 to 1795. The quote to which DeVane alludes exists in several versions. The one below was published in *The Literary Diary of Ezra Stiles, D.D., L.L.D., President of Yale College,* vol. 2 (New York: Charles Scribner's Sons, 1901), 209:

   My Election to the Presidency of Yale College is an unexpected and wonderful ordering of divine Providence. . . . I have no more resolved in my Mind whether I am qualified for such an office than for that of a prime Minister or Sultan, or whether I should on the whole be desirous of it; considering the Smallness of the Salary, and the great and complicated Difficulties & Labours which attend it. An hundred & fifty or 180 Young Gentlemen Students, is a Bundle of Wild Fire not easily controlled & governed—and at best the Diadem of a President is a Crown of Thornes.

2. In *Administration of Higher Education: An Annotated Bibliography* (US Department of Health, Education, and Welfare, 1969), Walter Eells and Ernest Hollis noted of the book that was published ten years earlier in 1959 by G. P. Putnam's Sons: "A report on the various roles of the college dean of students—as administrator, educator, counselor, disciplinarian, and benevolent guide. The dark side is not overlooked. Reference is made to some of the great deans of past and present. Written in cheerful and colorful style" (139).

3. DeVane refers to LeBaron Russell Briggs (1855–1934); Frederick P. Keppel (1875–1943); Herbert E. Hawkes (1872–1943); Frederick Scheetz Jones (1862–1944); Christian Gauss (1878–1951); and E. C. Norton (1856–1943).

Afterword

ANDREW ADAMS

It has been an honor to edit this book and, in so doing, to work with colleagues from across the country, most of whom I've never met. Together, we've shaped an edition that I hope will inform and inspire leaders just as ACAD's previous three volumes have done for more than two decades.

Preparation of this edition has been deeply rewarding for me personally. For the past year and a half, while editing a book in large part addressed to deans, I've served as the director of a school of music at a university in the rural mountains of western North Carolina. In my work, I studied every draft of every chapter from the perspective of someone who sought to learn from my colleagues. This opportunity was an example of the kind of professional development that ACAD has always afforded me. Through ACAD, I've found some of the best friends and most respected colleagues of my career.

I've been struck that many of the authors in this volume, like others who have written books and articles about leadership, describe program directors, department heads, associate deans, deans, and provosts as "leading from the middle." For me, this acknowledges our unfaltering dedication to shared governance. Few of us claim to be an absolute leader free from the gravitational pull of others. Rather, we seek to be nestled among the myriad voices around us who desire to take part in the conversation, no matter how truly momentous or seemingly trivial the topic. Whether we face a pandemic, a demographic cliff, or an overhaul of an academic program, every challenge is mitigated by the number of minds that unite to grapple with it and the number of hands that join together to fix it.

ACAD's seventy-five-year history and the historic sources on leadership it has produced have always intrigued me. For many decades ACAD printed yearly proceedings of its conferences, since 1999 we've published four handbooks, and we now offer an online newsletter, *The ACAD Leader*, that presents new and historic material. In my work for the *Leader*, it's been a pleasure to reintroduce sources from ACAD's archives such as Ruth Loving Higgins's 1947 deans survey; Elizabeth McKinsey's article from 1992 entitled "Political Correctness: The Metapolitics of Deaning"; and a fascinating speech by John R. Silber, "The Dean as Educator: His Doing and Undoing," given at the 1971 ACAD national conference, shortly after he stepped down as a dean and just before he became a university president. These articles and many others can be found on ACAD's website.

Given the uncertainties in the world in the past year and a half, it was important for me as the editor to anchor the central content of this book in a broad historical frame. Philip A. Glotzbach, author of the first chapter, accepted a deanship three decades ago, in 1992, and published the initial version of his remarks in the second edition of the *Resource Handbook* in 2007. William C. DeVane, author of the last chapter, was born in the nineteenth century, began his work as a dean nearly one hundred years ago in 1938, and first presented his remarks at an ACAD conference in 1964. Although the chapters they wrote were separated by six decades, we see through their eyes that some approaches to leadership are timeless.

At the conclusion of this fourth edition, I'd like to share a passage from an academic leader who came long before us but who faced challenges similar to our own. In 1959 Marten ten Hoor (1890–1967) was in his last year as dean of the College of Arts and Sciences at the University of Alabama. In the conclusion of "Personnel Problems in Academic Administration," ten Hoor moved from a recognition of the shared humanity of campus colleagues to a litany of searching hypotheticals that seek to lift us out of our egos. His antiquated use of the masculine pronoun demonstrates that profound truths can lie beneath the surface features of historic language. Near the end of the H2N2 influenza pandemic that raged throughout 1957 and 1958, killing an estimated 1.5 million people worldwide, ten Hoor articulated a transcendent vision of leadership in higher education, writing:

Educational administration is not a science and never will be. The basic reason is of course that it is concerned with the direction of a human activity which is not itself a science, namely education. Moreover, we are not dealing with perfect administrators or perfect professors. The fact is that we are all fallible and underlying all this talk about plans and procedures is the primary and inescapable assumption that we have to learn to live with one another's shortcomings. . . .

As for the administrator, let him not forget that the practice of educational administration is in itself an educational experience. If in the course of this experience he has learned not to mistake his own dogma for sound educational policies and his own comfort for the welfare of the faculty; if he has learned that a reputation with faculty and students for integrity is in the long run quite as important as routine administrative efficiency, and certainly more rewarding; if he has learned that in the use of democratic procedures the gain in faculty morale and cooperativeness usually offsets the loss in time and efficiency; if he has learned when to talk and when to keep silent, when to write a letter and when not to do so; if he has learned that the frank and prompt acknowledgment of mistakes disarms and frustrates critics, and eases his own conscience; if he has learned to bear the role of academic scapegoat with serenity; if he has learned cheerfully to accept the occupational risks of his job as the price of his glory; if above all he has learned to see his administrative functions in the perspective of their ultimate purpose, namely to create the most favorable conditions possible for education; if he has learned all these things and many more— then, over the long haul, he will have attained as good a measure of success as can be expected in the most complex and difficult of all human enterprises—participation in the direction of man's efforts to improve himself.[1]

NOTES

1. Marten ten Hoor, "Personnel Problems in Academic Administration," *Liberal Education* 45 (October 1959): 405–23.

Contributors

Andrew Adams is Director of the School of Music and Professor of Piano at Western Carolina University in Cullowhee, North Carolina. He earned the BM in Piano from the Kansas City Conservatory of Music and the MM in Vocal Coaching and Accompanying from the University of Illinois. He completed the DMA in Piano Performance at the University of Colorado. Adams served as Vocal Coach and Director of Collaborative Piano at Iowa State University from 2003 to 2006. He was a member of the editorial board of the *Journal of Singing*, the official publication of the National Association of Teachers of Singing, for twelve years. He has published articles and reviews in *Piano Professional* (England), *The American Music Teacher*, the *Journal of the International Alliance for Women in Music*, and the *North Carolina Music Educator*.

Cheryl Bailey, PhD, became hooked on science after viewing trypanosome parasites swimming under a microscope. Once she began teaching science, she found the same joy in helping students learn about and investigate the natural world. Her interest is providing opportunities and removing barriers for students to pursue their professional, personal, and community lives. Since 2014, Cheryl has served as the Dean of the School of Natural and Health Sciences & Education at Mount Mary University in Milwaukee. Cheryl also serves as the Chair of the Education and Professional Development Committee for the American Society of Biochemistry and Molecular Biology and cofacilitated an international meeting for educators on teaching science with big data. As a scientist, she sees the future looking very different from the one she was trained for and is interested in preparing students for new discoveries.

With increasing use of artificial intelligence analyzing large sets of data, the creativity of scientists will have even higher impact in the future, and they will bear increased responsibility for ethical actions.

Kelly H. Ball serves as Associate Dean for Graduate Studies and Associate Professor of Women's, Gender, and Sexuality Studies and Philosophy at Agnes Scott College. Ball holds a PhD from Emory University, having earned prior degrees at Transylvania University and The Ohio State University before joining the faculty of Agnes Scott College in 2014. An award-winning scholar, her research interests include continental feminist philosophy, feminist epistemology, and metaphysics. As the founding dean of the graduate programs at Agnes Scott, Dr. Ball oversees graduate and postbaccalaureate program development and design, academic policy, accreditation, admission, advising, curriculum, financial forecasting, enrollment marketing, and strategic planning and leads the graduate and postbaccalaureate faculty. Her recent projects include leading an institution-wide initiative focused on the professional success of undergraduate and graduate students, and leading the development of a new suite of graduate programs in the health professions.

J. Herman Blake's career spans more than five decades as a scholar, professor, and administrator. He received a BA in Sociology from New York University and an MA and PhD in Sociology from the University of California at Berkeley. He was the Founding Provost of Oakes College at the University of California, Santa Cruz, where he also served as Professor of Sociology. In 2007 he was appointed the Inaugural Humanities Scholar in Residence at the Medical University of South Carolina. His research focuses on academic achievement of minority students, Gullah Geechee communities in South Carolina, and Black militants. The video of his 1963 interview of Malcolm X has been widely viewed. In 1978 the American Council on Education named him one of the top one hundred emerging leaders in higher education. In 2021 the American Sociological Association presented him with its Distinguished Career Award.

Jamila Bookwala is Dean of the Faculty and Chair of the Diversity, Equity, and Inclusion Council at Lafayette College in Easton, Pennsylvania. Reporting to the Provost, she is responsible for all faculty hiring and also oversees staff hiring within the academic division. She is responsible for faculty diversity and retention, support, and personnel issues, including informal conflict resolution. She is Professor of Psychology and was the founding chair of the college's aging studies program and is former head of the Department of Psychology. Her teaching and research interests are in the subdiscipline of lifespan psychology. A primary focus of her research is social factors in health and well-being over the lifespan. She has published her research in leading peer-reviewed journals and has presented her research findings at national and international conferences. She is an elected Fellow of the Gerontological Society of America and the American Psychological Association. She completed her doctoral training at the University of Pittsburgh and postdoctoral training at the University of Pennsylvania.

Angela Bos is Professor of Political Science at the College of Wooster, where she has also served as Department Chair and Associate Dean for Experiential Learning. After earning her BA in Political Science at the University of Minnesota–Morris, she earned her MA and PhD degrees in Political Science at the University of Minnesota. At Wooster, she teaches courses on American politics, political psychology, campaigns and elections, media and politics, and gender politics. She also developed a program in which students study the US national political party conventions and then travel to the conventions to collect data for collaborative research projects. Her research focuses primarily on barriers to electing women to political office, including voters' gender stereotypes and how children are socialized to politics. As Associate Dean for Experiential Learning, she led a strategic planning effort to expand high-impact experiential learning opportunities to all College of Wooster students.

George H. Brown is the Dean of the David Orr Belcher College of Fine and Performing Arts at Western Carolina University in Cullowhee, North Carolina. Prior to his appointment in 2014, he served as the Associate Dean of the College of Fine Arts at Western Michigan University. From 2002 to 2012, Brown served as the chair of the Department of Theatre Arts at Bradley University in Peoria, Illinois. During his final year at the institution he concurrently served as interim chair of the Department of Interactive Media (2011–12). He has held leadership roles in the National Association of Schools of Theatre, the International University Theatre Association, and the Southwest Theatre Association. He served regularly as a mentor with the Association for Theatre in Higher Education Leadership Institute and with the International Council of Fine Arts Deans. He holds a PhD in Educational Leadership (Higher Education) from Western Michigan University and an MFA in Directing from Penn State.

Kendrick T. Brown is Provost and Vice President of Academic Affairs at Morehouse College in Atlanta. He served previously as Dean of the College of Arts and Sciences at the University of Redlands in Southern California for four and half years. For eighteen years, he was a faculty member, department chair, and Associate Dean of the faculty at Macalester College in St. Paul, Minnesota. His research focuses on the perception of allies by Black, indigenous, and people of color, as well as how skin-tone bias affects the psychological well-being of Black people and the ways interracial contact on sports teams can promote empathy and affect policy stances. He uses his training as a social psychologist to understand leadership dynamics, facilitate meaningful communication and interactions, and implement complex initiatives that promote institutional effectiveness, particularly within liberal arts contexts.

Ron Cole became Provost and Dean of the College at Allegheny College in 2015, where he served as a faculty member for twenty years and held leadership positions as department and natural science division chair, faculty moderator, a member of the trustees diversity task force, and chair of faculty council, the faculty review committee, and the finance and facilities committee. As provost he promoted data-informed change to improve student access and success that led to curricular revisions in STEM and humanities fields and increased first-year student retention. Cole is a speaker on campus leadership for the Council of Independent Colleges national workshop for division and department chairs and has been a panelist at national higher-ed conferences on a range of topics. As a teacher-scholar Cole teaches at all levels of the curriculum, has received an award for excellence in teaching, and established an active student-focused undergraduate research program in the geosciences. Before his career in higher education, he worked in the environmental consulting industry.

Del Doughty (PhD, Comparative Literature, Pennsylvania State University) serves as Dean of the College of Arts, Sciences, and Education and Professor of English at Texas A&M University–Texarkana. Prior to his appointment there, he taught English and held various administrative posts at Huntington University in Huntington, Indiana. He has published two award-winning chapbooks of poetry (*The Sound of Breathing*, Saki Press, 2000; *Flow*, Red Moon Press, 2004) and edited scholarly editions of Joyce's *Dubliners* and *Portrait of the Artist as a Young Man*. As an administrator, he's played a part in garnering more than $5 million in external funding over the past five years and has overseen regional and program-specific accreditations. His current abiding passion is promotion of the "Better East Texas" initiative, a suite of academic programs aimed at addressing mental health, intergenerational poverty, regional history, and economic development in the East Texas region.

Michele Yapsuga Ewing is Vice-President for Advancement at Goucher College. She leads Goucher's $100 million (Undaunted) comprehensive campaign, focused on diversifying revenue streams through individual, corporate, and foundation development. Previously, she served as Associate Dean for Development and External Relations at the Johns Hopkins School of Education, where she completed the school's $60 million portion of the Rising to the Challenge campaign. She specializes in formalizing turnaround and start-up fund-raising programs to increase support, strengthen board leadership, engage faculty, address institutional challenges, and secure transformational gifts for core, programmatic, and capital projects and education research. With a background in journalism and sociology, she also brings advancement experience from a variety of professional settings including engineering, law, pharmacy, education, and liberal arts at leading undergraduate and graduate institutions.

Maria C. (Cari) Garriga has served as Faculty Trustee; Department Chair; and Associate, Vice-, and Acting Provost at Thomas More University. In academic leadership, she has overseen multiple successful accreditations, implementation of an outcome-led student-learning core curriculum, sunsetting and development of programs, and adaptations to the pandemic. A professor of Spanish, she holds a PhD in Foreign and Second Language Education from The Ohio State University and degrees from the University of Cincinnati,

Paris IV (Sorbonne), and her native Universidad de Puerto Rico. In 2014–15, she participated in the Senior Leadership Academy presented by the Council of Independent Colleges and interned as special assistant to the VPAA at DePauw University. While evolving her administrative career, Dr. Garriga realized that to be truly effective as an academic leader, one must model and promote daily holistic health in support of all constituents. She intentionally builds time into the workday to cook, read, meditate, and do a rotation of practicing yoga (RYT200 and yin certified), paddle-boarding, CrossFit development, and running (2020 Boston marathon). She and her husband of thirty-five years live in Covington, Kentucky, and have three adult children and two grandchildren.

Philip A. Glotzbach became the seventh President of Skidmore College in 2003, serving until his retirement in July 2020. His presidency followed eleven years as an academic administrator at the University of Redlands in Southern California: first as Dean of the College of Arts and Sciences and then as Vice President for Academic Affairs. Previously, he was Associate Professor of Philosophy and Chair of the Philosophy Department at Denison University, where he taught for fifteen years. Glotzbach did his undergraduate work at the University of Notre Dame, earning a BA in philosophy with Highest Honors and Phi Beta Kappa. He undertook graduate studies at Yale University, earning the MA, MPhil, and PhD degrees. Over the course of his administrative career, he has written and lectured on a variety of topics centering on effective academic leadership and the importance of liberal education in today's world. He is currently working on a book—coauthored with Robert Weisbuch—on the role of higher education in addressing contemporary challenges to democracy.

Darla S. Hanley, Dean of the Professional Education Division at Berklee College of Music, holds an MM and a PhD in Music Education Research (Temple University) and a BM in Music Education and Vocal Performance, dual major (University of Massachusetts–Lowell). Hanley specializes in higher education administration, jazz and popular music education, professional improvisation, and teacher education. Prior to coming to Berklee, she served as Associate Dean of Graduate Studies, Professor of Music Education, and Director of the Shenandoah Singers at Shenandoah Conservatory of Shenandoah University. Hanley has presented sessions in nearly all fifty states and often works with teachers and students all over the world. Hanley is a former Jazz Education Network board member and founding member and past president of the Association for Popular Music Education. She is a published author on topics related to music education and arts administration, with a new book, *Jazz Is Elementary: Creativity Development through Music Activities, Movement Games, and Dances for K–5* (coauthored with Allison Kipp) launching in 2022 (Berklee Press/Hal Leonard).

Lilia Cuesta Harvey is Charles A. Dana Professor of Chemistry and Associate Dean for STEM Teaching and Learning at Agnes Scott College in Georgia, where she has served as a faculty member since 1994. She is faculty director of Agnes Scott's Science Center for Women, a STEM-focused center with cocurricular programs that contribute to student persistence and success by pursuing evidence-based best practices. At Agnes Scott she has served as Chair of the Chemistry Department and as Associate Vice-President for Academic Affairs and Associate Dean of the College. She has published articles on strategies for engaging students in the classroom, the use of collaborative cases for teaching organic chemistry, faculty approaches to undergraduate research, and other administrative topics, as well as scholarship in organic chemistry, her area of academic expertise. Dr. Harvey is a member of the Advisory Board for Project Kaleidoscope (PKAL), AAC&U's center for STEM higher-education reform. She earned a BS in Chemistry from Florida International University and a PhD in Organic Chemistry from the Georgia Institute of Technology.

Gina Hausknecht, John William King Professor of Literature and Creative Writing in the Department of English at Coe College, has served as Associate Dean of the Faculty and Associate Dean of Student Academics, directed Coe's First-Year Seminar program and Thursday Forum public lecture series, chaired the English Department and Film Studies program, and was the founding director of Coe's Learning Commons. She teaches early modern Renaissance literature, including Shakespeare, British Renaissance poetry, and Milton. She has published and presented on Shakespeare, Milton, seventeenth-century literature and culture, pedagogy and higher education, graphic novel memoir, and gender studies. She teaches and volunteers with Liberal

Arts Beyond Bars, the University of Iowa's college-in-prison program. Her ongoing research on the textual history of stage directions in editions of Shakespeare is reflected in the interactive online learning tool *All the World's a Stage Direction*.

Margaret Hunter is a sociologist and Senior Director of the Centers for Educational Justice and Community Engagement at the University of California, Berkeley. As a leader in the Division of Equity and Inclusion, she works on student success, retention initiatives, and leadership development for underrepresented students. Her experience at various institutions informs her perspective on equity, community partnerships, and educational ecosystems. She has extensive experience building strategic educational partnerships with community colleges, public school districts, and other four-year universities, both public and private. She earned a fellowship with the American Council of Academic Deans and has also completed leadership training with the National Equity Project. Dr. Hunter is also a leading sociological researcher on colorism in Black and Latinx communities, as well as the racial politics of education and knowledge production. She is a frequent media commentator on issues of race and racism in publications, including the *New York Times*, *Los Angeles Times*, *Boston Globe*, and *Chicago Sun-Times*. Her newest research concerns the racial attitudes of Gen Z, our youngest university students, and how they shape the youth activist agenda for racial justice.

Lisa Jasinski, PhD, is Special Assistant to the Vice-President for Academic Affairs at Trinity University. She is the coauthor of *Faculty as Global Learners: Off-Campus Study at Liberal Arts Colleges* (Lever Press) and the forthcoming *Stepping Away: Returning to the Faculty after Senior Academic Leadership* (Rutgers University Press). She is a 2021–22 American Council on Education Fellow. She served as a Fulbright Specialist to Finland. She holds a BA from Middlebury College, an MA from the University of Wisconsin–Madison, and a PhD in Higher-Education Leadership and Policy from the University of Texas at Austin.

Feng-Ling Johnson serves as the Dean of University College and Associate Vice-President for Student Success at St. Cloud State University in St. Cloud, Minnesota. She leads university-wide student success initiatives on student belonging, persistence, and retention, and oversees academic support services in the University College. She is a member of the Equity and Inclusion Council in the Minnesota State Colleges and Universities System Office. Prior to joining the team at St. Cloud State University, she served as Professor of English as a Second Language Education and Linguistics, Program Coordinator of ESL Education, Chair of the Department of World Languages, Chair of the Department of Interdisciplinary Studies, and Senior Dean of Academic Administration at University of Northwestern–St. Paul in St. Paul, Minnesota. As Senior Dean for six years, she oversaw the Center for Teaching and Learning, Global Initiatives, Education Abroad, Honors Program, Academic Achievement, Career Development, and other academic support and student services.

Bridget Keegan is Professor of English and Dean of the College of Arts and Science at Creighton University. Prior to serving as dean, she held a variety of leadership roles, including Chair of English, Chair of Modern Languages, Director of Scholarships and Fellowships, and Associate Dean for the College. After graduating from Harvard, she received her PhD in Comparative Literature from the State University of New York at Buffalo. A scholar of eighteenth- and early-nineteenth-century British poetry, she has published numerous essays and written and edited several books on the work of laboring-class poets, including the *British Laboring-Class Nature Poetry, 1730–1837* and *The Cambridge History of British Working-Class Literature*. She is a peer reviewer for the Higher Learning Commission (HLC), a member of Phi Beta Kappa's Committee on Qualifications, and an ACAD board member.

Claudine Keenan is Dean of Education at Stockton University in New Jersey, where she has been on the Academic Affairs team since 2006. She earned her EdD in Higher Education Leadership from the University of Massachusetts, Amherst; her MA in Rhetoric and Composition from the California State University, Northridge; and her BA in English and Education from Adelphi University in New York. She served as Director of Graduate Programs at the Marlboro College Graduate Center in Vermont in the early 2000s, and then completed a national academic consulting contract for SunGard Higher Education before coming to Stockton. Outside work, Claudine has served on local boards of education and on the New Jersey STEM team for the American Association of University Women, volunteering to organize a number of youth STEM programs every year. She cycles and takes long beach walks with her husband, discusses great books with their older daughter, argues economic and political theory with their son, and, whenever their younger daughter isn't looking, Claudine does her best to spoil her first granddaughter.

Josephine Mendoza Kershaw, PhD, Fulbright Scholar, Fellow of the American College of Healthcare Executives, and Dean of Health Professions at North Arkansas College, received her educational training at Florida State University, Harvard School of Public Health, and Johns Hopkins University. She is a past president of the Great Lakes Region for the Accreditation Council of Business Schools and Programs (ACBSP) and won the 2011 ACBSP International Teaching Excellence Award. Dr. Kershaw has been the principal investigator and administrator for over $2 million in grant funding. Her research interests are in the areas of quality and performance excellence, minority health disparities, and human rights. She began her academic career teaching at an HBCU where she received a Teacher of the Year Award and also served as Director of the Minority Resource Development Center. She became the Director of Assessment and the Health Care Management Program Director while on the faculty at a college of business. Before assuming the role of Professor and Associate Dean of Health Sciences at a college of nursing, she was Dean of Graduate and Undergraduate studies at a chiropractic college. In addition to higher education, Dr. Kershaw's work experience includes both government agencies and private sector institutions.

O. John Maduko is the Vice-President for Academic and Student Affairs at Minnesota State Community and Technical College. Prior to this, he served at North Central Texas College (NCTC) as Vice Chancellor for Student Affairs. He was also a Dean of Health Sciences and Dean for E-Learning at NCTC. At Rasmussen University, he served as an academic dean, as well as a Chair and Associate Professor for the School of Health Sciences. As a first-generation Nigerian American, John's career has been centered on advocacy and equitable outcomes for marginalized and underserved students, scholars, professionals, and communities. Domestically and internationally, he has supported medical and educational relief efforts. John is a fellow for the Aspen Institute College Excellence Program and a fellow for the Thomas Lakin Institute of Mentored Leadership. He serves as a member of the boards of ACAD, NASPA's James E. Scott Academy, and HERDI Innovate. John serves on regional and state-level education, health care, and economic development committees, including as a commissioner for Tri-College University's multi-institution consortium.

Margaret Brown Marsden is Dean of the McCoy College of Science, Mathematics, and Engineering at Midwestern State University, Wichita Falls, Texas. She holds a PhD in Biological Sciences from Purdue University and an MBA from Texas A&M Commerce. Dr. Brown Marsden previously served as a biology faculty member for eighteen years at the University of Dallas and in administration as an associate dean and Biology Department chair. She is a field biologist working in partnership with local, state, and national organizations at the interface between science and society, with applications to ecotourism and conservation. Having pursued research projects in Alaska, on Alcatraz Island, and Costa Rica, she currently studies the rare nonphotosynthetic orchid *Hexalectris* in Texas. She has consulted on exhibits for the Perot Museum of Nature and Science and the Dallas Museum of Art and on park design for Dallas, Southlake, Irving, and Wichita Falls.

Elaine Meyer-Lee is Provost and Senior Vice-President for Academic Affairs and Professor of Psychology at Goucher College. Before that, she was Associate Vice President for Global Learning and Leadership Development at Agnes Scott College and has been a senior academic administrator and international and intercultural leadership educator for eighteen years. Since earning her doctorate in human development and psychology from Harvard, she has also researched college student development within the context of intercultural higher education at the Harvard Facing History Project, Boston College, Yale, Cambridge College, and Saint Mary's College and has taught global studies, intercultural studies, leadership, and psychology. She has published and presented widely, serves often as an external evaluator, and is a past president and chair of the Board of Directors for NAFSA: The Association of International Educators. She has consulted for many colleges in the

United States, and provided academic dean and chair development for the Saudi Ministry of Higher Education. She has won numerous grants, including a Fulbright to France.

Emily L. Moore, Professor Emerita, Iowa State University, and Founding President, Scholars for Educational Excellence and Diversity, holds a BS from George Williams College in Illinois; an MA from Washington University in St. Louis; and an EdD in Health Education Administration from the University of South Carolina. Her career as a professor, chair, dean, provost, and vice-president in higher education also included leadership in medical and public health organizations. She was Coordinator for Health Education in the Detroit Hypertension Control Research Program. She was also Director for Health Education at Metropolitan Hospital, Detroit. Her scholarly interests led to research on health education intervention in HIV/AIDS in China, Zimbabwe, and the South Carolina Sea Islands. In higher education she was Associate Dean for Academic and Faculty Affairs at the Medical University of South Carolina; VP of Academic Affairs and Dean of Faculty at Concordia University, St. Paul; and Provost and VP of Academic Affairs at Dillard University, in Louisiana. An ACE Fellow from 1989 to 1990, she received the 2006 Faculty Award for International Achievement from Iowa State University.

Jamie L. Mullaney is Associate Provost for Faculty Affairs and Professor of Sociology at Goucher College. In addition to numerous journal articles, she is the author of two books: *Everyone Is NOT Doing It* (University of Chicago Press, 2006) and *Paid to Party: Working Time and Emotion in Direct Home Sales*, coauthored with Janet Hinson Shope (Rutgers University Press, 2012). Her research and projects largely focus on issues of time, emotion, and identity.

Paula O'Loughlin serves as the Provost and Dean of the Faculty at Coe College in Cedar Rapids, Iowa. Prior to coming to Coe, she served as Associate Provost and Dean of Arts and Humanities at Gustavus Adolphus College. Before beginning her full-time administrative roles, O'Loughlin spent sixteen years as a faculty member at the University of Minnesota–Morris. While at Morris, she served in a variety of leadership roles, including directing the Academic Center for Enrichment and as assistant to the dean.

O'Loughlin has presented nationally in recent years on best practices for recruiting and retaining underrepresented faculty, questions of academic freedom and civility, and the administrator as mentor. She is on the steering committee of the Consortium for Faculty Diversity and serves as a higher-learning commission reviewer. She received the BA in government from Smith College and the PhD in political science from the University of Minnesota.

Ross Peterson-Veatch has served as Vice President for Academic Affairs and Dean of the College at Southwestern College in Winfield, Kansas, since 2017. Before coming to Southwestern, he served Goshen College in Goshen, Indiana, for ten years as Associate Academic Dean, Associate Vice President for Academic Affairs, and Interim Vice President for Academic Affairs. In conjunction with his work in the dean's office at Goshen, he was Director of Curriculum, Teaching, and Faculty Development at the College's Center for Intercultural Teaching and Learning. Together with colleagues at Goshen, he developed and launched the master's in intercultural leadership and served as Academic Director for that program for its first two years. He has been a member of ACAD since 2008 and has participated in and presented at the Dean's Institute multiple times on various topics, including alternative program formats and margin-based program budgeting. He holds a BA in sociology/anthropology and Spanish from Earlham College and an MA and PhD in Folklore from Indiana University Bloomington.

Jeffrey Ratliff-Crain, PhD, is the Vice-Chancellor for Academic Affairs and Innovation at the University of Minnesota–Rochester (UMR). As UMR's chief academic officer since 2018, he has worked with faculty committed to the scholarship of teaching and learning at a campus devoted to health sciences undergraduates. From 2013 to 2018, he was Associate Dean for Curriculum and Enrichment at Augustana College, overseeing academic programs outside the classroom, such as student research, study abroad, and community service, and was Professor of Psychology at the University of Minnesota–Morris from 1989 to 2013. At each institution, he has focused on furthering the campus's diversity, equity, inclusion, and justice goals. Ratliff-Crain received the PhD in medical psychology from the Uniformed Services University of the Health Sciences, having researched stress, coping, and substance use, and the BS in psychology from The Ohio State University.

Hideko Sera is Director of Equity, Inclusion, and Belonging at Morehouse College in Atlanta. She previously served as Associate Dean of the School of Education at the University of Redlands in California, overseeing the school's operations, including internationalization efforts and management of the Office of Student Success, which provided holistic support for both undergraduate and graduate students in teacher education, counseling, and leadership and higher education programs. With her clinical psychology background, especially in the areas of psychological well-being and wellness of Black, indigenous, and other people of color (BIPOC), her professional contributions are heavily focused on educational and social justice. As a 2021 recipient of the American Psychological Association's Presidential Citation Award, she continues to forward equity, diversity, inclusion, and belonging initiatives to make significant changes at systemic, community, and individual levels. She currently serves on the American Psychological Association's Board of Educational Affairs. Clinical supervision and power differences between supervisors and supervisees, mentorship and mentoring relationships, and antiracism and racial justice in higher education are some of her recent scholarly focuses as they inherently involve issues such as power and privilege.

Pete Skoner has served as the Founding Dean of the School of STEAM (Science, Technology, Engineering, Arts, and Mathematics) at Saint Francis University in Loretto, Pennsylvania, since 2018. He has held several leadership roles at Saint Francis, including associate provost, interim vice president for academic affairs, president of the faculty senate, and department chair. His administrative responsibilities include institutional accreditation. He has published in engineering education and served as Associate Editor for *The Pentagon*, the journal of the Kappa Mu Epsilon (KME) National Mathematics Honor Society. He currently coordinates the Pennsylvania Statistics Poster Competition for K–12 students and is a member of the Pennsylvania Postsecondary Information Management System (PIMS) Advisory Committee. Before his academic career, he was a mining engineer with Bethlehem Mines Corporation, a research fellow with NASA, and a research observer with the Pittsburgh Public School System. Pete received his BS degree in Mining Engineering from the Pennsylvania State University, MEd from Saint Francis College, and MB and EdD from the Indiana University of Pennsylvania.

James M. Sloat is Associate Provost and Associate Dean of Faculty at Colby College in Waterville, Maine, where he has served since 2012. Prior to this position, he worked at Washington & Jefferson College as Associate Dean for Assessment and New Initiatives and as Founding Director of the Center for Learning and Teaching. He began his career as a political scientist at Dickinson College and served as Founding Director of the Center for Public Speaking. Along with other colleagues, Sloat organized the New England Small College Associate Deans and has facilitated numerous workshops on the work of associate deans. He received his training in political philosophy (with a focus on Christian political thought) at Washington and Lee University and Duke University.

Courtney B. Smith is Acting Dean of the School of Diplomacy and International Relations at Seton Hall University. His areas of study include international organizations, the United Nations, and peace studies. Dr. Smith has interviewed more than one hundred UN delegates and staff members for his research on the organization and its members. His book *Politics and Process at the United Nations: The Global Dance* was published by Lynne Rienner in 2006. Smith was a Faculty Consultant for the Secretariat of the UN Year of Dialogue among Civilizations and is a representative for the School of Diplomacy's NGO affiliation with the UN Department of Global Communications. He serves as Treasurer for the Academic Council on the United Nations System, and as an external reviewer for the Middle States Commission on Higher Education and the UAE Commission for Academic Accreditation. He developed and directs his university's United Nations Intensive Summer Study Program and is the faculty advisor for the Seton Hall Model United Nations Association and the school's student-run newspaper, the *Diplomatic Envoy.*

Tarshia Stanley is Dean of the School of Humanities, Arts, and Sciences at St. Catherine University. She focuses on developing programs and courses that engage the liberal arts learning process and embrace social justice across the university. Stanley developed and launched the Integrated Learning Series for St. Kate's to link curriculum and programming across the university. She has authored articles critiquing Black women in African, African American, and Caribbean cinema, as well as Black female iconography in American popular culture. She edited *The Encyclopedia of Hip Hop Literature* for Greenwood Press and a volume for the Modern Language Association's teaching series entitled *Approaches to Teaching the Works of Octavia E. Butler*. Her areas of focus are film and media studies and African American speculative fiction. Prior to joining St. Kate's, Stanley spent nearly two decades at Spelman College in Atlanta, where she served as director of the E. W. Githii Honors Program, and before that as the Chair of the Department of English. Stanley earned her bachelor's degree in English at Duke University. She attended the University of Florida, where she earned her master's and doctorate degrees in English as a McKnight Doctoral Fellow.

Jenna Templeton was appointed Vice President of Academic Affairs at Chatham University in 2015, after joining the university in 2011 as Assistant Dean (later Dean) of the School of Graduate Studies and the School of Continuing and Professional Studies. In her role as Vice President, she led the university's academic reorganization and curricular revisions as part of the institutional transition to undergraduate coeducation. Her prior work in higher education centered on online education as well as counseling services. She began her career working in alternative educational programs for at-risk youth, providing opportunities for high school diploma completion and job readiness training. Templeton's movement to higher-education systems aligns with her passion for assisting others in achieving their educational goals and developing skills for engaging work. Dr. Templeton earned a BA in Psychology and an MEd in Counseling, both from the Pennsylvania State University and a Doctor of Education in Higher Education Leadership from Nova Southeastern University.

Gregor Thuswaldner joined Whitworth University as Provost and Executive Vice-President in 2020. From 2016 to 2020, he served as Dean of Arts and Sciences and Professor of Humanities at North Park University in Chicago, where he was also Acting Provost in fall 2017. In 2006, he received Gordon College's Distinguished Junior Faculty Award. Dr. Thuswaldner is an elected member of the European Academy of Sciences and Arts, the Pen American Center, and Pen Austria. He is a Fellow of the Royal Society of Arts, the Royal Historical Society, and the Society of Leadership Fellows of St. George's House at Windsor Castle. He serves on the board of the American Conference of Academic Deans ACAD and is a past president of the Austrian Studies Association. A native of Salzburg, Austria, Dr. Thuswaldner studied German and English at the University of Salzburg, Bowling Green State University, the University of Vienna, and the University of North Carolina at Chapel Hill. He also holds a master's of higher-education administration from North Park University.

Ann M. Vendrely, EdD, DPT, is the Vice-President for Academic Affairs and the Academic Dean at Goshen College, where she is also Professor of Kinesiology. She holds a doctoral degree in physical therapy from Regis University Denver and a doctorate in education (curriculum and instruction) from Loyola University Chicago. Her master of science in physical therapy is from the University of Indianapolis and her bachelor of arts degree in education (physical education and science) is from Goshen College. She is a licensed physical therapist. Prior to her current position, she served at Governors State University for over twenty years in positions of increasing responsibility. She was a tenured faculty member, program co-director, program coordinator, and associate provost. She has served as a peer reviewer for the Higher Learning Commission since 2010, with responsibilities as a team chair since 2013. She is active in research on educational preparation in the physical therapy profession and undergraduate general education programs.

Mike Wanous is Provost and Vice-President for Academic Affairs at Northern State University in Aberdeen, South Dakota. He holds a BS degree in Agronomy and International Agriculture from the University of Minnesota–St. Paul, an MS in Plant Breeding from Texas A&M University, and a PhD in Genetics from the University of Missouri–Columbia. Wanous previously served as Vice President for Academic Affairs at Huntington University for five years. Prior to that, he worked at Augustana University for seventeen years, holding the positions of professor of biology, department chair, natural science division chair, and associate academic dean of the university. He taught in the areas of genetics, cell biology, and molecular biology, and his research focused on plant molecular cytogenetics and gene expression. Wanous's previous professional experience also includes completing a postdoctoral fellowship at the University of Missouri–Columbia and spending a sabbatical year with his family in Norwich, England, where he worked at the John Innes Centre on plant genetics research. Wanous is Chair of the Board of Directors of ACAD and past president of the South Dakota Academy of Science.

Wendy A. Weaver currently serves as Dean for the School of Humanities, Social Sciences, & Interdisciplinary Studies and Director for Core (general education) Assessment at Mount Mary University in Milwaukee. Before that, she served as Mount Mary's Dean for Academic Affairs. Her years as a tour guide in Alaska turned out to be surprisingly useful preparation for navigating the challenges of the classroom (she earned an MA from the University of Alaska–Anchorage). As a professor, she is deeply committed to promoting an actively engaged classroom and fostering an inclusive atmosphere. Wendy's commitment to these ideals continues to be reflected in her institutional work, as she supports faculty through seminars and workshops to promote teaching excellence and coordinates Mount Mary's first-year seminar Leadership for Social Justice. She served also as President of the Wisconsin Women in Higher Education Leadership.

Vincent Wiggins is the Dean of Career and Continuing Education Programs at Harry S Truman College, City Colleges of Chicago. Previously he served as Dean of Instruction at Harold Washington College in Chicago, where he worked with faculty and staff to support students' academic success. One of his current focus areas is looking at relevant education and programming to support students' academic goals that align with their desired careers. Dr. Wiggins completed his Doctorate of Education in Curriculum Design at DePaul University. As a Master Online Teacher (MOT) and Certified Online Learning Administrator (COLA), Dr. Wiggins's commitment to education includes researching multiple delivery modes for learning that include hybrid and online learning. He has presented on pedagogy, andragogy, and technology at professional conferences, including the American Association of Adult and Continuing Education (AAACE), the International Society for Self-Directed Learning, and the Mentoring Institute at the University of New Mexico–Albuquerque. Dr. Wiggins also participated in the Third Annual Research Conference in Adult, Community, and Higher Education (ARCACHE), held at Ball State University, Department of Educational

Studies—Teacher College, in Muncie, Indiana. His talk there, "Culture of Education: Connecting, Culture, Community and Campus," was captured in a *TedTalk*.

Angela Ziskowski is the Associate Dean of Faculty Development at Coe College. She is also an Associate Professor of History at the college, where she teaches courses on ancient Mediterranean history and archaeological method and theory. She received her BA in Classics from the University of Cincinnati and her MA and PhD in Classical and Near Eastern Archaeology from Bryn Mawr College. She also serves as the Assistant Director of the Lechaion Harbor and Settlement Land Project, an active archaeological excavation in the Corinthia, Greece. Her research areas focus on Archaic Greek history, archaeological methodology, Corinthian vase painting, and polis formation in ancient Greek states.

Index